Gothic Pride

GOTHIC PRIDE

The Story of Building a Great Cathedral in Newark

BRIAN REGAN

Rivergate Books

AN IMPRINT OF RUTGERS UNIVERSITY PRESS
NEW BRUNSWICK, NEW JERSEY, AND LONDON

Library of Congress Cataloging-in-Publication Data
Regan, Brian.
Gothic pride : the story of building a great cathedral in Newark / Brian Regan.
p. cm.
Includes bibliographical references and index.
ISBN 978–0–8135–5288–0 (hardcover : alk. paper)—
ISBN 978–0–81345346–7 (e-book)
1. Cathedral of the Sacred Heart (Newark, N.J.) 2. Gothic revival (Architecture)—New Jersey—Newark. 3. Basilicas—New Jersey—Newark. 4. Newark (N.J.)—Buildings, structures, etc. I. Title.
NA5235.N63R44 2012
726.609749′32—dc23
2011033053

A British Cataloging-in-Publication record for this book is available from the British Library.

Publication of *Gothic Pride* is made possible in part by generous financial support from the Most Reverend Peter Leo Gerety, Archbishop Emeritus of the Archdiocese of Newark; Thomas P. Higgins; the New Jersey Catholic Historical Commission; Eugene O'Hara; and Charles Scribner III. Additional support was provided by Pamela L. and Robert W. Ferguson Jr., John Pearson, and Shirley Smoyak.

Visit our website: http://rutgerspress.rutgers.edu

Manufactured in the United States of America

for

MY MOTHER AND FATHER

CONTENTS

PREFACE AND ACKNOWLEDGMENTS

This book began with a question, prompted by unexpectedly seeing a great stone church. It had picturesque towers, transepts, and a soaring copper spire. I saw it—what appeared to be a medieval cathedral—while traveling by train, not in France or Germany or England but in New Jersey, when I chanced to gaze toward the horizon as the train approached Newark from the east. Before I could take in this unlikely spectacle, a pair of apartment buildings in the foreground blocked it. As the train headed farther west, the extraordinary structure was momentarily back in view. Lit by raking sunshine—shimmering, and utterly improbable—it looked for all the world like an architectural apparition. Its apparent isolation heightened the incongruity of time and place, as if this Gothic wonder had miraculously risen up, or mysteriously been set down, on a weary patch of New Jersey. (Millions of television viewers of *The Sopranos* may have later unwittingly shared the experience of these flashing views of the cathedral during the opening sequence of images that preceded each episode of the popular series.)

I had seen the church before, as I often took the Morris & Essex Line of New Jersey Transit, and knew it as Sacred Heart Cathedral. Never had I considered it or connected it to other buildings I knew well and had long admired. For the rest of my train ride, one question persisted: What is *that* building doing *there*? This book aspires to answer that question. And I am pleased to acknowledge the many people who helped me do so.

Bernard Flanagan indisputably deserves first mention. I met him soon after the sighting I described, joining one of his lively tours of Sacred Heart and inaugurating the first of countless exchanges of research and insights.

Chronicling Sacred Heart has vocational purpose for him, and anyone interested in the cathedral's historical development, now or in the future, will be grateful for it. But no one could be more grateful than I. Flanagan's extraordinary research enriches all of *Gothic Pride.*

The Archdiocese of Newark Collection is preserved at the Monsignor William Noé Field Archives & Special Collections Center at Seton Hall University. Alan Delozier, director of the center, along with Kathleen Dodds, offered extraordinarily informed, collegial, and unstinting assistance. Monsignor Francis Seymour, archdiocesan archivist, gave helpful information about the Newark see and its personalities. The late Monsignor William Noé Field provided liberal, cheerful access to the holdings now named for him.

The Charles F. Cummings New Jersey Information Center at the Newark Public Library is rich in primary materials, and I appreciated the help provided by Dr. George Hawley and his colleagues there.

David Gauld answered questions about architecture and engineering with interest and limitless patience, providing understanding of the technical fields found in this history. As a practicing architect, he saw in this story timeless lessons about the excitement and challenges associated with working in the building arts. I am profoundly grateful for his generous, steady encouragement.

I am thankful for a research document on Sacred Heart by Monsignor Michael Gubernat. It comprises a notated transcription of Monsignor Joseph Brady's manuscript about Sacred Heart's history through 1950, as well as Gubernat's own study of the cathedral. The latter also provides a comprehensive mapping of the cathedral's symbolic subject matter. Detailed treatment of this topic is outside *Gothic Pride*'s scope; those with a special interest in it will find the research document essential.

Roy Horton introduced me to the buildings of A.W.N. Pugin, only one instance of his wide-ranging and lasting influence upon me and others. I honor the memory of this extraordinary person's joyful approach to life and learning.

I am grateful to Abbot Gerard Lair, O.S.B., for decades of commentary and exchange about virtually every aspect of the Western tradition and am also indebted to many of his confreres, past and present.

Virginia Chieffo Raguin, professor of art history at the College of the Holy Cross, provided both guidance and inspiration. Through brilliant research, writing, teaching, and exhibitions, Professor Raguin has done much to bring attention to the decorative arts found in American buildings, especially churches. Her close, astute readings of the manuscript yielded important commentary. I thank her warmly.

Charles Scribner III, art historian, author, and former publisher, demonstrated over and over again his multiple gifts and skills as well as his professional experience in offering me priceless advice while I was writing this book and bringing it to publication. Clarence Walker urged me always to "find the historical narrative." I tried to follow this esteemed scholar and professor's advice. Art historian and author Wheelock Whitney III offered recommendations on the critical apparatus to use in discussing art and architecture. He provided practical suggestions and, periodically, the encouraging words every writer needs to hear.

Monsignor Robert Wister, professor of Church history at the School of Theology at Seton Hall University, read the manuscript through the lens of his close familiarity with the Newark see and its history. His recently published *Stewards of the Mysteries of God* became a wonderful resource, one that sets a standard for institutional history of its type.

Troy Joseph Simmons, director of architectural patrimony of the Archdiocese of Newark, advanced my understanding of American Catholic architecture, particularly of the twentieth century. I benefited from many conversations with him about the buildings under his watch, and I am thankful for the many ways he extended his good offices in the interest of this endeavor. Together with Monsignor Wister, Simmons inaugurated the Newark archdiocese's groundbreaking architectural patrimony program.

Monsignor Raymond Kupke read the manuscript and provided excellent suggestions. His own *Living Stones* is an outstanding study of the development of Catholic and ethnic New Jersey.

Marlie Wasserman, director of Rutgers University Press, counseled me to sharpen some themes and to elaborate others, rightly calling for the broader forces that influenced the Newark cathedral project to be developed. This book's ultimate form resulted from her incisive, direct, often witty, and always kind executive shaping. I owe her much. I thank as well others at the Press who guided this work to publication: Jeanne Ambrosio, Marilyn Campbell, Allyson Fields, Lisa Fortunato, Anne Hegeman, and Bryce Schimanski. *Gothic Pride* was immeasurably improved by the alert, highly skillful editing of Beth Gianfagna.

The Archdiocese of Newark welcomed me and entirely respected my independence. Its upkeep of Sacred Heart Cathedral under Archbishops

Peter Gerety, Theodore McCarrick, and John Meyers is a model for all who are stewards of important buildings. I hope also that this book enhances appreciation for the Newark archdiocese's achievements in many realms and over many years.

As the recipient of a generous Watson Fellowship, I had rare opportunities for study and research; indeed, it was as a Watson fellow that I first read Kenneth Clark's *The Gothic Revival*, which excited my imagination about the Gothic Revival and its aesthetic validity, and from which much later inquiry stemmed. During my fellowship studies in England, I was privileged to be welcomed by a number of institutions. Especially hospitable were Downside and Ampleforth abbeys, in Somerset and Yorkshire, respectively; the latter's Saint Benet's Hall in Oxford; and The Queen's College, Oxford.

I taught early in my career at Saint Paul's School in Concord, New Hampshire, whose chapel is a masterwork of the Gothic Revival. In addition to its religious purpose, the chapel by Henry Vaughan provided me with important lessons about architecture's power to define a place. It is not only a building in which the community gathers. The high merit of its art and architecture heightens the aesthetic awareness and appreciation of those who experience it regularly. Moreover, these factors join to make the chapel the most important icon of the institution it serves. Similar points could be made about other churches in this history, including Sacred Heart Cathedral. I worked at Saint Paul's under two rectors, William Oates and the Reverend Charles Clarke, and I am happy to record my appreciation to them and my former colleagues and students.

The impetus to write *Gothic Pride* derives in part from a long fascination with what motivates people when they set out to create architecture with strongly aspirational aims. My work at the Morgan Library & Museum has offered the chance to participate closely in significant architectural ventures. The most extensive was a major expansion of the Morgan: its planning, an international search for an architect, design development of the scheme, and, finally, its construction. I had written much of *Gothic Pride* prior to that involvement, which in several instances provided insight into the types of circumstances discussed here, which then led me to reconsider some of my conclusions. Also, the capacity today of museum projects to attract patronage, talented architects, and public interest in many respects is a counterpart to church and cathedral building of a former age. I thank the Morgan's trustees, staff, and two directors, Charles Pierce and William

Griswold, for this and many opportunities. Morgan curators assisted with my study of rare holdings; library professionals provided welcome research assistance; and publications and photography department colleagues provided expert advice. Finally, the ties between two generations of Morgans and the Doane family, the latter critical to the Newark cathedral story, was a pleasing intersection between my work and the writing of this book.

My mother and father helped with, and took avid interest in, research that led to this volume. If at times *Gothic Pride* evinces respect for the legacy of the past and an appreciation for people and personalities, both largely come from them and the particular culture they inherited and kept alive. My mother, herself a skilled researcher and author of local history, assisted in practical ways. They both often provided the sheltering circumstances on which every author relies. For this and abundant reasons, this book is dedicated to them, in gratitude.

I thank others who helped along the way: John Bermingham; Charles Callahan; Mary Collins; Fred Denig Jr.; Helen O'Rourke Denig; John R. Ditmars; Pamela Ferguson; David H. Fox; Andrew Holroyd; Elizabeth Waldron Mitchell; Rory O'Donnell; John Pearson; Nancy Piwowar; Paul Waldron Reilly; Will Schwalbe; Jeanne Sheehey; Waddell Stillman; Jean Strouse; Dom Antony Sutch, O.S.B.; and Peter Wosh.

Gothic Pride

Introduction

Newark's Cathedral Basilica of the Sacred Heart is an exceptional example of American church building, and the long, important cathedral-building venture that it represents carries many distinctions. Its early leaders were the first American cathedral builders to search abroad for an architect and also the first Catholic cathedral patrons to conduct a formal architectural competition. After many challenges, when later generations finished and opened Sacred Heart in 1954, they helped to complete the largest church in New Jersey and the most expensive Catholic church ever built in the United States. And from the first intimations of the project in the late 1850s to the cathedral's completion almost a century later, it significantly reflects evolving social, economic, cultural, and religious circumstances.

A cathedral serves as the principal church of a diocese and is, literally, the place for the seat of its bishop. (Cathedrals serve an entire diocese, not just the city where they are located and for which they may be named.) When founded in 1853, the Diocese of Newark comprised all of New Jersey. The state's extraordinary development is an essential factor in Sacred Heart's history. Evolving business conditions and transportation modes and systems, exponential population increases, and the concomitant growth of cities, towns, and rural areas momentously changed the character of the diocese as much as other aspects of regional life throughout the cathedral project's span. For the Catholic Church this meant continual adaptation. It also prompted several administrative subdivisions by which new dioceses were carved out of the old statewide Diocese of Newark; one of these, in 1937, raised Newark to an archdiocese.

From first to last, the cathedral's history is intertwined with immigration and the profound changes it wrought. At the beginning of the nineteenth century, the need for, let alone the money required to create, a substantial Catholic cathedral anywhere in the United States was essentially unimaginable. This changed after huge numbers of immigrants, many Catholics among them, arrived in America. By the second half of the century, in Newark, as in other places, building a cathedral became both an aspiration and financially possible, demonstrating the interdependent forces of immigration and economic growth in the period.

Worship and devotion are the obvious reasons for creating churches such as Sacred Heart, yet they are scarcely an expression of only religious impulses. Such monumental buildings also manifest their patrons' social motivations, in this case pride in collective faith and identity, though the latter was sometimes fragmented. In a related matter, this history must confront America's sometimes troubling response to immigration and immigrants, especially when nativism and anti-Catholicism erupted. For Catholics, this adversity could also be a spur to grand gestures when they had the opportunity to express their presence, particularly by the buildings they raised.

As a work of architecture, the cathedral in Newark merits close attention. Taking into consideration size, cost, and architectural significance, it is positioned in the context of the most ambitious cathedral buildings in the United States, among which it undisputedly ranks very high. (A distinction between the Newark cathedral project and Sacred Heart Cathedral must be made because, as we shall see, the diocese attempted to build a new cathedral prior to Sacred Heart, a phase rich both in architectural history and for what it reveals about Newark's high ambitions.) A cathedral does not imply a particular style of building, but Gothic was always the preference in Newark, as it was for the majority of American cathedrals. The widespread revival of Gothic architecture that took hold in the nineteenth century must be explored to understand why designers and patrons in America looked back to the British and Continental Middle Ages for models of contemporary building.

The Newark cathedral project started just before the Civil War. Inaugurated by Newark's first bishop, its early driving force was George Hobart Doane, a Catholic convert and priest. His father, George Washington Doane, is a key figure in the Gothic Revival in America, and the extraordinary Doanes claim a prominent place in this history. The younger Doane's fruitful collaboration with Newark architect Jeremiah O'Rourke brought a special episode in the Gothic Revival, heretofore unexamined, and sets the stage for Newark's exceptional cathedral-building zeal.

Controversy, however, shrouded the first decade of Sacred Heart's construction. Principally (but not entirely) over the integrity of the cathedral's structural foundations, it far exceeded the tensions endemic in large construction projects. Grievous conflicts, peculiar circumstances, and possible scandal strained relations among the builder and O'Rourke and church leaders also became gothic in a literary sense, as did several later events. The dispute ended badly for O'Rourke, but difficulties did not cease with his departure. Recounting these troubles constitutes *Gothic Pride*'s longest chapter and in many respects is the cathedral story's climacteric.

Several byways are explored. For a short time in the 1890s, O'Rourke held the position of United States supervising architect. His service in Washington becomes a pertinent digression because it occurred at a watershed in both American architecture and the architectural profession. Moreover, it sheds light on O'Rourke's character and makes a turning point in the cathedral's history less mysterious. Events that directed or altered the cathedral project's progress, such as the drama at Saint John's Church in Orange, which ensued from the 1870s economic collapse, are retold.

Sacred Heart eventually became the work of multiple designers—O'Rourke, Isaac E. Ditmars, Paul C. Reilly, Gonippo Raggi, and others—and a succession of diocesan leaders. And its history richly illustrates how the personalities and values of the individuals who join to create religious structures affect them no less than any human venture.

Newark, as a city and forge of identity, is a central force in the cathedral's story. This place, quintessentially and revealingly American, grew into a major industrial center in the 1800s and for about half a century enjoyed a golden age of urban culture. The Newark cathedral project thus also participated in a broader impetus by established and new Americans to create architecture that supported and conveyed their emerging sense of civic life. Like Brooklyn and other places that struggled to hold their own in the shadow of a metropolis such as New York, Newark's natives and denizens often developed an intense identity with their city and pride in its abundant accomplishments. The second half of the twentieth century, however, brought reversals. Diminished first by an exodus to the suburbs, shifting ethnic and racial mixes further altered Newark's financial and social economies. The shattering events of the summer of 1967 eviscerated a city that had been in decline for decades. In all, these later developments made

Newark an unlikely setting for a great neomedieval cathedral, one raised in 1995 to the rank of a basilica church. But the destinies of Sacred Heart and the place in which it arose—once flourishing, later troubled, recovering, always aspiring—are closely bound.

The construction of a cathedral in Newark took a crooked path. As it ran along for nearly a century and added new protagonists, it became, by turns, a story of great expectations; a morality play; a classical tragedy; a layered, multigenerational saga; and, finally, a tale of a grand hope fulfilled but with quixotic aspects that persist. Seldom in the chronicles of cathedral building do those who first draw the plans live long enough to light candles at the altars. And to tell the story of Sacred Heart, therefore, I return to the 1850s and to those whose dreams for Newark took Gothic form.

PART I
Gothic Vision in Newark

1

Destination: Newark

On a Sunday afternoon in the late fall of 1869, a young priest known for his flair for oratory stood before a small crowd gathered in Newark. In a big, passionate voice, he proclaimed: "Newark has done wonders in the past . . . and here today in this hallowed spot there is laid the foundation of the Cathedral not to be surpassed in beauty by any in the land. . . ."[1] Then he urged, "Don't be afraid my friends of doing too much. . . . Let Newark not be behind the other cities of the land and let her Cathedral spire, rising high over a magnificent stone edifice, rear its lofty peak as high if not higher than those of New York, Philadelphia, Albany, and Buffalo."

Those listening to Father Pierce McCarthy had gathered to witness the blessing of the cornerstone of a little church that Newark's Catholic leaders called a "cathedral chapel," a diminutive forerunner of the great cathedral they imagined. Although the cathedral chapel was temporary, and even though the site for the future cathedral that it foretold would ultimately change, McCarthy's high hopes for Newark never died.

Father McCarthy in many respects embodied the change that had occurred in New Jersey in the nineteenth century. He was the son of immigrants employed in a succession of iron mines scattered around the western part of the state. His father, originally from Ireland, did back-breaking toil in damp, filthy mines, and the family's home was in one after another of camps and settlements inhabited mostly by other immigrants. From hardscrabble beginnings, the vocational path of the Church carried the talented priest to the center of diocesan affairs.

McCarthy made his appeals in behalf of the diocese and the City of Newark itself. His rhetorical bravura echoed the chest-thumping vogue of the period. But there was also a strain of pride in his words, pride in his Catholic faith and pride in Newark. These themes would recur, undisguised and unembarrassed, as plans for the new cathedral went forward. The civic aspect of McCarthy's boasts were similar to those heard often from Newark's leaders, and they pointed to an underlying feeling that their city had something to prove, especially by trying to be David to Manhattan's Goliath. It galled many locals, for instance, when business operators demanded that "Made in New York" be stamped, etched, or sewn into goods produced in Newark, merging its identity with that of the better-known city. In their chauvinism, locals ignored the fact that Newark was one-tenth the size of New York City and half the size of Brooklyn. Yet they had bragging rights. Although Newark's population ranked it in the lower range of nation's top-twenty cities, its industrial output catapulted it to third place after the Civil War, qualifying it indisputably as an emerging powerhouse.

Spread out on a flat expanse and gentle hills mostly west and south of a sharp bend in the Passaic River, this old Puritan settlement and colonial center was transformed by the transportation revolution. Newark was connected to Manhattan by toll roads and rail lines over the marshland known as the Hackensack Meadows and a ferry or boat trip across the Hudson River. The Passaic's waters carried sail and steam ships eastward, out four miles to Newark Bay, and through the Kill van Kull narrows to New York Bay and the Atlantic. To the west, the rising and falling locks of the Morris Canal, conquering geography across New Jersey, linked Newark, and hence New York, to the Delaware River and then Pennsylvania, as well as to the mining resources along the way. Train routes soon vied with, then eclipsed and extinguished, the canal and opened access to the west and south.

Newark's bigger businesses made clothing and carriages and brewed beer. Yet by far the largest enterprises were in the leather trades: tanning and making shoes, boots, saddles, and harnesses. But by no means was Newark a one-company, or a one-industry, town. Newarkers produced fertilizer, India rubber, zinc oxide for paint, varnish, carriages, furniture, and dozens of other items. Along with the big firms in these businesses, hundreds of smaller ones formed a broad economic base. The steam engine transformed many operations, creating factories with an irreducible need for abundant, cheap labor. Immigrants, in successive waves, provided it. Water routes brought these immigrants to Newark; jobs kept them there and attracted tens of thousands more. They began arriving in substantial numbers in the late 1830s, and a two-decade swell followed. In the 1840s, New Jersey's population increased by almost a third. By 1850, about 10 percent, or fifty-six thousand, of the population was foreign born, a ratio that kept climbing for decades and was always higher in the state's northeast.

Almost all immigrants in this first great wave were from Ireland or Germany. The tragedy of Ireland's potato crop failures is well known; it is a grim fact that about one million Irish fled their homeland at the Famine's peak years in the late 1840s and early 1850s. In the same period, an equal number died from starvation, disease, or both. Those who came to New Jersey for the most part labored on the canals and railroads and at other unskilled tasks. In 1850, of those born abroad, more than half, thirty-one thousand, were from Ireland, and that figure doubled in a decade.

In the nineteenth century, Germans increasingly fled economic stagnation, along with political and religious hostility and persecution. They arrived in the United States in smaller numbers than the Irish during this phase and for more complex reasons.[2] In other parts of the country, especially the Midwest, Germans opted for farm life, but in New Jersey they tended to settle in towns and cities. Like the Irish, they toiled on canals and railroads; however, generally arriving with more skills, they soon became bakers, carpenters, masons, brewers, and the like and worked in the tanning and textile trades—and thus joined the middle class.

The majority of these immigrants to New Jersey were Catholic. The Famine Irish in this period were virtually all Catholic. The Protestant Reformation rendered Catholics a minority in Germany; of German immigrants now in the state, a third to a half were Catholic. These large Catholic numbers were a profound change from the start of the century, when there were fewer than a thousand Catholics in the entire state, a sliver of a religious minority that was tolerated but had little legal protection. These earliest Catholics to live in what became New Jersey were skilled German and Irish glassworkers employed in Salem County starting in the 1740s and Irish immigrants laboring at ironworks in the northwest. After the American Revolution, Catholic refugees also arrived from France, fleeing the French Revolution, and from the West Indies. They were served by priests who traveled to the area from New York and Pennsylvania.

The first Catholic church in the state was not built until 1814, in Trenton, and Newark's first parish was organized in 1826, with a church built two years later, mostly to serve a modest influx of the early Irish immigrants.

The growing number of German Catholic immigrants in Newark led to the founding of a church to serve them in 1842. This was also the first national or language parish established in the diocese. (National parishes were created for those living in a concentrated area with shared foreign origins or language or both; a traditional parish covered a designated geographical territory.)

A Slippery Welcome Mat

In this period and for the next seventy-five years, in fits and starts, immigration defined and continuously transformed the United States—and especially places such as New Jersey, where newcomers arrived in vast numbers. Always, immigrants found both work and prejudice here. And Catholic immigrants were twice foreign: born in another country and having a religious faith unlike that of the Protestant American majority. This produced a backlash of anti-Catholicism that began with escalating immigration in the 1830s. For the next two decades, riots, church burnings, and physical attacks on Catholics were a fact of American life. The torching of the Ursuline convent near Boston in 1834 was the first major flare-up. Outbursts in an Irish Catholic neighborhood in Boston followed in 1835, and the mid-1840s brought ugly scenes in Philadelphia. Nothing fanned fear and hatred more than the publication of *Maria Monk's Awful Disclosures,* which first appeared in 1836. An allegedly personal account of a girl's narrow escape from a convent, the book was a catalogue of atrocities: captive nuns, fornicating priests, murdered babies, and bizarre rites. *Maria Monk's Awful Disclosures* fed the suspicions of those ready to believe the worst about Catholics. Although entirely fabricated, it and similarly salacious tales found an eagerly receptive readership for decades.

Seen through a prism of ethnic and religious prejudice, Catholic immigrants had wildly fantastic fears projected onto them. Many Americans objected to religious practices that they did not understand (because most Catholic rites were conducted in Latin, this was literally true), Catholics' apparent superstitions, and a general sense that they were in some way morally deficient. Some feared that Catholics posed a risk to American democracy, believing that the pope, through bishops and priests, controlled them and their voting. Many believed it was impossible for Catholics to be loyal U.S. citizens, and Protestants and Catholics experienced real and imagined rivalries over jobs, usually menial and low-paying ones. But what is undeniable about this phase of American life is that the huge influx of immigrants, especially in major cities, severely burdened the housing supply, while underdeveloped infrastructures (sanitation, safety, and health services, such as they were) bowed and buckled under the weight of fast, heavy population growth. The sheer number of new immigrants indisputably upended the status quo in the places where they settled, and many Protestants resented them for it.

In 1853, a Vatican official, Archbishop Gaetano Bedini, came to the United States as part of a tour to prop up Catholic unity. Instead, his mission largely sowed terrible sorrow, provoking a rash of church torchings and vicious assaults. A luckless priest in Maine was tarred and feathered, causing physical and mental torments that killed him not long after. Nativism coalesced into a national political movement by 1854, when "Know-Nothings" stood upon a political platform of bald anti-Catholicism. Rancor and violence came with it. Widely fluctuating economic conditions and heavy immigration in these decades proved to be a toxic combination, and nativists, demonizing the foreign born, lashed out.

Newark Becomes a Diocese

In these years of unprecedented immigration, Catholics formed the largest single religious group in the country, outstripping in numbers each of the numerous Protestant denominations. In response to this swell, in 1853, ten new Catholic dioceses, or jurisdictions, were created; one comprised all of New Jersey, where there were thirty-three Catholic churches already established, most very recently.[3] Though clearly growing quickly, these Catholic churches represented a mere fraction of the more than eight hundred churches throughout the state at the time.[4] Newark, by far New Jersey's largest city (and among the twenty biggest in the nation), was made its administrative center. The Catholic Church hierarchy appointed the Reverend James Roosevelt Bayley, then serving in New York City, as the Diocese of Newark's first bishop. He was consecrated in Saint Patrick's Cathedral, on Mott Street in lower Manhattan, on October 30, 1853.

The City of Newark, where Bishop Bayley would live, had recently experienced phenomenal growth; its population of about forty-eight thousand was three times what it had been in 1840.[5] Though on the rise and among the nation's twenty largest cities, it was hardly a metropolis. Its tallest commercial buildings stood four stories high, made of wood and brick and a popular local brownstone. Its main thoroughfare, Broad Street, was the city's only paved road, and its cobblestones had been laid only a year before the bishop arrived. Church towers and spires, as elsewhere, formed the peaks of its silhouette. Following a common practice, Bayley selected one of those churches, Saint Patrick's, as the cathedral for the new diocese. (This made it Newark's pro-cathedral, short for provisional cathedral church.) Opened in 1850, it was the newest of the city's three Catholic churches.[6] Rendered in a highly simplified Gothic style adopted in Ireland in the decades before it was built, Saint Patrick's was a pleasing brick structure, with an imposing, dignified presence near the center of Newark. It was also in the vanguard of a growing number of Newark churches and other buildings in the emerging preference for the Gothic style.[7]

ALL SAINTS DAY, 1853

Just two days after his consecration, James Roosevelt Bayley rose early in New York, crossed the Hudson by ferry to New Jersey, and boarded the train for Newark. The journey, only about nine miles, passed plains of water and vast flats of grassy reeds growing in the Hackensack Meadows. The train soon traveled over a long bridge spanning the dull currents of the Hackensack River and a shorter one above the Passaic, arriving in Newark at about ten o'clock. Thousands came to welcome Bayley as the new—the first—bishop of Newark. On a perfect autumn day, a mile-long procession of children, church societies, clergy, and brass bands escorted him from the station and through their city and to another Saint Patrick's, this one in downtown Newark. For Roosevelt Bayley and those who greeted him it was a history-making, pride-filled day, the first of November, All Saints Day, 1853. And it was a day that many others in Newark lamented.

Protestants thought there was more than enough Catholic presence in Newark without a bishop and all that went with him—the miter and crosier, popish processions, Latin rituals, and Catholic idolatries—let alone the more official presence of Romanism in the form of a diocese and a Catholic bishop of Newark. Acutely aware of such feelings and the anger (and, indeed, the violence) they could incite, many Catholic clergy were chary about too much display, too celebratory a welcome for their new superior. It seemed antagonistic, teasing the bull of anti-Catholicism with the papal flag. But the priest organizing the day's events would hear none of that. Tough, blunt, and not to be crossed, Father Bernard McQuaid put Catholics on notice. In a word-of-mouth campaign and in a printed program, he instructed, "It will be the duty of every Catholic, either in the procession or on the ground, by his orderly and religious demeanor to do honor to the Bishop, and reflect credit on the Catholic body of Newark; even at the sacrifice of his own personal gratification."[8]

On Bishop Bayley's first day in Newark, he spent much of it blessing the jubilant but obedient Catholic crowds. Though there were taunts from Protestants along the parade route, most of that portion of the community, the majority, went about its business—business that was making Newark a thriving small city. But in Bayley's early years as bishop, there were many tribulations. At one point, he wrote in frustration to a local newspaper that "every week almost we read of some violence committed against Catholic property."[9] A day of reckoning came when several thousand rabid anti-Catholics participating in a demonstration (locals later said that most came from New York) marched around the city in early September 1854, to the appalled glare of Catholic onlookers lining the streets. This combustible mix exploded when a small mob, thought by some to have targeted the pro-cathedral, headed instead to Saint Mary's Church, the German Catholic parish. It stormed and sacked the interior, chopping the head and hands off the statue of Mary. The mob went for the organ, yanking out pipes and bending and twisting them until, as one observer said, they looked like pretzels. Moving on, these hooligans pillaged the rectory and set a school building ablaze.[10] Police stood by during a rampage that left several Catholics badly hurt, one dead, and another who eventually died from blows received that day. Bishop Bayley poured oil on the waters, and Newark did not again reach a boiling point over religious prejudice. But many Catholics were left feeling wary about their new country. And this tended to strengthen bonds to what was familiar and affirming, especially religious ties.

The riot incidents seared Newark's Catholic leaders, but Bishop Bayley and his fellow priests were largely consumed by starting and staffing parishes for the mounting Catholic population in this period. They discussed eventually raising a new cathedral for the expanding diocese, but Bishop Bayley, ever prudent, pushed these plans into the future in preference to building parish churches and other institutions in service to Catholic interests.

Episcopal Restraint

James Roosevelt Bayley descended from the families whose illustrious names he bore. Educated in New England, his early career choices reveal a shifting purpose. He was commissioned as a midshipman in the navy, but forsook it for college. He then decided on medical studies (his father and grandfather were physicians), only to be pulled, after about two years, to theology, in preparation for becoming an Episcopal clergyman. Shortly after his ordination, and to most of his family's disgust, Bayley converted to Catholicism. In this he imitated his revered aunt, Elizabeth Ann Seton, who became a Catholic and a nun after the death of her husband and founded the religious order, the Sisters of Charity, which inaugurated the parochial school system in America. Still, the Newark *Sentinel* had earlier played its nativist hand, writing that Bayley had been "[s]educed from the faith by a deluded female, his aunt" and that in becoming a Catholic he paired himself with the "Mother of Harlots."[11] This "deluded female," however, became the first canonized saint born in the United States.

Bayley's deep, balanced, spiritual and intellectual life was as much a product of Enlightenment philosophy as the early writings of the Church, both of which he read closely. In conversation, Doctor Johnson's worldly phrases came to Bayley as readily as those of the Doctors of the Church. With the acuity and manners of a diplomat, he generously contended with poor immigrants and a region that felt besieged by them. He was also a natural mentor. Bayley counseled other bishops to lead firmly but not lose their humanity. "Drink a little claret with your dinner," he told a new prelate, "study to be quiet and you will grow fat & do much good in your generation." In dealing with strong-willed priests, he urged, "Don't let those exacting Padres press you too much."[12]

Born to wealth, Bayley was wholly prudent and unprepossessing. It fazed him little, for instance, that he was disinherited from a fortune as a price for becoming a Catholic. His grandfather took him out of his will on the mistaken belief that, as a Catholic priest, he could not inherit property. An uncle more intentionally disinherited him. Always taking the long view, Bayley commented, "It will all be the same a 100 years from now." (The bequests that Bayley lost went to the Union Theological Seminary and Roosevelt Hospital, both in New York.) In another instance, when Bayley was trying to help the institution known as Seton Hall take root, he hopefully noted that a "good many persons have been out to see it." But, he added, "as is always the case, some of our friends in New York are doing all they can to help us downwards"—his wry way of admitting that they were competing for students who might otherwise choose colleges in New York.[13]

As Bishop of Newark, however, Bayley allowed one extravagance in the early, lean years. He commissioned John Jelliff, a gifted Newark furniture maker, to craft an ornate new cathedra in which he would sit in Saint

Patrick's sanctuary. The word *cathedral,* in fact, does not indicate a church's size, but derives from *cathedra,* Latin for "chair," and is literally the place for the bishop's chair, from which he officiates as spiritual leader within his diocese's boundaries. The black walnut ecclesiastical throne that Jelliff produced is a masterful work of Gothic cabinetry that brought credit to both artisan and bishop.[14] It hinted as well that a grander setting for it might be expected in Newark.

Search for the Perfect Site

About a half-dozen years after arriving in Newark, in January 1859, Bishop Bayley took the first step toward building a new cathedral, purchasing a site at the intersection of High (now Martin Luther King Boulevard) and Kinney Streets on the south side of the city, which was no farther than a long walk or quick carriage or buggy ride to and from the neighborhoods with the highest Catholic numbers. (The diocese purchased the land from a Catholic couple, James Dougherty and his wife, who themselves purchased the land on the same day from John H. Stevens; it was not uncommon in these antagonistic years for Catholic lay people to serve as intermediaries in buying real estate intended for use as a church site.)[15] Bishop Bayley thought it would be a good site for "a cathedral one of these days."[16] The Civil War delayed and then dashed these plans, but in 1867, with the country recovering and a frothy postwar economy giving confidence, Bayley and his advisers thought the times more promising for fund-raising. They also found what they regarded as a more congenial site several blocks from the one chosen previously. The new location, at LaGrange Place, faced a pleasant, triangular green known as South Park (later renamed Lincoln Park) and looked up Broad Street, which had been laid out in Puritan days on a Native American trail and now stretched up in boulevard-fashion past the residences of the city's burghers and to a mixed district of three- and four-story residences and businesses fronted by awning-covered sidewalks.[17] A writer visiting Newark about this time by chance compared the former site for the cathedral on High Street with the new one: "High Street is certainly a handsome avenue. But I must confess I consider Broad Street to be one of the finest streets in the United States. . . . When the long shadows of the late afternoon cover it, pen cannot paint the brilliant scene here presented—the fashionable turnouts, the fast trotters; the beauty, elegance, and wealth displayed on wheels and on horseback."[18] Lower Broad Street was, in other words, a fine, convenient, proud place for what the diocese said would be called "The Newark Cathedral." Bishop Bayley thought that a "proper Cathedral Church" would "serve as a crown," writing to his clergy when he began to appeal for help in financing it: "I know that you are all busy with your own good works for the advantage of Religion, in your various missions; but, as a Cathedral is a Diocesan and not merely a parish church, I am confident that you will take an interest in the matter, and make such a collection as shall be an evidence of your zeal, and the zeal of your people, in providing a Mother Church for the Diocese of Newark."[19] A couple of years later Bayley concluded that "every day's experience shows how much we need a proper Cathedral, and Bishop's House for the Diocese of Newark."[20]

It was this need that had brought Father McCarthy to the site on lower Broad Street and inspired his lifting oratory about the cathedral venture they were starting in Newark—marked by the laying of the cornerstone for the cathedral chapel.

2

Gothic and the Context of American Cathedral Building

From the inception of the cathedral project, Bishop Bayley and other Church leaders in Newark imagined that the building would be in the Gothic style. Three of the four structures, for instance, referenced by Father McCarthy at the cornerstone ceremony of the Cathedral Chapel were Gothic. Though famously authoritative and centralized, the Catholic Church did not dictate the choice of style for churches or the architects to design them. The very name *cathedral* brings to mind the spectacular structures of the Middle Ages, but cathedrals are in fact defined by neither size nor style. They could be large or small, classical or Gothic—whatever was preferred. In this period, however, there was an overwhelming preference for Gothic for both small and large churches. Gothic's embrace was the most passionate of the stylistic revivals that virtually defined nineteenth-century architecture. Buildings rendered in Egyptian, Greek, Roman, Romanesque, Gothic, and American Colonial were among the styles that took a turn (though by no means in chronological order) as the style of choice. Part of a broader cultural movement that romanticized the Middle Ages, the new interest in Gothic became the most idealized of the stylistic revivals, set apart by a robust theoretical underpinning.

Pugin and His Principles

The Englishman Augustus Welby Northmore Pugin fundamentally shaped this transformation in taste in the English-speaking world. Other European lands saw similar phenomena, yet it is the Gothic Revival in Britain that is most relevant to the Newark cathedral story at this juncture. Pugin's buildings, decoration, and especially his provocative writings, produced between 1836 and 1843 (*Contrasts, True Principles of Pointed or Christian Architecture, The Present State of Ecclesiastical Architecture in England,* and *Apology for the Revival of Christian Architecture in England*), made historically accurate Gothic style widely popular.

True Principles presented his essential theories, which he said were deduced from studying medieval buildings. "An old English parish church, as originally used for the ancient worship," Pugin waxed, "was one of the most beautiful and appropriate buildings that the mind of man could conceive; every portion of it answered both a useful and mystical purpose."[1] He summarized his theory on the first page: "The two great rules for design are these: 1st, that there should be no features about a building which are not necessary for convenience, construction, or propriety; 2nd, that all ornament should consist of enrichment of the essential construction of the building."[2] Clear as they are at face value, these rules do not make Gothic style obligatory; but about that Pugin was unequivocal. For him, Gothic's superiority rose from its fusion of form and function and because it developed during the Middle Ages, when the Catholic Church, to which he converted, was pervasive and dominant.

The prevailing taste for Neoclassicism stood as the opposite pole of Pugin's aesthetic axis. Seeing it as descending from pagan ancient Greece and Rome, he crusaded against classicism with blinding fanaticism. His polemics and antics notwithstanding, Pugin truly mastered the Gothic style and taught many to follow his lead. And his higher aim is lost if one does not grasp how profoundly he believed—and inspired others to believe—that a church building achieved unending good.

Pugin earned his fame with outstanding Gothic-style buildings: houses, churches, cathedrals, and academic and institutional buildings. His designs for Saint Chad's Cathedral in Birmingham and Saint Barnabas Cathedral in Nottingham especially spread his reputation, and his extravagant Saint Giles Church in Cheadle, in the English Midlands, became the best-known early Gothic Revival church in the English-speaking world. Pugin's interiors for the new Palace of Westminster displayed his total command of the Gothic idiom.

The Oxford Movement and Ecclesiology

Other Englishmen also laid the groundwork for a broad-based Gothic Revival. Beginning in Oxford in 1833, in sermons and pamphlets, clergymen

John Keble, John Henry Newman, and kindred spirits began urging theological and liturgical reforms that led to a transformation within Anglicanism. It became known as the Oxford Movement, and reclaiming the elaborate ceremonies of the Middle Ages became one its chief interests. This led almost inevitably to a desire to revive the type of building in which these old practices were conducted. New societies at Oxford and Cambridge universities brought dogma and youthful zeal to these changing ideas about theology, liturgy, and architecture. They analyzed and promoted the merits of medieval churches, both as historic treasures and models for contemporary building. These zealots called their study "ecclesiology," which meant for them the science of church architecture. Derivative forms of this unwieldy term defined the movement's followers (ecclesiologists) and the style of church they preferred (ecclesiological).[3] Pugin and these groups, parsing the Gothic style and at times exchanging charged feelings, took pains to enunciate their differences. Yet they played variations upon the same theme: the English medieval parish church was an unsurpassed paradigm.

At midcentury, the ideas and influence of these diverse Gothic partisans combined and mutated, and preferred design characteristics emerged and solidified.[4] They believed that the church's site must be the key determinant of the design and the building fabric, preferring local materials, especially native stone. Asymmetrical plans and the simpler Early Pointed (unadorned arches for windows and other wall openings) and the Decorated (window tracery using simple geometric shapes) phases of Gothic became ideals. Pugin also loved timber roofs whose interior beams were exposed to view, rhapsodizing: "The construction of these, so far from being concealed, is turned into ornament. The principle tie-beams, rafters, purloins, and braces, which in modern edifices are hidden at vast expense by a flat plaster ceiling, are here rendered very ornamental features, and this essential portion of a building becomes its greatest beauty."[5]

Catholics, especially Pugin, asserted that their rights to the Gothic style were more legitimate than those of Anglicans and others, claiming the ground of its first flowering in the Catholic society of the Middle Ages. They insisted, too, that the faith that they believed motivated the medieval builders must inspire those working in Gothic again. "There are a great many modern Catholics," Pugin warned, "who admire Pointed architecture but they do not admire it on true principles as the result of Catholic feeling. . . . We must have the real spirit of Catholic churches as well as their ornaments."[6] For their part, some Anglicans feared that being too receptive to this inspiration was a slippery slope: it might lead to abandoning Anglicanism for Roman Catholicism. They pointed to Pugin and Newman, who also eventually and famously converted, as proof of the perils.[7] Other types of hazards lurked. Intelligent as it often was, the new work in the Gothic style was filtered through contemporary aesthetic preferences and understanding of its old models. A return to earlier architectural forms is as fraught with challenges as is the attempt to retrieve any aspect of the past.

THE GOTHIC REVIVAL AND NATIONAL AND ETHNIC IDENTITY

In nineteenth-century Britain and Europe, stylistic revivals also had a nationalist dimension. Historical building styles of a region, nation, or kingdom were seized upon to represent a society's past achievements—and its future promise. Architecture, like language, was seen as a means to convey common history, identity, purpose, and destiny. The completion of Cologne Cathedral, for instance, was also seen as a unifying symbol of German nationalism for those whose loyalties had been to many individual princes, dukes, and lords but who shared German lineage and language. But architectural style and its meaning is often contentious. Just as some leaders and designers mined the Middle Ages for building forms and theories to rally around, others called up classical idioms as more appropriate.[8]

In the United States it was a different story. Because there was no indigenous formal style and structural technique to evoke, from the first colonizers onward buildings were in some form of imported style. For Catholic builders here, historical references were sometimes drawn—round-arch style for German churches, central European architectural devices for Poles, even Baroque in the American Southwest, where Spanish explorers and settlers came—but the most important prerequisite was that a church's architectural style had some form of Catholic precedent. This meant that they had many patterns to claim. And yet the prevailing taste of the period was usually the more determinative influence.[9]

SETTING THE CATHEDRAL STANDARD IN AMERICA: BALTIMORE

At the cathedral chapel's cornerstone ceremony in Newark, when Father McCarthy urged that its cathedral should eventually "rear its lofty peak as high if not higher than those of New York, Philadelphia, Albany, and Buffalo," he cited most of the notable cathedrals then extent in the United

States, yet he omitted Baltimore's cathedral, perhaps because it had no spires. Yet it was exceptional. The Cathedral of the Assumption served the United States's premier Catholic see and was the first purpose-built cathedral here. Designed in the classical style by Benjamin H. Latrobe, and begun in 1804, it was the largest house of worship in the country when it was dedicated in 1821 and arguably the most sophisticated architectural work in America. As sublime and important as Latrobe's Baltimore cathedral was, the upsurge of American cathedral building that began in the late 1840s coincided with the sweeping rise of the Gothic Revival, which set the stylistic expectation in this epoch.

The next cathedral to be conceived on a grand scale and built later than Baltimore's was Albany's Cathedral of the Immaculate Conception, whose cornerstone was laid in 1848. The Albany diocese retained Patrick C. Keely, based in Brooklyn, to design it. Keely, in fact, designed Saint Patrick's Church in Newark, adopted as the pro-cathedral at the Newark diocese's founding.

Patrick Keely's Dominance of Catholic Building

As the number of Catholics in this country, especially on the Eastern Seaboard, swelled, thousands of churches were built to serve them. Smaller buildings were often the work of local architect-builders. The greatest share of the larger buildings were designed by Patrick Keely.[10] Church commissions in this era predictably aligned along denominational lines, and when Keely began, he was a rare professional: a Catholic architect. Born in Ireland, he settled in Brooklyn and after initially working as a carpenter-builder, acquired architectural skills, rising to meet the demands of a burgeoning market for Catholic churches and ancillary structures: schools, rectories, convents, and institutional buildings. Keely's early entry permitted him to gain dominance in the field; he was the only Catholic architect with a truly national practice in this period. Keely's churches were in a variety of revival styles. His Gothic designs reflect Pugin's general influence without a rigorous commitment to ecclesiological principles and historic correctness.[11] Some of his major commissions were of immense scale, with interiors rather like vast halls richly embellished with architectural and decorative ornament, and they achieved an attention-grabbing monumentality.

Albany was Keely's first cathedral commission, and he intended to make a mark. Though smaller than the cathedrals abroad, the English Decorated Gothic–style building was vast by American church standards: a cruciform structure whose original length was about 210 feet and 96 feet across the transepts, with seating for 2,500. Its initial cost was estimated at $100,000, and ultimately at least $250,000 was spent on outfitting the interior with extravagant appointments: stained glass by an English firm that produced some of Pugin's glass, abundant statuary, and a large pipe organ by Henry Erben of New York City. The diocese expended still more to raise the spires and enlarge the chancel and sacristies.[12] Although Keely's almost contemporaneous commission for a smaller cathedral in Cleveland was finished first, when Immaculate Conception in Albany opened in 1852, it was acclaimed as the largest and most imposing in the country. (Both spires were not completed until a generation later; worry about the stability of the soil conditions on the site led Keely to reduce their height from 300 to 210 feet. Still, they were the highest points in Albany's skyline.)

Father McCarthy's reference to Buffalo was to the Cathedral of Saint Joseph, also by Patrick Keely. Started in 1851, this far more modest Gothic building was dedicated in 1855 at a cost of $150,000, but one of the spires was never erected.

OTHER MAJOR CATHEDRAL PROJECTS

Although a passion for Gothic style spread far and for many years, classical modes never lost their appeal entirely, and Catholics often elected styles that called to mind the great churches of Italy and, especially Rome. Philadelphia's Cathedral of Saint Peter and Saint Paul was distinctly patterned on such buildings and later ones they inspired.[13] Made of brownstone, it was 250 feet in length, 136 feet wide, and 101 feet high, with seating for about two thousand. Napoleon LeBrun, of French ancestry and trained in America, was the principal designer.[14] Constantino Brumidi, whose work also appears in the U.S. Capitol building, painted murals for the cathedral. Though not in a building idiom that had spires, the cross on the top of its central dome reached 209 feet.

The original Saint Patrick's Cathedral building in New York City, dedicated in 1815, had been the nation's second cathedral built for that purpose and bore hints of the Gothic style. The structure that was designed to replace it, begun in 1856, cast a shadow in which all later American religious building—by any denomination—rose.

Archbishop John Hughes conceived the second Saint Patrick's Cathedral. Hughes always fought hard and thought big for American Catholics and was determined that there should be a great cathedral in New York, a symbol of the emerging Catholic presence in the United States. He hired James Renwick, an accomplished Gothicist, to realize his hopes. Renwick gave him a design that integrated Continental and English medieval models and reflected the influence of two major building projects in nineteenth-century Europe: the completion of Cologne Cathedral and the rebuilding of the west facade of Saint Ouen in Rouen (about which more will be said later). Hughes provided Renwick with an entire block for the building, though the location between Fiftieth and Fifty-First Streets was thought by many to be too far north from the center of city life. Hughes and others, however, saw Manhattan expanding vigorously northward and, in retrospect, were visionaries.

When Saint Patrick's cornerstone was laid in 1858, the *New York Times* said that when finished, it "would have no parallel" in America.[15] The project survived substantial changes to critical elements of Renwick's design: eliminating plans for an apsidal choir and Lady Chapel (to make room for residences on the eastern side of the site) and a large masonry crossing tower, and the decision not to construct authentic stone vaulting. These compromises were a bitter pill for the architect, and Protestant critics pounced on them when the opportunity arose. (The matter of stone vaulting is particularly pertinent to any assessment of American cathedrals: none of Patrick Keely's were built with stone vaulting, the constructional system that was a defining aspect of the great medieval cathedrals. Keely used roofs of wood and iron construction, along with lathe and plaster, creating a Gothic-style shell but not true Gothic construction.) Yet the conception and reality of Hughes and Renwick's marble structure was truly monumental and, when it was blessed in 1879, minus the spires, it was a staggering achievement: the largest church in the country and a sophisticated, coherent Gothic composition. The completion of the spires in 1888 crowned it, adding another $200,000 to the earlier construction costs, which Renwick said ranged between $2 million and $2.2 million.[16]

The Diocese of Brooklyn, established at the same time as the Newark see, began building a cathedral in 1865, its own riposte to Manhattan. It was then little more than an excavated site, but its scheme, again by Keely, was huge: more than 350 feet long and with spires higher than those planned for Saint Patrick's Cathedral.[17]

Cathedral building always brought challenges and often severe difficulties. In Pennsylvania, the Diocese of Pittsburgh overreached in its aspiration to construct an elaborate Gothic cathedral. Put up relatively fast and opened in 1855, the design by John Welch was estimated to cost $60,000, but the Pittsburgh diocese eventually spent about $300,000, five times as much as originally conceived. Even so, brick was substituted for stone as the building was finished. The Cathedral of Saint Peter had three towers, two spires at the facade rising to 220 feet, and a 285-foot spire above the crossing tower. But the latter spire soon developed structural problems and required remedial support systems, and ultimately it was taken down and replaced with a central lantern.

American bishops long remembered the tribulations in Pittsburgh, in part because the troubles with the cathedral plagued that diocese's finances for decades. Philadelphia's cathedral project moved forward only once funds were in hand, fiscally prudent but protracting progress. In Newark, Bishop Bayley, despite exhortations in his ranks to build boldly, repeatedly told those directly helping him with the cathedral project that they should not attempt too much. He instructed, "A small Cathedral—with clear strong lines—solidly built is all we want," and added that it should be "simple" and also one that "we can easily preach in."[18] He insisted, "There is no use in our attempting to rival New York or Brooklyn."[19] But others in Newark had more lofty aspirations.

A START: THE CATHEDRAL CHAPEL OF OUR LADY AND SAINT PATRICK

When construction teams finished the Cathedral Chapel in Newark at whose cornerstone ceremonies Father McCarthy preached his appeals to the city's Catholic residents, a reporter described it as "a neat, handsome, unique little edifice."[20] Although small and simple, it was blessed as the "Cathedral Chapel of Our Lady and Saint Patrick." Its poetic dedication, intended for the future cathedral, reflected renewed devotion to Mary among Catholics as well as the strong Irish presence in New Jersey.

The Newark priest with chief responsibility for the cathedral project, Father George Hobart Doane, gave the sermon at the chapel's dedication, attended by Newark luminaries, including former governor Marcus L. Ward, and many Catholics from around the city. When Bishop Bayley had written to another bishop a few years before, saying that he wanted Father Doane "to begin my new cathedral which is much needed," he acknowledged both the diocese's hopes and the priest's gifts.[21] With a sophisticated appreciation of all the arts, and especially architecture, few clergy in America, and certainly no Catholic, was better suited to the work of church building than Father Doane. He, if anyone, could judge an architect's ability and serve as a discerning client. However, there was more to it than that.

Sensitivity about the religion of the architects and builders chosen for such projects was acute. It reflected the ethnic and denominational divides of the era and yet also arose from the building of Saint Patrick's in New York, whose architect, James Renwick, was not Catholic. Although Renwick's work was admired, hiring across denominational lines in this sectarian period, especially for such a visible commission, raised hackles. But New York's Hughes daringly recognized that at the time no American Catholic architect could realize his ambitions.[22] This did not shield him. When the Brooklyn diocese announced its own cathedral plans, the *New-York Freeman's Journal and Catholic Register* took the opportunity to sling arrows at the New York archdiocese and laud the sagacity of Brooklyn Catholics in having selected "a Catholic architect to build their Cathedral." "For there is one thing that cannot be done: A Protestant mason may build up a substantial wall. A Protestant carpenter can do decent wood-work. But, a Protestant architect can never build a Catholic Cathedral that will not be a jest and failure! It is a lie on the face of it."[23]

Father Doane knew that the Newark Catholic who designed the cathedral chapel, Jeremiah O'Rourke, could provide plans equal to those of any American. That was not enough. Doane urged that the diocese look to England, whose influence on the American architectural scene remained preeminent and where there were a good handful of well-trained Catholic architects. Doane believed that O'Rourke should work in conjunction with a British firm, joining in design development and providing local supervision. This arrangement won on all fronts. It held promise for the design's artistic merits, the diocese avoided the opprobrium Catholics would heap upon it if a non-Catholic were selected; and a British firm would give the project cachet. At the same time, O'Rourke's membership on the team was another pennant of Newark pride: a local resident would be a partner in an international venture to plan and build the cathedral.

Higher Ground

The Newark cathedral project veered in another direction even before the Cathedral Chapel of Our Lady and Saint Patrick was finished. Father Doane learned that a pair of Newark banking and real estate investors, Peter H. Doremus and Hiram M. Rhodes, had several lots in the northern part of the city for sale. Newark's lovely topography stretches over a low-lying expanse of long ridges that ascend gently higher as they progress westward. The parcels in question—on one of which Newark's cathedral would ultimately be built—were on one of these rises, prominent enough that it was known as "Mount Prospect." Father Doane said that the cathedral site commanded "a view of the Orange Mountains on the West and Newark Valley, the hills of Staten Island and New York on the East."[24] A writer for the *American Architect and Building News* in this decade described an elevation close by: "The view is vast and of peculiar beauty. On the east, the natural front, is a bird's eye view of the entire city of Newark, which lies in the valley below, dividing into East Newark and Newark proper by the Passaic River. At the lighting of the lamps the scene is magnificent. The smoke and blaze of many factories, together with the crossing lines of street lamps, repeated for miles, present an illuminated picture of ideal brilliancy. Over beyond Newark, . . . across Newark Bay, nine or ten miles away, lies the ocean, narrowing into New York Bay, and at its head the city of New York."[25]

Views from this location would certainly be impressive. But with the open swath sweeping around it—low-lying Newark proper, the Meadowlands, the Passaic River basin—and with light spilling onto the plain between the Watchung Mountains to the west and the Palisades to the east, a monumental building erected on the small promontory would be visible for miles and miles.

These undeveloped parcels intrigued Bishop Bayley when he heard about them, and he asked Jeremiah O'Rourke to evaluate them and other parcels in north Newark. A further reason for finding another site had also emerged. Diocesan leaders concluded that few Catholics lived, or were likely to live, near the South Park area.[26] And the smart money thought that north Newark would see greater development. This consideration underscored a cathedral's double purpose. It functions both as the bishop's own church and a local parish, serving a congregation from the neighborhood around it. A spike in real estate values in downtown Newark added another incentive: the diocese could sell the parcel there, pay off the mortgage, cover improvements made on it, and net a surplus to put toward constructing the new cathedral.

The new location seemed to offer spectacular promise. No decision would be more fundamental to the visual impact of the cathedral that would be erected than this one. And broader influences came into play in this critical matter.

Siting of Cathedrals

Church officials in the United States were well aware of the potential symbolic effect of large churches and what they said to Catholics and non-Catholics alike. These structures proclaimed in architecture the Church's growing presence and power. Catholics might have a low, fragile place in the social order of their new country, but they could rally behind building big, high-reaching churches, symbols of pride and instruments of promotion. Maximizing the effect of new cathedrals was a frank desire of many bishops, especially by the selection of a prominent site and, whenever possible, one with a high elevation relative to its surroundings. The cathedral in Baltimore stood on a hill overlooking Baltimore Harbor. Bishop McCloskey in Albany chose land that assured that his cathedral would be seen from the Hudson River (just as it would look down on it), and that its spires would reach higher than any structure then in the city. Archbishop Hughes in New York wrote that the site for the new Saint Patrick's was "the most elevated and most central in the city."[27] The location of the future Brooklyn cathedral was on a hilly prominence in a fashionable section of the city.

The impetus for such siting might be traced to Charles Borromeo, the Counter-Reformation cardinal and reformer, who urged that major churches be in a prominent location and, when possible, on an elevated site.[28] Although the custom of arranging churches with an east-facing altar had arisen early in Christendom, no Church directive prescribed this, and, once a location for a new cathedral was identified, the persistent goal was to dramatize the presence and architectural impact of the great structure. And this, we shall see, became the intention in Newark.

We now must look at why Bishop Bayley had special confidence in Father Doane to lead the planning for a great cathedral for New Jersey.

3

Gothic Passions

The Doane Family

George Hobart Doane recalled his boyhood home in New Jersey as an American center for "the dissemination of the views which took their origin in Oxford, and were first broached in the 'Tracts for the Times,'" a reference to the Oxford Movement. This rightly credits his father, George Washington Doane, as one of the most influential forces in both the High Church wing of Episcopalianism and the Gothic Revival in America.

The elder Doane was rector of Trinity Church in Boston when his first son was born in 1830. Elected the Protestant Episcopal bishop of New Jersey several years later, he moved his family to Burlington, situated on the Delaware River between Trenton and Philadelphia. As the bishop of New Jersey, George Washington Doane pushed tirelessly for the opening of new parishes and church-affiliated institutions. Widely perceived as brilliant and fantastically energetic, he published tracts, sermons, stories, and poems at a furious rate. His hymn texts (including "Thou Art the Way" and "Softly Now the Light of Day") became interdenominational classics. The bishop knew a host of leading Anglicans: John Keble, Edward Pusey, Henry Edward Manning (later a Roman Catholic cardinal), and the poet William Wordsworth. The first American invited to preach in England since the Revolution, Doane, in the words of an admirer, "could out-preach, out-vote, and out-work the whole of his brethren in the Episcopate."[1]

Bishop Doane and the American Gothic Revival

By fostering the High Church movement in the Episcopal Church, Bishop Doane helped stimulate a vibrant new interest in reviving the Gothic style.

He zealously studied English Gothic churches, closely followed the ecclesiological movement, and joined in establishing its outpost here, the New-York Ecclesiological Society. For his interest and efforts, ecclesiologists of the Cambridge Camden Society elected him a patron member, the first U.S. citizen so honored.[2]

The son of a builder, Bishop Doane himself irrepressibly commissioned buildings—churches, chapels, schools, residences. And he sought the best architects available. He had the Philadelphian John Notman plan an Italianate villa as a family residence and a chapel for a nearby Episcopal girls' school.[3] He hired Richard Upjohn, in many respects America's preeminent architect, for a new church for his parish in Burlington, where Doane served as rector from the time that he became bishop of New Jersey.[4] And he promoted Frank Wills, another English-born designer and the first official architect of the New-York Ecclesiological Society, who returned the complement by dedicating his influential book *Ancient English Ecclesiastical Architecture* to the bishop. (Upjohn and Wills, born in England, and Notman, originally from Scotland, were on the short list of architects approved by the Anglican Ecclesiological Society.)

The bishop's wife, Eliza Greene Callahan Perkins Doane, from a wealthy Boston family, helped fund these building projects and other institutions.[5] She was known and revered for quiet acts of charity to the needy—providing for the care of infirm neighbors (she was chronically unwell herself), secretly dispatching gifts and holiday meals to poor families, sending support to less well-off clergy working under her husband—compassion and altruism that registered permanently on Mrs. Doane's alert sons. Mrs. Doane's independent means also assured those sons a childhood of privileges and pleasures. Not long after the family moved to New Jersey, the artist Henry Inman painted a double portrait of George and William, capturing in oil the charmed world of their youth.[6] More than that, on a distant horizon behind the Doane boys Inman also added, with a few brush strokes, the prophetic imagery of a little Gothic church.

The bishop's magnetism drew a host of Episcopal and Anglican leaders to "Riverside," the name he gave to the stylish villa that Notman designed for him on the banks of the Delaware. In its Gothic rooms, religious and architectural matters were discussed with knowledge and enthusiasm. And as his sons, George Hobart Doane and William Croswell Doane, grew up, they joined in this High Church salon.[7] In this milieu, and by watching the construction of a series of outstanding structures owing to their father's initiative, they came to appreciate the role of architecture (and architects) in realizing the vision of Bishop Doane's Christian—Gothic—utopia.

Doctor, Then Deacon

George Hobart Doane attended Burlington College, the local church school his father established to provide "a thorough preparatory and university training."[8] An honors student intent on becoming a doctor, he proceeded to Jefferson Medical College in Philadelphia, where he was a pupil of the highly regarded Dr. Thomas Dent Mütter. Jefferson, in addition to its renown as a center for medical study, would be immortalized by Thomas Eakins's paintings of the Gross Clinic and the Agnew Clinic, two of the greatest American nineteenth-century paintings. And Dr. Mütter's anatomical and pathological specimens would form the nucleus of the amazing Mütter Museum at the College of Physicians of Philadelphia. Not long after going to Jefferson, George told his father that he wanted to leave to prepare for the ministry, but Bishop Doane urged him to complete his medical training. George dutifully finished Jefferson's rigorous lecture and clinical course (with emphasis on chemistry and surgery) and went on from Jefferson to advanced training under specialists in eye disease in Paris and Vienna, then the world's leading centers for such study.

Doane never treated ocular pathology or practiced any medicine.[9] Beset by the first of two crises of vocation and identity, he persuaded his father, by this time willing to be convinced, to allow him to begin theological studies in preparation for ordination to the Episcopal priesthood. His younger brother, William, had already been ordained deacon, joined the New-York Ecclesiological Society, and was on a fast track to a bishop's seat of his own. George read theology, and briefly taught chemistry at his old school, Burlington College. Ordained a deacon (by his father), he went to Grace Church in Newark as an assistant. Grace Church, designed by Richard Upjohn and dedicated by Bishop Doane, was a locus of High Church activity in the largest city in his father's diocese. Here, upon a path offering vistas of a brilliant future as an Episcopal clergyman, the new deacon fell into a chasm of doubt about the legitimacy of Anglican theology and priestly orders.

In Newman's Steps

The story of Doane's second personal crisis began with an episode that entered Newark lore. On a Saturday evening, having just visited his father in Burlington, he was returning to Newark by train. It stopped in Rahway and, by chance, Newark's Catholic bishop, James Roosevelt Bayley, boarded and took a seat in the same coach. Doane silently watched the bishop as the train rattled north, but they did not exchange a word and, arriving in Newark, went separate ways, Bayley to his residence at the cathedral and Doane to the Grace Church rectory. A little later, preparing for the next day's service, George was overcome with anxiety and, telling no one, rushed out and hurried north through downtown Newark to Saint Patrick's Cathedral, in search of Bayley. He found a sexton closing up after confessions and was directed to the rectory on Bleeker Street. The priest who came to the door refused—at eleven o'clock on a Saturday night—to summon the bishop. The agitated visitor insisted that he had to speak to him. Told of the caller, Bayley sent word for Doane to make an appointment. The young man would not leave.

Doane had reason to expect a sympathetic ear. Both Bayley and Doane were from affluent Episcopal families and, as we have seen, Bayley had also studied medicine before being drawn to religious service. He fast became a major figure in the American Catholic Church. On that momentous August 1855 night in Newark, as other priests in the Bishop's House had backstairs talk about the uninvited visitor, Roosevelt Bayley capitulated and met with Doane, conducting an emotional interview that ended in the small hours.

On the other side of the state, in the days after this drama, Bishop Doane said that only two days after seeing his son happy and tender at home in Burlington, he was "a Papal petrifaction: his fine feelings all frozen up, and his beautiful features hardened into marble."[10] His father insisted that he take a vacation in Newport, Rhode Island, presumably hoping that its ocean air and proper society would bring his first-born to his senses. In Newark, Bishop Bayley called for prudence and discernment. Untethered, Doane found himself in a spiritual and emotional no-man's land: "Most unwillingly I found myself afloat, adrift, no longer a Protestant, nor yet a Catholic. God only knows Who led me safely through what I endured—the thought of the grief at home, the breaking up of ties, and of associations which were dearer to me than life itself, the imputation of false motives—everything . . . which the heart most dreads, stood before me to keep me back."[11]

But he would not be kept back, and Bayley agreed to receive him into the Catholic Church. Doane thus forced his father's hand.[12] As the Episcopal bishop of New Jersey, George Washington Doane had to depose his son, effectively excommunicating him. It dealt a heart wound, the parent cried, that "must go with me, into the grave, and bring me sooner there."[13] In his fastidious grammar, aggrieved Bishop Doane wrote, "If I am asked to explain this strange and instantaneous transmutation, I must do so in his own words; and leave it, to whoever will, to frame the theory. To one, he said, that, 'it flashed across his mind, in the train . . . that his ministry might not be valid,' To another, that he 'felt something snap, in his head.' To me, that he left the house of his Rector, to whom he gave no word or sign of intimation of his doubts, 'in a state of perfect frenzy.'"[14]

What snapped in George's head and brought on a state of perfect frenzy? In religious terms, it could be described as a moment of revelation and grace. It was surely more. The Catholic Church's tradition and authority were moorings for some set spiritually adrift in the aftermath of the Enlightenment and the scientific and industrial revolutions; an unusual number of Protestants converted to Catholicism in this period.[15] And whatever else it may have been, young George's break was an oedipal revolt: a strong son's flight from a titanic father and the institution he embodied. Other conscious and unconscious motivations probably played a part, but now only the urgency and authenticity of the young man's life-changing feelings seem knowable. What is certain, however, is that George's actions inflicted a deep trauma on the Doane family. That blow was compounded because it involved a promising cleric and a prominent bishop who had already struggled with fellow Episcopalians over matters of theology, liturgy, and administrative practice. As in England, those opposed to the High Church movement warned that inclinations toward the ways of Rome could lead there; much of the nastiness between the Ecclesiological Society and Pugin, who shared many aims, had been the result of the designer's conversion. And there was always the example of John Henry Newman, young George's new hero and exemplar, and the most brilliant Oxford Tractarian, who had famously converted to Catholicism. After George's break, in order to deflect reproach or worse, Bishop Doane broadcast that "there is not a house, on earth," that had less "sympathy with Rome" than Riverside.[16]

Although George claimed later that his doubts about Anglicanism coalesced slowly and that seeing Bishop Bayley in the Newark-bound train was the catalyzing moment that brought action, the abrupt turn shocked all who knew him. A reconciliation between father and son occurred after several years. Even this transpired with the Doane panache. Father George was a popular preacher throughout the diocese, and the news that he was coming to Burlington for Sunday mass caused a stir in his hometown. When the local Catholics entered their small church that morning, they saw altars laden with flowers sent from the bishop's lovely garden at Riverside. Rapprochement was achieved but turned out to be short. Hastened or not by the breach, as he feared it would, Bishop Doane's death a few years later closed an anguished chapter in the life of a distinguished family. Mrs. Doane died the next year in Italy, where she had been living.

New Priest and Parishioner: Doane and O'Rourke

On Newman's path, James Roosevelt Bayley trod; not far behind him walked George Hobart Doane. Bishop Bayley sent Doane to France for study and then to Rome, where he enrolled at the Collegio Pio, founded just a few years before for converts and dominated by Englishmen.[17] Here, Doane not only explored Roman Catholicism at its institutional heart, but in keeping company with British seminarians, he encountered a Catholic culture unlike any he had known. The Doanes were ardent Anglophiles, and the rarified world of the cultivated, companionable English Catholics living in Rome merged the Doane fondness for English ways with George's fresh religious feeling. In many respects, it was a milieu of perfect happiness that suited George Hobart Doane as none in the United States could.

Doane was ordained a Catholic priest, and Bishop Bayley made him his secretary (marking him immediately for possible advancement in the Church) and assigned him to Saint Patrick's Cathedral, Newark, where Jeremiah O'Rourke was an active member of the cathedral parish.[18] If the new curate had not known Jeremiah before, they would surely have met in 1857. When Jeremiah opened his own architectural practice two years later, it would be apparent how significant their association had become.

4

Father Doane and Jeremiah O'Rourke

Architectural Collaborators

JEREMIAH O'ROURKE, a refugee from the Irish Famine, in 1850 came to Newark, where his extended family settled. For the O'Rourkes, immigration was a relatively brief reversal of fortune. Jeremiah's father ran a successful tailor shop in Dublin, where Jeremiah was born in 1833. Just a few years before, Irish Catholics had won civil liberties following centuries of oppression, and enterprising men like the elder O'Rourke entered the economic mainstream. It placed his family apart from most Irish, who remained rural-dwelling and desperately poor. Jeremiah attended a Dublin school run by the Christian Brothers, who rigorously inculcated Church doctrine and taught all subjects through a Catholic lens. Thus, at home and at school he absorbed the extreme religiosity of nineteenth-century Irish Catholicism and its deep moral imperatives. There was even an ecclesiastical side to his father's business. Steps from the O'Rourke's combined household and shop stood the gates of All Hallows College, a Catholic seminary whose faculty and students came and went from the O'Rourke establishment to be fitted in the black cassocks that Jeremiah's father made. This bounded, Church-oriented environment channeled the young O'Rourke's artistic interest into a desire to become an architect of Catholic buildings.[1]

Jeremiah enrolled in the Royal Dublin Society's school of drawing, Ireland's foremost institution for the study of art and allied subjects.[2] Its students pursued a curriculum divided into four schools (or areas) of draftsmanship: figure, landscape and ornament, architecture, and modeling.[3] Aspiring architects were expected to apprentice later with established architects or builders to learn the science of building. For about a year, his studies enthralled O'Rourke, but the Famine forced him to leave them and Ireland behind. Jeremiah's entire immediate family eventually settled in Newark. His father opened a grocery, and, pushing through the rough passages of immigration, the O'Rourkes' lives soon matched the modest gentility they knew in Dublin.

Jeremiah's own professional ambitions were tested but not shaken by leaving Ireland. He was hired by a Newark designer and builder, Jonathan V. Nichols, whose office produced commercial, residential, and institutional work and some of the region's firehouses. At the time, the architectural profession in America was in its infancy. There were no architectural schools, societies, or journals, and designer and builder were often the same. Nichols, for instance, advertised himself as both. At one of his drafting tables, Jeremiah, disciplined and exacting, undertook what was known as office training. Measuring and drawing, consulting established formulas for calculating weights and loads, he worked out the visual and textual instructions by which an idea for a building is transformed into a practical guide for builders.[4] Visits to building sites grounded the neophyte designer in construction methods and practices. About the time that O'Rourke started with Nichols, the *Advertiser* carried a note about local architectural developments and Nichols's firm: "The residences in our suburbs have also undergone a change in character. Many of them are of the so called Gothic style first introduced here we believe by Mr. Jonathan V. Nichols."[5] O'Rourke thus participated in spreading the Gothic cause in his earliest professional activity. Many of O'Rourke's work tasks manifested talents and skills—design, measurement, precision—that were intrinsic to his father's tailoring. And as his father had made priests' cassocks, he would make their churches.

Opportunity Taken

For Jeremiah, the double adversity of leaving Ireland and arriving in a place of doubtful hospitality gave way to opportunity. Catholic immigrants created a need for more and more new churches and ancillary buildings: rectories, schools, convents, and affiliated institutions. There was never a more propitious moment in the United States, and New Jersey specifically, to start a career in ecclesiastical architecture.[6] O'Rourke later claimed that when he opened his office in 1859, it was the first firm in Newark operating under "modern conditions"—offering architectural services exclusively, with none of the blended role of designer and builder common earlier.

Two years after opening his office, O'Rourke married Elizabeth Cecilia Dunn, the daughter of William Dunn, a pre-Famine Irish émigré who prospered in the leather trades. Transforming animal skins into a usable commodity was hideously slimy and fetid work. But because of low barriers to entry (it more required ambition and a stomach for the task than investment capital), it was then a promising route to financial independence in Newark, where many streets and stretches of river reeked of odors of a trade that could make business owners and independent operators prosperous. O'Rourke's father-in-law leveraged his success by gaining a stake in local financial firms, including the Howard Savings Institution. The Howard opened in 1857 to provide banking services to a neglected market of working-class people who, with their small savings, were becoming homeowners and starting businesses. It was a strategy that turned it into a top regional financial house and provided for the comfort of Dunn's extended family. In his orbit, O'Rourke could not have married better; income from his father-in-law's investments over the years steadied the volatile revenue streams typical of an architectural practice. Jeremiah soon settled his family at 45 Burnet Street, on a block of pleasant two- and three-story row houses, not far from his architectural office on Broad Street and a short walk from Saint Patrick's Cathedral, where Father Doane lived.[7]

O'Rourke's first independent commissions emerged from the expanding Catholic presence throughout New Jersey. The earliest were chapel-size structures in Mendham and Phillipsburg. Mendham, a Morris County hamlet nestled amid farms, small mills, and factory operations, had a mission that had grown enough by 1858 to require a building. It was served at that juncture by Father William McNulty, who was working at the new institution of Seton Hall, then located outside of Madison. McNulty previously was in Newark, where he almost certainly knew both O'Rourke and Father Doane. O'Rourke provided a scheme that resembles any number of churches put up on both sides of the Atlantic in the previous fifteen years, and yet it has direct parentage: Saint James the Less in Philadelphia and Christ Church in Newark.[8]

The journal of the New-York Ecclesiological Society carried an article in 1849 about planning small churches that was accompanied by an illustration captioned "First Pointed Church."[9] The designer was Frank Wills. On the list of designers approved by the society, Wills was the author of *Ancient English Ecclesiastical Architecture,* which he dedicated to Bishop Doane. This model church supplied the pattern for the design of Christ

Church in eastern Newark, spawned by Newark's Grace Church, to which the Doane family, as we have seen, had strong ties.[10] O'Rourke, in turn, carried them over for his early works. Although constructed of wood, an expedient often accepted by America congregations, the Mendham church conveyed clear aspirations: prominent buttresses fronted the facade, which held three lancet windows and a bell cote. Visible in the dim light of the interior, a modest display of roof beams articulated its structural bones and hinted at ecclesiological ideals. A similar approach was taken for the Phillipsburg church near the same time.[11]

Within a year of these preparatory exercises, O'Rourke received the commission for a new church in Boonton that provided the opportunity to realize more fully the Wills-derived scheme, this time built of local stone, the preferred material of the ecclesiologists. Boonton was founded on the basis of iron ore and related businesses, and its many Catholics worked in local mines. From these they brought the stones for the church's rubble walls. Thus the geological formation in which parishioners extracted iron ore, the source of their livelihoods, also yielded their church's fabric. Symbolism is the bedrock upon which the architectural movement that produced Our Lady of Mount Carmel rose. It never went deeper than in Boonton.

Seton Hall Projects: Come War or Fire

Two projects for Seton Hall in South Orange lifted O'Rourke's fledgling practice. The first, a chapel built of dressed local brownstone, was a more elaborate rendition of the Boonton church, with decorated window tracery, a side porch, and a deep chancel.[12] O'Rourke completed plans for the chapel, but building it was another matter. The Civil War upturned the diocese and Seton Hall no less than other American institutions. Many regional businesses had ties to southern markets, and the Union cause at first met local resistance. Father Doane (and Father Bernard McQuaid, too) is credited with being among the first to persuade Newarkers of the necessity for the war. As men began enlisting, Doane jumped into action, insisting to Bishop Bayley that he be sent as a chaplain. With his appointment to the New Jersey First Regiment, Doane joined the Union's earliest soldiers to enter the war. Newark was well represented among those who mustered at Trenton and took boats south to dig fortifications along the Potomac to protect Washington. It was there that the men of New Jersey's First spent virtually all of their three-month tour. Father Doane, saying mass and hearing confessions, was quartered with Newark's Brigadier General Theodore

Runyon and other military brass. With only three days of duty remaining, out of the blue came the First Battle of Bull Run. Doane rushed to the action in northern Virginia and, at times under fire, attended the wounded, dying, and dead, many of them hardly out of boyhood. He knew the gore of the surgeon's table from his medical school days, but the gruesome ministry in the blood-soaked fields and camps around Bull Run horrified him. He wrote to Bayley to say he was safe. "I do not enter into the details of the battle as the newspapers will give you these. It was a terrible one on both sides, and the carnage has been dreadful."[13] The experience was shattering for Doane, and after recuperating, he did not reenlist but returned to Newark to help Bayley run the diocese.

After the war and just as life at Seton Hall was stabilizing, the diocese faced another kind of fire. A conflagration destroyed the villa that served as Seton Hall's main facility. Out of its ashes arose an opportunity for O'Rourke to work on a large scale. The varied elevations, belfry, and quiet embellishments that he gave his new Main Building formed a picturesque profile that, when it opened in 1867, displayed O'Rourke's competency in handling bigger projects.

When Seton Hall's chapel was finally consecrated in 1870, it was appropriate that Father Doane was called on to preach at the dedication, for the design descended from the same Doane-connected models as O'Rourke's previous churches. The timber roof's hammerbeam system and tracery was a particular glory. As mentioned, Pugin exulted in the medieval roofs, saying, "The construction of these, far from being concealed, is turned into ornament . . . this essential portion of a building becomes its greatest beauty."[14] That certainly held true for this building. The Seton Hall chapel, with an interior both monumental and warmly intimate, became O'Rourke's thesis in the Gothic style. Located at the heart of Newark diocesan affairs, it became a demonstration piece that propelled his career as a church architect.

CHURCHES IN CAMDEN, ORANGE, AND PRINCETON

While the Seton Hall projects were under way, O'Rourke received a commission for a new church in Camden, New Jersey. The refined lines of his Church of the Immaculate Conception adhered to ecclesiological models for a large parish. The idea for the detached, flanking tower probably came from Saint Mark's in nearby Philadelphia, an important Episcopal church by John Notman, who, as we have seen, had received commissions from George Washington Doane, again attesting to this family's influence on

O'Rourke's early architecture.[15] The Camden parish at the time only had enough money to put up the nave and chancel, yet Immaculate Conception was admired. It amazed Bishop Bayley, who gave the pastor credit for creating such a beautiful building "with such poor means."[16] And a writer from New York thought that it was "[a] gem of architectural taste. It shows a unity of design, and fertility in detail, for the promotion of piety, that is worthy of adoption elsewhere. Father Byrnes [*sic*] . . . has few that are not the poor. But, from their devotion, he has been enabled to build, on the finest square in Camden, a church that, if it were in one of the oldest Catholic countries, would command attention for its elegance."[17]

Orange, a Newark suburb, prospered in the 1860s with the brisk growth of local light industry, especially hat making. In 1864, its Catholic parish, Saint John the Evangelist, welcomed a new pastor. Father Edward Hickey's previous assignment was at Saint Patrick's in Newark, where he came to know both Father Doane and his prominent parishioner, Jeremiah O'Rourke. He quickly began planning a larger church for his burgeoning parish and asked O'Rourke to design it. *The Advertiser* reported on the church they envisioned: "Situated upon a rising ground . . . it will, when completed[,] present a beautiful sight for miles around, with its graceful tower of two hundred feet in height. The length of the building will be one hundred and sixty feet, and seventy the width. The estimated cost, it is believed, will reach $100,000. It cannot fail to prove an adornment to the city of Orange, whose citizens justly boast of many sumptuous public and private buildings."[18]

The $100,000 estimate for Saint John's was double the cost of a typical stone church from this period, an amount that seemed manageable when the project was born. Adding to the sense of good times and architectural distinction in the vicinity was Llewellyn Park, the first planned suburban village in the United States, whose villas and cultivated grounds were developed the decade before. The brownstone masonry used to build Saint John's, in fact, came from local quarries owned by Llewellyn Haskell, who developed Llewellyn Park and which Haskell, a Protestant, donated.

In designing Saint John's, O'Rourke again called upon ecclesiological models for large parishes, including Pugin's Saint Giles Church in Cheadle, along with French features.[19] The Cheadle church prompted John Henry Newman to say that it was "the most splendid building I ever saw."[20] Saint Giles's two hundred–foot tower and spire, with its distinctive tabernacles and crocketing, appear in another guise in O'Rourke's Saint John's design. "A heaven-pointing spire surrounded by clusters of pinnacles," Pugin thought, formed "a beautiful and instructive emblem of a Christian's brightest hopes."[21] What Pugin wanted for all major churches, O'Rourke wanted in Orange, New Jersey. The latter's interior ornament aspired to match the richness of its most elaborate models.[22] Three years after Saint John's was started, and though its tower, spire, and porches were left undone, it was ready for use. Father Isaac Hecker, the brilliant founder of the Missionary Society of Saint Paul (the Paulists), who also had close ties to Father Doane, came from New York to preach at the dedication service. Hecker, from the pulpit, said that many people in Orange were surprised that the parish had erected such a beautiful church, conjecturing that it probably puzzled them how poor people had the resources to raise "churches so capacious and magnificent."[23] Soon (as will be discussed in chapter 7), it became evident that there was good reason to have been puzzled.

Father Doane was a popular preacher at church ceremonies. When he gave the sermon at the 1869 cornerstone laying for a new church in Princeton, his "presence . . . attracted many, who came to listen to this great convert priest."[24] Saint Paul's had regretted that its church was "not in keeping with the architectural beauty of other buildings in town" and now able to afford a new one, the parish wanted it to compare favorably with the architecture around it.[25] Princeton's Catholics were right to recognize that they lived amidst distinctive buildings. Among the fine houses was "Prospect," which eventually became the residence of the president of Princeton University, and was designed by John Notman, architect of the Doane family's Burlington villa.

O'Rourke's design for Saint Paul's Church, very different from his previous work, broke from the ecclesiological models that he had employed. Like many architects in this period, he heard the call of John Ruskin, who persuaded his fellow Englishmen and their American imitators of the beauties of Italian Gothic. Ruskinian Gothic, as it became known, was often built in brick with polychrome patterns, and this is what O'Rourke specified for the Princeton church.[26] Picturesque and unique, Saint Paul's conveyed the intention of parish and architect to keep pace with the world around them, but it was so unlike Princeton's other churches that it must have looked anomalous.

On Pugin's Wing

Although the Princeton church's syntax probably seemed foreign, in fact, all Catholic churches in America were typologically a world apart. Most Protestant churches were likely to be in some form of a comparatively straightforward meeting house or assembly hall, which ranged from a simple box to quietly elegant, from vernacular to stylistically proficient.

A Catholic church's elaborate altars, tabernacles, relics, statues, murals, stained glass, candles, bells, incense, flowers, and other sacramental and symbolic accoutrements and devices were part of a separatist religious culture and "helped to create the sense that one was in a sacred space where familiar intercourse between this world and the other world could take place.[27] And O'Rourke's opinions were pronounced, if Catholics chose Protestant-style structures for their churches.[28] When a scheme that he regarded as particularly deficient was being considered by a pastor in the Newark diocese, Jeremiah ranted that if it was built, the church would be "another of those Methodist barns, the erection of which throughout the Diocese is enough to make the spirit of the elder Pugin wing its way across the Atlantic and ring in our ears his noble and thoroughly Catholic 'Plea for the revival of Christian Architecture.'"[29]

O'Rourke's early churches, more than those of any Catholic architect in the United States, closely followed the designs favored by Pugin and the ecclesiologists. They thus constitute a distinct episode in the American Gothic Revival and in Catholic church building in this country. Like their English Catholic counterparts, Doane and O'Rourke also believed that they were returning this style of building to its original—and proper—use: for Roman Catholic worship. Indeed, for such men, these structures were more than architectural ventures. Building them was infused with religious purpose, fulfilling what Pugin claimed: "The greatest privilege possessed by man is to be allowed, while on earth, to contribute to the glory of God: a man who builds a church draws down a blessing on himself both for this life and that of the world to come, and likewise imparts under God the means of every blessing to his fellow creatures."[30]

Doane and O'Rourke, and others like them, believed wholly in a church's mystical use and meaning, certain it was nothing less than the house of God.

It was in the ardent context of Doane and O'Rourke's church planning that they took up the Newark cathedral project, the ultimate religious and architectural expression of their ideals. They spared nothing. Doane arranged an ecclesiastical grand tour to cull ideas for the new cathedral, charting a course of old and recent Gothic buildings through England and Europe. They also met with possible architects in England (and with Father Doane's friends along the way). Their aim, indeed their obsession, was to return to Newark with a design that would be worthy of the expanding Catholic presence in New Jersey and in America, and one that would serve as a symbol of religious and civic pride in the vigorous city that they had adopted as home.

5

Newark's Gothic Pilgrims Abroad

Boarding the steamer *Russia*, Cunard Line's newest and first all-propeller-driven ship, in May 1870, Father Doane and Jeremiah O'Rourke headed off on their mission. Doane wrote lengthy letters home for publication in the *Advertiser* that made Newarkers fellow-travelers on a journey that the priest was sure would lead to the creation of the finest building in their city. His telling installments recorded their course and what caught their eye and interest.

Old Gothic

Having seen two of Britain's most glorious medieval cathedrals, Doane wrote from the north of England: "One day York, the next Durham with an architectural feast of the greatest abundance. The one the splendour of Gothic architecture, the other the majesty of Norman, choose—there is no choice. Each is perfect in its way and he must be narrow-minded who cannot accept and enjoy them both."[1] In Durham Cathedral they cast their eyes on the arcade's decorated shafts and up to the rib vaults rising from them, the earliest surviving example of such vaulting. And outside they saw what has delighted many others: the cathedral's hillside site overlooking the River Wear valley. This would—if they could secure the land on higher ground that they had discussed before leaving—become a model for Newark. From Durham, they headed north to Scotland. Doane described the train's approach to Edinburgh for his Newark audience, including its picturesque hills and the medieval castle. But by this time he was Gothic-tipsy and said in disdain that the view toward the castle was marred by "a rage for classical architecture which seems to have seized the good people of Edinburgh, as it did the people of other places some years ago, and which spent itself peppering Calton Hill with two or three very ugly monuments, and erecting two long buildings . . . which catch and distract the eye."[2] It distressed Doane, as he could see in Edinburgh, that classicism had once been favored. He regarded this instance of classical architecture in modern Britain as a lapse in good taste made worse because it spoiled the prospect of a Gothic landmark.

They went to Melrose to see the ruins of the medieval monastery, a favored outing for the romantically inclined Victorians.[3] The survival of parts can convey the essence of a structure as it once was, the skeleton revealing the methods and materials used to create the former whole. Studying the vertebrae of this monastic complex, Doane (and presumably O'Rourke, too) came to a startling conclusion: "Nothing can be of a greater condemnation of most of the modern work than the details of Melrose Abbey."[4] Doane had encountered real Gothic architecture and seen the style as if for the first time! Pugin himself confessed to such an awakening, "When I have done my best and when compared with the puny and meager abortions of the day I have produced a sturdy effect, yet how terribly do my efforts sink when tested by the scale of ancient excellence."[5]

Pugin wrote persuasively in *True Principles* about the value of careful study of actual medieval work, and on that Scottish heath, Doane and O'Rourke could see the master's wisdom. Melrose, Doane declared, was "a perfect study in all its parts and details."[6] He also noted, "The stone is red sand-stone, almost the same as our Paterson sand-stone, but what an eye for beauty the architect must have had!" The sculpting of the stone amazed them. Comparing modern Gothic to its models, Doane reported: "The designs are to a certain extent imitated, but the depth upon which everything depends is wanting." Doane drew an important conclusion from their study of Melrose Abbey: "It would be well if our modern Gothic architects would go there to learn the depth to give their window and door moulding if they would in any way reproduce buildings like those of the olden time."

From Melrose they went to see Walter Scott's nearby home, Abbotsford House, and his grave at Dryburgh Abbey. More than any novelist, Scott cast the medieval spell over the English-speaking world in the nineteenth century and their detour to his shrines was the literary counterpart of visiting Gothic Revival architectural sites.

New Gothic

The Newark pair were equally alert to newer buildings, particularly Catholic churches. In Manchester, they saw Salford Cathedral, "one of the finest of the new Gothic buildings in England."[7] Its architect had more recently done an interior scheme for it, by which time he was assisted by a young designer called George Goldie, who will figure in Newark's plans. Visiting Preston, they ducked into Saint Walburge's Church, whose hammerbeam roof, springing from full-figure sculptures standing on corbels, makes it one the most wonderful of all Victorian churches. Doane ranked Gilbert Scott's nearby new Gothic town hall "noble," and its interior, he thought, "beautiful beyond conception." In Oxford, Doane's contacts at the highest reaches of the university summoned a vice-principal (a senior Oxford administrator) to act as their guide. They took in the customary highlights and the "New Museum," with its Italian Gothic arches and structural polychrome—a seminal building that pointed to a new direction in the Revival and that O'Rourke had already incorporated into his design for Saint Paul's in Princeton.

They gave Pugin's works special notice. At Nottingham, in the Midlands of England, they went to Saint Barnabas Cathedral, a large cruciform church with ancillary structures. They also spent time at educational institutions, places that corresponded to their own Seton Hall. Near Birmingham, they stayed at Saint Mary's College, Oscott, where Pugin was appointed to the faculty and Doane informed his readers, "Most of the architectural work is by the older Pugin."[8] Oscott College, as it is known, was one of the theological and liturgical engine rooms of the revival of Catholicism in Britain in the nineteenth century; every aspect of what Newman called the "Second Spring" of English Catholicism transfixed Doane. Indeed, in Birmingham he noted, "I had the pleasure of seeing Dr. Newman who was as cordial and child-like as I had remembered him thirteen years before. I found him at the Oratory where he has a much frequented church and a school of some sixty seven boys."[9]

Outside Durham, the travelers surveyed Ushaw College, for which Pugin composed a chapel and where his son later did work. (In Ireland, they ventured to the leading Irish seminary, at Maynooth, where Pugin built the imposing principal building, and the correspondent thought it "the most splendid ecclesiastical seminary I have ever seen.")[10]

The pair made special arrangements to see Oulton Abbey, a cloistered convent north of Stone that had ties to Doane's influential friend Bishop

Bernard Ullathorne and Pugin, and whose chapel was an early work of Pugin's son Edward. Here, at this Benedictine convent in the English Midlands—deep in the heart of Pugin country—a window to their minds was unlatched. Doane admitted to his Newark readers: "Of all that I have seen in England, nothing has equaled this. It is small but exquisitely beautiful—nothing better than this chapel was ever done in the ages of Faith. The carving, brass and iron work are each perfect in their way. It seems like a bit of Heaven let down upon earth."[11] Heaven on earth, for Doane and O'Rourke, as for many of their generation, took Gothic form. The Chapel of the Immaculate Conception at Oulton Abbey, with its subdued light and cloistral hush, fine and very complete decoration, including rich stained glass, held the most heartening lesson for them: Despite the obstacles, it was possible in their time to equal the old Gothic builders.[12]

Doane and O'Rourke's itinerary also hinted at the decorative arts that they contemplated for the Newark cathedral's interior. They visited John Hardman & Company in Birmingham, the leading British maker of stained glass, metalwork, furniture, and fittings. Hardman and Pugin had formed a partnership to manufacture and distribute Pugin's designs, and Doane told his Newark readers: "We were shown works executed and in the process of execution. Besides the stained glass works there were works in silver and gold for chalices, etc. in brass, and in wrought iron each very perfect in their way. Hardman, the elder, was a colleague of Pugin in the revival of Gothic architecture in England."[13] Their diversion to Stoke-on-Trent and the pottery region was almost certainly to visit the famous Minton firm, where fine tiles and encaustics were produced. It executed both Pugin's custom designs and those for mass production and distribution. Both Hardman and Minton thus had direct ties to Pugin and continued to offer materials based on his designs (and through overseas distributors) that served the American church market.

On the Continent

On the Continent, Doane and O'Rourke juggled their itinerary and hurried to Rome, so not to miss the 1870 Ecclesiastical Arts Exhibition. The nineteenth-century church building boom, like the Western economy that made it possible, was at a peak, and a diverse, international industry had risen up to supply it. The exhibition spread out in the large cloister of Santa Maria Degli Angeli in 1870 was its consummate trade fair.

The two stayed in Rome for almost a month, and there Doane had a signal honor. Pius IX, now nearing the end of the longest pontificate in history, received him. In an audience in the fabled chambers of the Vatican, Doane said the pope welcomed him "with the greatest cordiality and kindness, and in the most absolutely informal manner."[14] The pope proceeded to present Doane with a cameo of Saint Peter, in gratitude for his work in behalf of the North American College and as a souvenir of the visit.

In Rome, they paced labyrinthine streets and passages until they found the studio of Friedrich Overbeck. The German-born Overbeck shared with Pugin and the English Pre-Raphaelites a Romantic vision of the Church in the Middle Ages. The Americans' visit to his former workplace (the painter had died the previous year) confirms again the alignment of preferences between the Newark pair and Pugin, who called Overbeck "Prince of Painters."[15] Doane's appreciation for religious themes led him to say about Overbeck (not well known today outside of art historical circles) that he was "the master of his time," and he described the works they saw still hanging in the studio as "matchless drawings full of the spirit of faith finding expression in the highest form of art."[16]

The travelers moved north through Tuscany, arriving in Florence, where at the Royal Florentine Manufactory they marveled at newly made mosaics, which invites speculation that the Italian inflection that John Ruskin's influence was giving contemporary English Gothic architecture might have appeared in the new cathedral's interior. From Florence, they headed north to Pisa, Genoa, and Milan, taking in their cathedrals and other sites.

Crossing into Switzerland, at Geneva they learned of tensions and the likelihood of war between France and Germany. The brewing trouble thwarted their plan to boat down the Rhine to Cologne and then proceed overland to Paris. Doane lamented, "the recollection of our own war deepened the regret with which we see the approaching armies . . . on the banks of the Rhine."[17] The Franco-Prussian War would prove as atrocious as Doane feared, and the escalating conflict meant that they could not see Cologne Cathedral, whose completion was the best-known, large-scale Gothic project on the Continent in the nineteenth century and whose influence stretched to New York, where it strongly marked Renwick's scheme for Saint Patrick's Cathedral.

In addition to the letters published in the *Advertiser*, Doane commemorated their tour with an album of *cartes de visite* that depicted scenes of what they had actually visited and also what they had been prevented from seeing. Among the pictures are seven views of Amiens and six of Cologne, both of which were clearly among the cathedrals and potential models they hoped to study.[18] Doane's letters make no mention of Notre Dame in Paris or Chartres, which he knew from his years of study in France. In any event, Doane, on another occasion gave his own ranking of the High Gothic cathedrals: "to Amiens must go the plume."[19] (Many years later, and under different auspices, some of Amiens's features would be incorporated into the cathedral in Newark.)

The impressive roster of workshops and studios that Doane and O'Rourke sought out is evidence that they were well informed about where to source much of the finest decorative arts currently being produced. It held enormous promise for the new cathedral's interior, just as examining Gothic models for themselves and exchanging ideas about them became a traveling seminar that immeasurably refined their architectural perceptions.

An English-American Architectural Partnership

They visited London twice. While there, they attended sessions in both Houses of Parliament. The sumptuous interiors of these government buildings were principally Pugin's work, so they saw that his genius for Gothic had a secular expression. There, too, they heard Gladstone hold forth on the Irish Land Bill and were stirred, like many others, by the prime minister's oratory. Most important, O'Rourke and Doane were joined in London by Bishop Bayley, and together they met and interviewed the English architects with whom they might work.

As Doane and O'Rourke surveyed it, Pugin still hovered over the English and Irish architectural landscape. But Pugin had been dead for eighteen years, and there were now diverse strains of Gothic. To whom could they turn for the Newark project? Candidates included Pugin's sons, Edward Welby Pugin and Peter Paul Pugin. The Pugin name remained popular in Catholic circles, and Edward Pugin's practice would soon push across the Atlantic; he briefly kept an office in New York.[20] But their focus fixed instead on George Goldie. Goldie was a London architect well known in Catholic circles who was then riding a crest of major commissions in England and Ireland. He had been a student at Ushaw College (mentioned earlier as one of Doane and O'Rourke's stops), where he met A.W.N. Pugin and tried to become his pupil, but Pugin recommended that he go to Hadfield and Weightman's firm.[21] There was, therefore, a connection, though indirect, between Pugin and Goldie that doubtlessly appealed to the Americans. Goldie had recently gained two major Irish projects, and a pair of English churches had brought particular notice: Our Lady of Victories in Kensington, in central London, and Saint Wilfrid's in York.[22] Shortly after the Kensington church was finished it became the Cardinal Manning's pro-cathedral, and consequently England's premier Catholic church. Doane and O'Rourke also saw Saint Wilfrid's in York. Father Doane remarked that it was much admired: "It stands next to the Old Minster, and Cardinal Wiseman said of it, that it seemed as if the old Cathedral had sent a shoot which had sprung up with this beautiful structure—great and deserved praise. I can only say that if we succeed in Newark as well as they have in York, we will be perfectly satisfied."[23]

Higher Expectations

They completed, with Bayley's consent, arrangements for the transatlantic design partnership between Goldie, his partner, Charles Edwin Child, and Jeremiah O'Rourke.[24] The influential London *Tablet* reported on their visit and architectural errand, and confirmed what was known at home about Doane's role: "This splendid undertaking has been taken up with the utmost zeal and energy by the Reverend Mr. Doane whose name is well known as a distinguished Catholic convert and now a devoted priest of the Catholic Church."[25] The *Tablet*'s coverage, reprinted in the Newark *Advertiser*, expressed the command held by Bayley and Doane in the wider Church, and went on to offer an opinion, in the context of the Newark project, of American Catholic church architecture: "The Cathedral will, when completed, be one of the most remarkable modern ecclesiastical structures in the United States, where immense sums have been expended on ecclesiastical buildings by the zeal and energy of both clergy and laity, without the results which should have been expected."[26] This was a polite way of putting what the great American Gothicist Ralph Adams Cram wrote later in the century in an *Architectural Review* article titled "Good and Bad Gothic." Cram's splenetic lines about one of Patrick Keely's cathedrals bashed all Catholic work. Cram called it "R.C. [Roman Catholic] Gothic," which he deemed "the worst thing in the architectural world. For sheer shapelessness, poverty of line, utter lack of dignity and meagerness of parts it is a masterpiece. 'Trade Gothic' is all you can call it, cheap, thin, and futile. It is exactly wrong at every point."[27] Cram's view contained a degree of bigotry and overlooked both the challenges and achievements of the

Catholic Church in America. But some Catholic building (and allowing for notable exceptions such as the Latrobe's Baltimore cathedral and Renwick's Saint Patrick's), judged on the grounds of historical accuracy or overall refinement, was wanting. Men as sophisticated about architecture as Doane and O'Rourke were unusual in America and exceedingly rare among Catholics. They understood, as the *Tablet* had said, that a great deal of money had been spent, "without the results that should have been expected." Doane said as much when he explained his approach to commissioning churches and regretted that some thought they could do as well by hiring a builder or an inadequately trained designer (revealing also his respect for what professionals offered): "My way always had been to leave things in the hands of the architect and to be governed by his advice—that when I wanted law, I went to a lawyer—medicine, to a Doctor, etc."[28]

Newark's Gothic pilgrims were determined to avoid the artistic insularity that compromised much American Catholic building. Before leaving England, they commissioned a watercolor of the proposed cathedral by Henry W. Brewer, an accomplished artist who specialized in architectural renderings and exhibited often at the Royal Academy and the Society of British Artists. A Newark newspaper, presumably echoing Doane, described Brewer as "one of the first water color artists in England."[29] As far as Doane and O'Rourke were concerned, the drawing had to be—as with everything else about the new cathedral—nothing but the best.

6

"The Newark Cathedral"

Gothic Pilgrims at Home

EXHILARATED BY ALL THAT THEY HAD SEEN and accomplished and by their dreams for Newark, priest and architect came home, triumphant. The *Advertiser* painted this brightly lit scene of Doane's return:

> The serenade to Rev. Father Doane last evening in honor of his return home from his travels on the continent of Europe, was a complete ovation. A torch-light procession was formed in New Street, near Washington, a little after eight o'clock, and after marching down Washington to Market streets, down Market to Broad, and then down Broad below William, it countermarched up Broad and then proceeded to the parochial residence in Bleeker Street, where a tremendous crowd had already gathered to witness the proceedings. The procession was headed by Reinhard's Silver Cornet Band, which discoursed lively and familiar airs. . . . In the procession was borne a transparency, on one side which were the names of St. Patrick's Temperance Societies Nos. 1 and 2, and the following inscription in Irish: "Cead mile failthe soggarth aroon," which in English means, "A thousand times welcome our beloved pastor." On the other side were the words, "Welcome home to our Reverend President, Y.M.C.A." Arriving at the parochial residence, . . . a speech of welcome was made by Rev. Father Reilly . . .
>
> The welcome [had] commenced immediately upon his arrival, for as he was making his way quietly up from the Centre street Depot, thinking that no one would see him, a shop window was thrown up and some of the good girls who were working there shouted out, "Welcome home." A smile of pleasure and astonishment came over the faces of the children as he met

them, one after another, and now the whole had culminated in the magnificent spectacle which he saw before him."[1]

The report of Doane's response to the throng shows his wonderful knack with people and how skillfully and subtly he imparted important lessons:

> He [Doane] hoped however, that the enthusiasm would not spend itself in shouts and cheers, and music and torchlights, for there was the unfinished hospital [Saint Michael's Hospital] on the hill, which he had come home to help finish. . . . He excused himself from any lengthy remarks by the Horation plea that he was *lassus maris et viarum*, and that many of them know from experience the fatigue of a sea voyage, and how one feels when first on shore. At the same time he would show them that he had redeemed a promise he had made before leaving home that he would bring them a Shamrock, and lifting up the flower-pot in which it was planted, he said here it is. He had brought it in his own hands from Dublin. The Shamrock was received with deafening cheers, and then after saying that he had not brought it from the North or from the South, but from Dublin between the two, and repeating the words of the poet:
>
> "The Shamrock the Shamrock
> The green immortal Shamrock
> Chosen lead of bard and chief
> Old Erin's native Shamrock,"
>
> and wishing them good night he retired.

The next day Doane and O'Rourke's pride burst upon the pages of the local press. A *Newark Evening Courier* headline declared: "The new Cathedral—To be the most magnificent temple in the Country." The article announced: "The building will be in the Early English Gothic style, and will be larger than the magnificent cathedral now being erected on Fifth Avenue, New York, and even more grand and beautiful. . . . Suffice it to say that it will probably be the grandest edifice erected in this country."[2] The report suggested that the design partnership had worked out much of the exterior. Its dimensions truly were grand. The total length was to be 300 feet; the width at the transepts, 120 feet. The *Advertiser* proclaimed that "lofty spires will rise to a height of nearly 300 feet"—spire to spire, a match to those of

Saint Patrick's, which at this point were, like Newark's, at that height only on scaled drawings.[3] As Pugin would have wanted, the Newark cathedral was to be built of a local brownstone.

The Cathedral's Ultimate Site

Soon after their return, Bishop Bayley, still in Europe, cabled O'Rourke through Doane: "Heartily approve your selection."[4] O'Rourke had recommended, after he and a surveying firm examined four plots for sale and their subsurfaces, that the diocese purchase property in north Newark that had come under consideration before their trip. In the report that O'Rourke filed, he saw the merits of each of the four, tipping his hand in favor of those on the summit of the hill; he thought, too, that the cathedral should be positioned facing south, toward Newark proper. O'Rourke liked that the location was adjacent to what was then called Fifth Avenue, which he thought "will always be a first class thoroughfare direct to Orange."[5]

He also indicated what the investigation of the subsurface showed: "There is not the slightest danger of water in the cellars of this locality and, after a careful examination of the ground made this day, I have no doubt of a solid and uniform foundation." Referring to the lot that was immediately adjacent to the one that would be chosen, O'Rourke noted, "A well dug . . . was sunk thirty feet before meeting the rock and, water is not found at a less depth than forty feet from the present surface."[6] Two months later, and doing all that they could to optimize the prominence of the site, O'Rourke and Father Doane attended a meeting of the Street Committee of the Newark Common Council and together "urged upon the Committee the importance of establishing as high a grade as possible for Fifth Avenue."[7]

Doane and O'Rourke were delighted, realizing the glorious Cathedral of Our Lady and Saint Patrick was clearly in sight. This plot of land, a geological prominence dating to the Triassic Era and rising up from the Piedmont Plain in New Jersey, was assuming, in the minds of these starry-eyed Victorians, its God-created purpose: nature's plinth for the Newark cathedral. What is more, the diocese reported in the newspapers that, unlike the superseded site, it was "near a large Catholic population." It meant, or so it seemed at the time, a pastoral as well as an architectural advance. And yet, as one account said later, the "verdict of the people was against the bishop's action" in purchasing the new site.[8] These skeptics regarded it as too distant from the city's heart; their doubt was not unfounded, but the stage was set.

THE CATHEDRAL OF OUR LADY AND SAINT PATRICK

The project moved ahead in the summer of 1872. The architects refined the drawings and released a description of the cathedral that said the design was in the High Gothic Rayonnant style that originated in fourteenth-century France. The term *Rayonnant* derives from the handling of the Gothic tracery, and the description stated that the windows in the new cathedral would be "rich in flowing traceries."[9] It had a clerestory, transepts, and what they called a "transept tower," almost certainly a flèche, or small metal spire, crowning the intersection of the transept and nave. The press account implied that although the interior decoration was only partially developed, important decisions had been made. The columns were to be Aberdeen granite, aligning it with Goldie's other recent major works. About the roof, the article said, "The groined work of the nave and other ornamentations, usually of plaster, will be of black walnut and other hard wood." It was thus to be similar to the roof in Goldie's Kensington church. Although it was to be without the stone vaults of the Rayonnant specimens to which they looked for models, it was an elegant compromise. Keely's numerous American cathedrals had roofs that were merely scaled-up versions of those in his churches. And about this time, New York cathedral authorities were fretting over the vaulting composition of Saint Patrick's. The cost of stone vaults, and the scarcity of masons able to build them, led to plaster substitutes—and to architect Renwick's everlasting regret.

The 1872 description mimics the one that Doane and O'Rourke returned with from London two years before, but in some respects, it was very different. The stated emphasis on French Gothic models over English Gothic models revealed an ascendant interest in Continental styles as the Gothic Revival progressed in England and America. The dimensions were also reduced, and the tallest of the towers was to be two-thirds as high as that first planned.[10] Publicity for the cathedral also reined in the immodest early claims, saying it "will undoubtedly be the grandest church edifice in New Jersey."[11] This time, Bayley's dictum about size and cost prevailed.

The account also described the bishop's house to be built adjacent to the cathedral (which they planned to construct first) that would "afford a model of what such an establishment should be . . . in a modified and simple treatment of domestic medieval architecture."[12] The plans for the bishop's house were published in London in *Building News*, which said, "It will be the first example in America of an Episcopal residence built with a definite expression of its object both as to plan and architectural character, the ordinary type of dwelling-house of the better class having been hitherto employed."[13]

As design development continued, Charles Eastlake's *A History of the Gothic Revival* was published simultaneously in London and New York. Eastlake was the first to assess critically the revival of Gothic in the past generation; generally unflattering to Catholic work, he included George Goldie in the small group of architects who "had in their several ways done their best to secure honest and substantial work—and to keep clear of the tawdry superficial style of design which brings discredit on the Gothic cause."[14] Eastlake thought Goldie was a moderate standing on a middle ground between the strictly ecclesiological and freer High Victorian style. About the pro-cathedral of Saint Mary's in Kensington, he saw shortcomings yet conceded that "[e]very detail throughout the work . . . bears evidence of artistic care." Eastlake's verdict on Goldie must have heartened Newark authorities.

In early July, the *Advertiser* carried news that put the estimated cost for the cathedral at $1 million and the bishop's house at $250,000. After Bayley's warning that the buildings were not to be unnecessarily grand or to burden the diocese, the piece made a stir. The next day, through Doane's initiative, the *Advertiser* declared that the cost would be much lower. The chastened journalist added: "We very cheerfully make the statement on Father Doane's authority, but it is just to the reporter to say that he derived his facts from the architect and one of the trustees, whose statements as to the details were deemed high authority."[15] O'Rourke was never shy with reporters, and this time got ahead of his client.

A great many people would have the opportunity to inspect the cathedral plans for themselves. In 1872, Newark organized the nation's first industrial exhibition. Modeled on similar promotional fairs in England, it celebrated locally produced goods. The *Sunday Call* declared it "the grandest enterprise ever undertaken by the people of Newark."[16] President Ulysses S. Grant and Horace Greeley, the famous newspaperman who was then running against Grant, were among the 130,000 people who pulsed through the fifty thousand square feet of exhibitions laid out in the Skating Rink to see the fruits of Newark's hugely diverse labors: saddles, trunks, jewelry, machinery and castings, lamps, cutlery, pianos, goldsmith work, clothing, oilcloth, and even paintings by local artists and plans drawn by its architects.[17] Shortly after the exhibition opened, the *Advertiser* noted how the drawings of the proposed cathedral stood out among the architectural renderings displayed:

> Our architects exhibit plans of buildings, already erected or about to be erected, which are highly creditable to their skill, indeed they show that they are not inferior in intents to those of New York and Philadelphia. The most prominent among these plans are those of the new cathedral, to be built on the lot recently purchased by Bishop Bayley at Clifton and Fifth Avenues. These plans were executed by Messrs. Goldie, Child and O'Rourke. In the works representing the interior of the proposed cathedral, the altar and ornaments, the many columns and richly decorated arches are all brought out with remarkable distinctness, while the lights and shade is so distributed as to make the picture beautifully harmonious as well as grand.[18]

Newark's cathedral-building initiative thus ranked high among its civic enterprises; moreover, it could be seen as such by an immense throng of local and out-of-town visitors.

(The plans and renderings of the Cathedral of Our Lady and Saint Patrick appear to be lost, but Goldie's manner can be seen in his firm's successful competition entry for Saint James Church, Spanish Place, in London.[19] A rendering of this, published in the *Building News* a decade after the Newark plans were completed, shows many features described in the publicity for the American project, providing more than a hint of what Goldie and his collaborators intended for the Newark cathedral; one must imagine a second spire added to the London church's scheme.)[20]

Other Fruits of the Tour

Father Doane, as we have seen, wrote of an epiphany about the nature of true Gothic construction while walking with O'Rourke amidst the ruins of Melrose Abbey in the Scottish Borders countryside. Jeremiah must have asked himself (perhaps it was he who raised the question) if he was among those "modern Gothic architects" who only "imitated" the historic work. His architecture gave the answer. It was transformed. In short order after the tour, his commissions revealed an artistic awakening.

In designing Saint Joseph's Church in Newark in 1872, O'Rourke, as with the Princeton church, brought together aspects of the revival styles found in England and Ireland with those popular here. He also devised a fine hammerbeam roof system inspired by models of Doane-connected architects Notman, Wills, and Upjohn that he would use again to excellent effect, including for Saint Mary's Church in Plainfield, to which he gave a full Ruskinian treatment.[21]

When Father Pierce McCarthy became pastor of Saint Mary's Church, nestled in the heart of the iron mines in the Dover hills of Morris County where his family lived, he needed a bigger church and hired O'Rourke. It was McCarthy who preached the thumping sermon at the cornerstone ceremony for the Cathedral of Our Lady and Saint Patrick chapel in 1869, and he was now getting his own chance to build boldly, of not being "afraid . . . of doing too much."

Jeremiah began at the drafting board with his Princeton scheme and added richer ecclesiological elements.[22] Over a four-stage tower, he drew a handsome spire. This nicely integrated composition prompted an observant reporter to comment, "Mr. O'Rourke, the architect, while adhering to the stern rules of the order of architecture to which the edifice belongs, has here and there thrown in touches of his own which may be considered original."[23] As in Boonton, the Dover church's stones were taken from local mines. The same reporter described it in a vernacular that would have warmed any ecclesiologist's heart: "From the aspect of the building and its location it presents to the traveler a very inviting appearance—being massive yet unpretentious. . . . It is in the shape of a cross, and but for its modern trimmings, closely resembles those venerable fanes of medieval times described by historians and tourists. . . . Nearly all the materials used in the construction of the church remain in a comparatively primeval condition."[24]

The rustic treatment was brought inside, where thick, chamfered beams form an open timber roof that would have sung to Pugin. O'Rourke was sufficiently pleased with Saint Mary's that he gave it a special gift-in-kind: a stained-glass window depicting a bearded, brooding "Jeremiah the Prophet" in the north transept. The glaziers painted "J O'Rourke, arch't" in Gothic letters on the donor panel.[25]

Father Doane joined in officiating at Saint Mary's dedication in 1873 and took in what Jeremiah had achieved. He could also see what a newspaper reporter noted. The church had no spire. A financial panic on Wall Street in 1873, while the church was under construction, sent rippling fears everywhere. Father McCarthy was worried enough that he had a temporary roof put on the tower from which the spire was to rise. The reporter explained that the parish intended to raise it when better able to "sustain the expense," assuring readers that it would be completed "at an early day."[26] That day never came: Saint Mary's capped tower, elegant as it was, would be neither temporary nor the last emblem of an economy in free fall.

7

Bust

Crisis and a Grand Hope Deferred

No place dropped further in the fiscal descent than Saint John's Church in Orange, O'Rourke's church that had opened only a couple of years before. What happened there is one of the most extraordinary episodes in American church building, and it brought the Diocese of Newark to its knees. Moreover, it forever altered the course of the cathedral project.

When the church opened in 1869, Orange's factories were beginning to feel the slowdown that followed the post–Civil War boom. With slackening demand, manufacturing plants contracted, inducing wage and job loss. Like other Catholic churches of the day, Saint John's relied on the contributions of working people. Though modest, their gifts were a substantial percentage of their discretionary income and in aggregate serviced mortgage payments on often ambitious parish buildings. Most Catholics in Orange, formerly living in genteel subsistence, now got by in sharply reduced circumstances. As collections plummeted, Father Hickey scavenged for funds, taking whatever he found. Piece by piece, he mortgaged all of Saint John's property: church, school, rectory, convent, and land belonging to the church. This raised cash but meant more new fixed payments.

When Hickey's woes could hardly seem worse, they deepened. The church caught fire. Starting on a votive altar, flames flashed from the altar to a statue to the vaulting above before fire brigades saved the church. Disaster was averted and insurance covered most losses (an errant burning candle was thought the cause), but Hickey had to ask for donations to complete repairs.

An odor of burnt wood still lingered in the church when Hickey presented a new money-raising scheme. He proposed that collectors make weekend visits to parish homes and requested that everyone put ten cents in the collection at Sunday masses. Just how low the high-flying parish had fallen was clear when Hickey urged girls and boys in the parish schools to offer a penny daily in their classrooms. Whether desperately hopeful or delusional, Hickey assured his flock that their cooperation with these measures would eliminate Saint John's entire debt. His credulous parishioners began speaking about the imminent consecration of their church (possible only when the building is debt-free).[1] The men of Orange might as well have dug the church's foundations with spoons as relied on Hickey's fund-raising pitches to meet the parish's huge obligations. In one more desperate act, Hickey took out life insurance policies on himself, naming Saint John's as the beneficiary.[2] The insurance premiums added yet another recurring expense to the parish ledger.

By late fall 1872, the parish also fell behind with its regular expenses. With nothing left to mortgage, Hickey—unknown to diocesan superiors and all but a few parishioners—raised funds by borrowing still more. Month after month he signed notes for floating (short-term) debt of thirty-day maturities, financial instruments prudently used only to sustain current operations. In other words, he borrowed short-term to pay long-term obligations. Never wise, escalating interest rates meant that they were taken or renewed each month at ever higher rates. Saint John's total borrowings reached $280,000.[3] Under this staggering mound of debt were land and developments whose original mortgaged value was $79,000.

For seven months beginning in November 1872, Father Hickey recorded in the parish minute book that he was authorized by the board of trustees to sign new debt agreements. The resolutions, stating no financial terms, were signed by Hickey and Saint John's two lay trustees, one of them an elderly fellow who signed the papers in a trembling hand as feeble as the judgment that approved the new debt. This trio also authorized a mortgage loan of $11,000 from Newark resident and former New Jersey Governor Marcus L. Ward, and another one of $38,000 from John O'Rourke (no relation to Jeremiah), whose construction firm built the church.[4] With these actions, Hickey ignored a regulation that he secure written consent from the diocese to sell or mortgage church property or increase parish debt by more than $500.

Church authorities heard thunder from Orange as early as summer 1872, when Bishop Bayley, elevated to archbishop of Baltimore and preparing to leave Newark, discussed his worries about Saint John's with his successor in Newark, Bishop Michael A. Corrigan.

BISHOP CORRIGAN STEPS IN

Michael Corrigan, son of a quickly prosperous Irish immigrant living in Newark, had succeeded Bernard McQuaid as president of Seton Hall after study in Rome. His intellect, phenomenal memory, copious knowledge of theology and canon law, and his sanctity overcame his youth (at thirty-three, he was the youngest American bishop). He was also a person of fastidious habit and manner. Born for the cloister or quadrangle, his focus and drive nonetheless allowed him to grab the levers of temporal affairs in the diocese, especially in relation to the Orange disaster. Soon after taking over, the new bishop took up matters with Father Hickey, and a little later the priest confessed his "financial embarrassment" about certain mortgage agreements to Corrigan. Although there was frank talk on the bishop's part, Hickey withheld (if he knew) how much debt had piled up.

Seeing clouds that darkened by the day, Corrigan threatened to remove Hickey. Saint John's people rallied around their pastor, petitioning the bishop to leave him in Orange. Galling to Corrigan, the *New York Freeman's Journal*, which had a big Catholic readership, began a campaign of support. In the face of their own desperation and financial hardship's bitterest fruit—shame—parishioners said that Hickey was not to blame, that he was doing the best that he could in hard times. It was to no avail. In June 1873, Corrigan, not an overly forgiving superior, dispatched Hickey unceremoniously to another parish.

In his place, Bishop Corrigan sent Father Winand Wigger into the maelstrom of Orange. Wigger did his best to put accounts in order so an accurate picture of the financial condition could be assessed. He also arranged for the resignation of first one, then the other, of the lay trustees who rubber-stamped Hickey's fateful decisions. The son of German immigrants, Wigger had the unenviable task of taking the reins from a popular Irish priest and winning over an Irish enclave. He appealed for more donations, but the Catholic wells of Orange were dry, and he and the bishop increasingly reached out beyond the parish to Catholics of means.

Meanwhile, with Doane and O'Rourke among those working behind the scenes, discussions with creditors (insurance companies, local banks, individuals, and contractors on the new church) intensified.[5] To raise cash, the parish agreed to sell its undeveloped land and give the proceeds to creditors.

It made headway when two private lenders agreed to take a discounted amount on debt they held, in some cases as much as half the nominal figure. It proved a false dawn. The bigger creditors, fearful of their exposure and besieged on all fronts by an economy in fast recession, began litigation to force Saint John's liquidation.

To Bishop Corrigan's new regret, Father Wigger, after less than a year at Saint John's and feeling it was an Augean stable in which he could no longer toil, pled to be relieved. Grateful for the efforts Wigger had made, the bishop consented. About this time, news concerning the depth of the crisis reached the press. An editorial in the *Newark Daily Advertiser* adopted a puzzled tone: Saint John's had recently seemed prosperous; it had raised so much money; why was it now in trouble? The piece tip-toed around the possibility of scandal.[6] Four days later, a letter to the editor in the same paper, signed "Orange," chastened the diocese, saying it had not done enough to help Saint John's. Stung, Bishop Corrigan responded with a letter to the editor, "fixing the blame where it rightfully belongs"—with Hickey.[7] But the priest's role was immaterial. The diocese's legal and financial counselors declared that Saint John's obligations, all of them, were binding.

Institutional creditors, especially the Republic National Bank and several individuals who held notes, demanded liquidation. Newspapers reported that the church would be auctioned. Twice the sale was scheduled. Twice it was postponed. Corrigan feared that the second delay bought time for the creditors to "crush us completely." A new date for the auction was set: Tuesday, February 24, 1874. Everything was to go: church, rectory, convent, schools, land for the cemetery. Adding insult to misery, a news story noted that a serious bidder for the church had surfaced: a company that planned to convert the church into a theater for popular entertainment. On the Sunday before the public sale, Saint John's parishioners, certain that all was lost, wept openly at mass.

Just days before the scheduled auction, Corrigan and his advisers learned that bankruptcy law gave them the right to have it postponed for a month, and exercised it. The prospect of plays, musicales, and dancing in the church's chancel and nave sharpened the bishop's determination to rescue the parish. He beseeched every Catholic pastor in New Jersey to take up special collections: "Surely in all New Jersey there is not a single Catholic without the wish, as there are few, without the means, even in their poverty, to give something to save Church and graveyard, and sacred vestments and chalices from the hammer of the Sheriff, from the cry of the Auctioneer! If the contributions be generous and general, Saint John's will yet be saved!"[8]

BOLD ACTION AND THE BROADER COSTS IT INCURRED

The young bishop consulted Archbishop McCloskey of New York throughout these agonizing months. They grasped that more than the Orange church was at stake, seeing that the situation might make lenders to other parishes wary. A call on loans would be disastrous. And if churches in general were thought not creditworthy, the Church's building program, reliant on mortgage financing, would be jeopardized. They had to contain the panic.

Bishop Corrigan's urgent appeal, combined with the earlier efforts, brought $45,000 in gifts or pledges and was offered to creditors in proportion to their aggregate claims. Corrigan himself and Father Doane, both able to draw on family money, made large personal contributions, and Jeremiah O'Rourke gave $1,000, one of the largest single gifts. Still the creditors pressed in, threatening to move against Saint John's. After tense negotiations, on April 15, 1874, there was a breakthrough. The debt holders, in a kind of collective bargaining agreement, consented to a restructuring and payment plan that had as a condition that they not force the sale of Saint John's. It was a dubious victory for the diocese. Even to meet the revised schedule of payments required almost $70,000 in new funds on top of the $45,000 already raised.

Understanding that donations alone would not feed the wolf at the door and encouraged by his vicar general, Father Doane, and others, Bishop Corrigan called a meeting of all the pastors in New Jersey. Corrigan and Doane entered the session with a plan that levied every Catholic congregation in the state with assessments ranging from $100 to $5,000.[9] They projected that this would eliminate the floating debt, leaving Saint John's with the original mortgaged amount, which they believed that the Orange parish could adequately service. In presenting the plan, Corrigan shrewdly asserted that a broader Catholic honor was at stake: "Though most unjustly and recklessly incurred, nevertheless, as it stands, it is now a legal debt; and not only the honor of the Diocese, but the good name of Catholics at large, would be seriously compromised, did we neglect in paying it."[10]

In a show of solidarity, clergy agreed to meet the goal, though many of the parishes they led bore their own debt burden and all were gripped by the bigger economic vise squeezing Orange. Astonishingly, some parishes had to borrow to meet their assessment. The appeal, in general, struck a deep chord that was heard as well by non-Catholics, with substantial gifts offered by Protestants in Orange and Newark.

Although the plan to save Saint John's succeeded, almost every debt restructuring leaves someone feeling short-changed. Several individual creditors thought it was them, but neither they nor institutional creditors again sought judgment against Saint John's.[11]

And how might Father Hickey be judged? A good priest by most accounts, nothing prepared him for a pastor's business responsibilities, let alone management of a major building project. Although a few creditors seemed to have been eager to proffer cash at usurious rates, Corrigan wrote later that he was "egregiously deceived" by his subordinate. This deception thwarted the controls in the well-crafted articles of incorporation for parishes, clauses that Father Hickey himself had transcribed into the parish minute book. A better economic climate might have spared Hickey, but the harsh winds of recession, panic, and depression laid bare his financial ignorance and his pride. The latter led Hickey to bury his worry and his risky course when he might have consulted, or at least apprised, his superiors. He might also have saved his place in the diocese if he had not kept mum on the $38,000 loan from John O'Rourke. Inevitably, Corrigan learned of it and in a fury banished Hickey from the diocese forever.

Remarkably, by the early 1880s, Saint John's had recovered sufficiently to complete the spire, yet this too brought trouble. O'Rourke was asked to prepare drawings, and he added more Pugin-inspired features. However, when workers began to finish the tower, they found that it had been originally constructed with substandard materials and methods.[12] They and O'Rourke concluded that it could carry no additional load. Saint John's pastor placed the blame on the earlier construction firm, O'Rourke and Moran (no relation to Jeremiah), which had won the job with a low bid and may have cut costs and quality as a result. The pastor concluded that the builder and architect shared responsibility, even if Jeremiah O'Rourke's culpability was that he trusted too much in the builders. O'Rourke offered the new plans and the supervision of the new construction free of charge, but to the pastor's ire the contractor refused any restitution. The tower was partially removed and rebuilt, and only then could the spire, an echo of both Saint Giles Church and Senlis Cathedral, be raised. On a small scale, this incident of faulty construction and the uncertainty of responsibility foreshadows problems with the Newark cathedral's ultimate construction. Despite it all, in later years, O'Rourke pointed to Saint John's Church as the one that mostly fully expressed his ideals.[13]

Against the worrying and absorbing trials of Orange, Bishop Corrigan, tenacious and detail-obsessed, particularly hoped to keep diocesan projects, especially the cathedral project, moving. In summer 1872, a newspaper report said that construction on the Cathedral of Our Lady and Saint Patrick would begin "early next season." Signs appeared in mid-decade that the cathedral project might still have life. A construction team graded the site, and Church officials made expectant talk. But the economic crisis continued, not hitting bottom until 1877. It even grounded the high-flying real estate investors who sold the diocese the land for the cathedral in 1871: Peter Doremus and Hiram Rhodes landed in trouble over their more speculative banking activities.

The locust years of the 1870s, known for decades as the Great Depression, pulled diocesan fund-raising prospects under, and the debacle in Orange sealed the cathedral project's fate. Despite Newark's vaulting ambitions, grand plans, and soaring rhetoric, the Cathedral of Our Lady and Saint Patrick, designed by the Englishmen with local support from Jeremiah O'Rourke, constituted nothing more than a set of drawings and a leveled lot.

PART II

Interludes

8

O'Rourke in Washington

JEREMIAH O'ROURKE became supervising architect of the United States in 1893. He had a rocky time in the post, and several episodes during this public service (as well as other interactions with the supervising architect's office) elucidated his professional motivations and personal character. O'Rourke's interlude in Washington bears closer scrutiny than would ordinarily be called for here because of its value in interpreting a later turning point in the history of the cathedral.

As his career advanced, O'Rourke rose to prominence in Newark, taking his father-in-law's seat on the board of managers of the Howard Savings Institution and as a trustee of the cathedral parish and other institutions.[1] In his sixtieth year, his long-standing loyalty to the Democratic Party and professional competence put him within reach of the position of supervising architect.

SUPERVISING ARCHITECT OF THE UNITED STATES

The supervising architect's role grew out of the national government's need to manage federal buildings projects: post offices, courthouses, customs houses, and the like. Its responsibilities were formalized in the 1850s as a bureau or department under the secretary of the treasury. When O'Rourke set his sights on the office, in 1893, it had been entered through a revolving door for a decade. Party politics unseated previous recent incumbents and created the vacancy that he wanted to fill. He seized his chance when political heavyweight (and, often noted, an enormously heavy man) James J. Smith, a newly elected United States senator, fellow Newarker, and parishioner of Saint Patrick's, promoted his candidacy to John G. Carlisle, the treasury secretary in Grover Cleveland's second administration.

Jeremiah O'Rourke viewed American politics as two polarities: Democrats were selfless and devoted to the public good; Republicans were self-serving and corrupt. He always had political views, and everyone within earshot knew them. But this now seemed to be paying off in a way that he could scarcely have predicted. Peers in the American Institute of Architects (AIA) raised an eyebrow that someone who had been a sole practitioner doing mostly ecclesiastical commissions was under consideration. But this did not deter O'Rourke or Senator Smith's Democratic machine.

For O'Rourke, it was the realization of an American Dream whose prize was professional eminence. And in dreaming about it, he would have had in mind the extraordinary, hyperbolic claim made in the *American Architect and Building News* six years before: "[T]o the future historian of American art, the succession of Government Architects will be nearly as important as that of the kings of England in British secular history."[2]

O'Rourke left his Newark office without regret, saying later, "had I foreseen that I would have died in the poorhouse, I would have accepted for the sake of my native land and my religion."[3] Lifted from a narrow prominence, O'Rourke eventually received a nod from the *American Architect and Building News*, when the editor noted that his selection "will be accepted by the profession as a more than usually satisfactory appointment, as the new incumbent is known generally as an architect of more than average capacity and information, who, during the last twenty years, has enjoyed a larger practice than has fallen to most of his fellows. The fact that the greater portion of this practice has consisted in the construction of ecclesiastical buildings of various kinds for the Roman Catholic Church does not, under the changed conditions attending the design of Government buildings, affect the propriety of the appointment."[4] These "changed conditions," a sudden shift in architectural taste, and internal politics in the Treasury Department and the supervising architect's office blew arctic headwinds at the new appointee.

Prominence and Politics

The year 1893 unfolded as a watershed in the history of American architecture. A fantastic fair in Chicago marked the four hundredth anniversary of Columbus's discovery of America. The World's Columbian Exposition, as it was called, drew more than 27 million visitors to its pavilions, halls, and monumental water features, many designed by a rising generation of American architects influenced by the classicism taught at the École des Beaux Arts in Paris. The pageantry of this world's fair and its showcase of colonnades and capitals, pediments and architraves helped make Beaux-Arts classicism the new cynosure of American architecture. The AIA's national convention and a World Congress of Architects were held consecutively in Chicago during the fair. When O'Rourke addressed a joint session of the groups on the topic "Architectural Practice of the United States Government," he was on a roster of such notables as Bannister Fletcher, the British architectural historian; landscape designer Frederick Law Olmsted; and architects Charles McKim, Louis Sullivan, and Daniel Burnham.

At O'Rourke's new office in the Treasury Building, he surveyed a staff of 145, both men and women, including scores in the vast drafting room, constituting, he said, "the largest and best equipped architectural office in the United States, perhaps in the world."[5] The job also meant managing about 180 construction supervisors at federal projects across the country.

O'Rourke defined his major tasks quickly and broadly, and attempted to rationalize the office's structure and reporting methods. Logan Carlisle, the secretary's son, served as the chief clerk of the Treasury Department and exerted enormous influence over its affairs. (The Carlisles, to all appearances, treated the Treasury as a family-run business, dispensing appointments with a liberality that, even by prevailing patronage standards, was surprising.) Facing resistance in his attempt to take charge, O'Rourke dismissed a senior employee. This proved unpopular, as was his determination to function autonomously from the Carlisles and the department's bureaucrats. O'Rourke was soon battling with Logan, who joined with both the chief clerk of the supervising architect's office and its in-house law clerk, to counter him. He tried to weaken the troika of insiders by suggesting to Secretary Carlisle that the Law and Contract Division be eliminated because legal counsel was "properly the province, as I understand, of the Solicitor of the Treasury, or the Attorney General" and that its other functions be absorbed elsewhere.[6] Rearguard action thwarted this and other O'Rourke initiatives.

Competitions for Federal Buildings and the Tarnsey Act

It frustrated many American architects that federal buildings were designed in the office of the supervising architect and that the profession at large could not compete for the work. The AIA had been lobbying for years for competitions.[7] It argued that a closed system produced, at best, mediocre federal architecture as well as scheduling and financial inefficiencies. Of course, it was no secret that such projects, and many were large, were a source of fees for which the profession hungered.

Just prior to O'Rourke's arrival in Washington, sentiment shifted sufficiently for Congress to pass a bill, called (after its congressional sponsor) the Tarnsey Act, that permitted architectural competitions for federal projects; although, and this became a sticking point, it did not make them mandatory. Shortly before O'Rourke was appointed, Secretary Carlisle received AIA leaders. He seemed receptive to the idea of opening commissions to the private sector and asked the institute's leaders to suggest a method for administering competitions. O'Rourke, an AIA fellow and in a position to push implementation of the Tarnsey Act, also appeared sympathetic, and his professional colleagues thought that, as the sitting supervising architect, he would be an advocate. But Carlisle and O'Rourke, to different degrees and with different motivations, were not resolute in introducing competitions. The office staff had firm views. They saw the most creative facet of the office's tasks—design—slipping away, and began counteraction.

Nine months after O'Rourke took over as supervising architect, an illustration of a scheme for a new post office for Buffalo was published in a local newspaper, crediting O'Rourke, as supervising architect, as the designer. It became a lightning rod jolted by two of the architectural profession's preoccupations at the time: implementing the Tarnsey Act and the embrace of Beaux-Arts classicism.

In a sharp letter that Carlisle forwarded to O'Rourke, Daniel Burnham, president of the AIA, pounced both on the failure to use the competitive process and on the design itself. Bristling, O'Rourke penned an arch response that tried to refute its contents. AIA leaders took offense at his retort, and both sides began a posturing, petty exchange. O'Rourke idealized the institute as a kind of medieval guild bound by fraternal codes of loyalty, so the rebuke from its leadership hit hard; the more so because it also served to undercut him in the supervising architect's office.

Members of the institute's executive committee visited Washington to plead directly to Carlisle to stop or suspend the Buffalo project. Carlisle asked O'Rourke to receive the delegation in his place, which O'Rourke was prepared to do, but they refused to meet with him until he retracted his censorious letter. They were seen instead by the assistant treasury secretary, who took them through multiple reasons for the delay in starting competitions.[8] At the meeting, and in a follow-up communication, the AIA's leaders thought they had provided answers and assurances that removed roadblocks to implementing the Tarnsey Act. They were wrong.

Secretary Carlisle believed that not all of the problems had been addressed and told Daniel Burnham that the plans for Buffalo were to proceed and that the competitive process could be tested on a future federal project. Burnham's piqued response posited, "The obstacles are not real ones and never were."[9] In trying to force Carlisle's hand, Burnham overplayed the institute's. It would take several years, new legislation, a new presidential administration, and the departure of Carlisle before it became common practice for the supervising architect's office to administer design competitions. This tempest was reported in the pages of the *American Architect and Building News*, which also published the combatants' overheated correspondence. Before it was over, the journal's editors acknowledged that O'Rourke's initial umbrage with the institute was understandable.

Architecture under O'Rourke

O'Rourke was in essential agreement with the AIA about the aesthetic quality of much American architecture—federal and otherwise—and the need to raise standards. But, now in place as supervising architect, he protected the position's prerogatives. During this feud he wrote to the AIA president, signaling his willingness to talk about the issues.[10] But this gingerly proffered olive branch disclosed his conflicted feelings. What had seemed right as a loyal member of the AIA now felt self-abnegating. Given the chance to put his mark on the country's building and leave an architectural legacy of his own, he could not release the opportunity. Rather than directing his full energy toward persuading Carlisle of the Tarnsey Act's merits, he focused on raising the quality of architecture that came out of the office and on trying to introduce an educational function in the office.[11]

The turbulence swirling around, and in, the office did not prevent respectable architecture from being designed on O'Rourke's watch. The vast work load and heavy administrative duties had made it difficult for a long time for the supervising architect to be involved in the planning details of new buildings, and schemes coming out of the office should be regarded as done under rather than by him. And yet the supervising architect generally set the stylistic thrust of the office, and for O'Rourke it was a historicist mode rendered in his moderate approach.

The design to which the AIA objected was an intelligently composed Romanesque Revival structure with Gothic detailing that descended from H. H. Richardson's public buildings. Ridicule was heaped on O'Rourke's design largely because he did not fall immediately in line with the obsession for classicism that followed from the Chicago exposition. Having given himself over to Pugin's Gothic, and gradually adjusting to changing historical styles over the years, the precipitate triumph of the new Beaux Arts style took O'Rourke by surprise. He sang the old hymns louder as influential professionals took up the new anthem of American classicism. It cost him their good will at a time when he sorely needed it.

Cut Short

Although most of the underhanded politicking in the supervising architect's office was played out behind closed doors, O'Rourke had at least one face-to-face encounter with outright (attempted) corruption. A United States senator came to see him at the Treasury Department to inquire about a federal post office that the office was designing. He asked about the building and the type of construction material that would be used for it. O'Rourke reviewed the specifications and explained that it had not yet been chosen. The congressman then offered him $10,000 in return for specifying a particular source for it. Eyeing him (with what was called a dangerous glint), O'Rourke asked the senator to repeat what he said. The bribe was repeated. O'Rourke blasted him as a dishonest scoundrel and, showing him the door, warned him not to return.[12] To such a proposition, as to other conduct that in his mind did not measure up, O'Rourke would not back away. Incapable of suffering the failings of others silently, he felt obliged to tell them their sins and pronounce a penance. The worst who received this treatment, like the contemptible senator, deserved the dressing down, but all who displeased him were subject to reproach.

O'Rourke's plans for the supervising architect's office were inchoate when he lost the platform from which he might have persuaded others of their merits. His tangle with bureaucrats in the supervising architect's office, Treasury Department politics, the tussle with the AIA, and the capricious patronage dealings that had put him within reach of the position, all played a part in upending him. Eighteen months after taking over, a curt letter from Carlisle abruptly ended O'Rourke's government career. Stunned, he appealed to the secretary:

> I beg to remind you of a promise made to me some months ago, that in case of accusations against me, which I anticipated, you would send for me and give me the opportunity of being heard before taking any action. . . . I know I have made enemies in my endeavor to raise it [the supervising architect's office] to a higher plain of professional tone and integrity than it has hitherto occupied in the Treasury Department. . . . I am well aware of the dishonest, untruthful and bigoted conspiracy. The exposure of it now, in the event of my resignation, will cause a grave public scandal, and I ask, in simple justice to me, to yourself and to the Treasury Department, to postpone your request for my resignation, until I have had an opportunity of being heard.[13]

The Carlisles turned a deaf ear.[14] O'Rourke, in concession, soon wrote again, putting the blame on the operatives in the office and asking only that Carlisle choose as a successor "a regularly trained Architect, of experience and character."[15]

His departure produced a ripple, mostly among Republicans who saw it as more evidence of corruption in Carlisle's Treasury Department. The rabidly partisan *Chicago Tribune* mischievously reported:

> Washington, D.C. Sept. 18—Carlisle late yesterday asked for the resignation of O'Rourke, the supervising architect. O'Rourke didn't resign at once. He wanted to talk it over with Carlisle. O'Rourke is a good architect. He is also a New Jersey Irishman with a temper like a gale of wind. Smith, the sugar man of the Senate, had him appointed. Carlisle says he sliced off O'Rourke's head because his office was demoralized. Carlisle disclaims any thought that O'Rourke is personally deficient in either honesty or skill in his business. . . . O'Rourke is Smith's man. A blow at O'Rourke is a blow at Smith. . . . Carlisle has never loved O'Rourke. Carlisle has had rows with Eckels, O'Rourke, Treasurer Morgan, Revenue Collector Miller, and a dozen other treasury bureau heads. This was in each instance because of their opposition to Carlisle sticking some favored incompetent into their bureaus. As a result of Carlisle's and Logan Carlisle's mismanagement in this matter of appointment the treasury department is rotten from skin to core.

O'Rourke's termination stirred up New Jersey Democrats, but not because of any high-minded loyalty to O'Rourke. Raw politics again reared up. A New Jersey politician's request to Carlisle once more called attention to the special-interest pressure that influenced the selection of the supervising architect: "Can't you give the place held by Mr. O'Rourke to some other Jersey man—we have several good men—who would fill the place to your satisfaction—and they want the job. It would help us much in the pending campaign. Please let me hear from you in reply—and although I am ill will try and come and see you."[16]

Despite the unceremonious departure, O'Rourke considered himself a distinguished emeritus, with "Ex-Supervising Architect of the U.S." thereafter engraved on his business stationery and routinely mentioned to the press. He later said that his principal objections to the Tarnsey Act were about how to implement it, not its intent. O'Rourke regained the good graces of the AIA and took part in trying to have legislation passed that explicitly opened federal projects to architects outside the supervising architect's office, which he had been unwilling to do while in Washington.

"O tempora! O mores!" O'Rourke

One more episode bears noting in this account of O'Rourke's government service. Two years before he became United States supervising architect, he was embroiled in a dispute over the construction of a new Newark post office, for which Monsignor Doane, in his persuasive way, had been an advocate. O'Rourke had initially served as local supervising architect for the post office (the field representative of the supervising architect in Washington) but, after repeated disputes over its construction, stepped aside. He nevertheless looked over the shoulder of his successor, carping that the structural brick and the construction methods were substandard.

When his complaints were brushed off, he sent alarmist letters to the supervising architect's office in Washington, alleging dangerous failings and misuse of public funds. He also published them in a Newark newspaper. O'Rourke succeeded in fixing the government office's attention on the situation. The local supervisor now had to formally address the allegations, and he assured officials that the materials and the workmanship were entirely to specification. O'Rourke's alarm bell nonetheless brought federal inspectors to Newark. They found conditions that were not as poor as O'Rourke said nor as good as the local supervisor claimed. The local supervisor attributed it to O'Rourke's anger at having been dislodged from the job and contempt for his successor. The net result, however, was that greater attention was paid to construction practices. Even so, the chagrined supervisor wrote to Washington officials when it was over that he never doubted the outcome, saying about O'Rourke: "I am not a stranger in the city, and the people of Newark also know a thing or two about Mr. '*O-tempora O-mores*' O'Rourke."[17] (The former supervisor here referenced a Latin lament by Cicero that O'Rourke used unsparingly: "*O tempora o mores.*" Translated figuratively and as delivered by O'Rourke, it bemoans a culture of low morals and corruption: "Oh what times! Oh what morals!")

O'Rourke's shrill complaints understandably irked the local supervisor, but his suspicions about malfeasance and misuse of public funds, however, were grounded in the tawdry prevalence of boss-style politics and corrupt or tainted contracts for public works. And though he was governed by profound moral imperatives, it would be incorrect to attribute them wholly to his dyed-in-the-wool Catholicism. His views on religious and ethical obligations of those who raise buildings—architects and builders—derive as well from Pugin and Ruskin's writings. His beliefs were also tested and sharpened over many years of dealing with contractors and vendors susceptible to inventive forms of cheating. The passion of O'Rourke's views—Jeremiah's jeremiads—suggest that for whatever direct, inverted, or derived causes, he felt morally superior to a healthy share of his fellow men. Such rectitude earned him respect in some quarters, but it occasionally made it hard, sometimes impossible, for O'Rourke to operate in a world inhabited by those with more elastic principles. And this would come to the fore at a crucial juncture in the Newark cathedral story.

9

Monsignor Doane

IF A DUTCH-STYLE GROUP PORTRAIT of Newark's eminences had been painted in the late nineteenth century, George Hobart Doane, in the ecclesiastical attire that he wore grandly, would have been in it. On an arc of advancement since his ordination, Doane succeeded Bernard McQuaid as pastor of Saint Patrick's Cathedral parish. Doane built on a strong legacy. His humanity permitted him to reach everyone in the parish—and beyond. His Oxford Movement sensibility imparted a care for liturgy and music that befit the diocese's premier church.

On a Mission

When traveling, Doane habitually arranged to tour libraries and hospitals; the latter attracted him because of his medical training. He was always on a mission for ideas to bring home that might enhance Newark's quality of life. As the prime force propelling Saint Michael's Hospital, the city's first full-service health-care facility, he joined with Jeremiah O'Rourke to develop a scheme for a building of 150 beds. In a region experiencing a population explosion, it met a begging need for medical services that the government or other organizations had not yet addressed. O'Rourke designed a Gothic chapel on the back of Saint Michael's, and Father Doane organized a cornerstone ceremony for it on the Feast of Saint Michael in 1869. Upwards of fifteen thousand people turned out, and the *Evening Journal* thought it "really astonishing how order was maintained among such an immense concourse," adding: "Here was shown how greatly beloved was one at least of the local clergy, whose name it is not necessary to mention. More potent than a thousand uniform policemen to quell disorder or open up a passage was a single wave of his hand, or a gentle command from his voice."[1]

The local clergyman, Father Doane, also instigated another historic event that transpired that day. In the paradelike procession that preceded the ceremonies, a group of African American Protestants from the Friendship Benevolent Society joined the line of march. Newark's newspapers reported it as the first racially integrated parade in Newark and alluded to more national significance, as the *Advertiser* pointed out: "Perhaps the most notable feature of the great procession was the participation of a society of colored men. We understand that these colored men are Protestants and joined in the procession in accordance with the general invitation extended by the committee on arrangements. . . . We believe this to be the first time that such a scene has been witnessed in any procession in the North, and we are glad that the example had been set."[2]

At a reception following the hospital's later inauguration, Father Doane rose and reviewed Saint Michael's history, from its start in a house with seven beds. He seized the moment to pressure the city to help fund the $40,000 building, twisting the arm of an elected official in the room. "Father Doane insisted," a reporter commented, "that the Common Council should make an appropriation, and Alderman Gurney was understood to say that he would recommend it to the Council."[3] Because religious affiliation played no role in whom Saint Michael's would serve, Doane thought of it as a true city hospital, which therefore deserved municipal support. Newark's Common Council, in the end, did not agree. But Doane tried. He also drove the creation of (and O'Rourke designed) institutions that functioned as social safety nets: an orphanage, a home for the indigent poor, and several others. Doane found time to organize a nationwide Catholic Young Men's National Union, patterned on the Protestant YMCA, and to forge ahead as well with the Catholic Union, a countrywide group for sectarian interest. He also advocated the temperance movement.

Doane's rectory looked like a gentleman's house, with fine furniture, art, and conversation pieces. He filled its rooms with books and displayed a growing collection of etchings by important contemporary artists, including Ruskin and Whistler, chosen with a connoisseur's eye. Portraits of John Henry Newman, both copies and engravings, had pride of place. All this, and his courtly hospitality, made the Bleeker Street residence, as his boyhood home Riverside had been, a magnet for visitors from here and abroad. But whether an English lord or a parishioner in distress, everyone received the same warmhearted welcome.

Priests who served with Doane admired him unconditionally, and while it was not unusual for Catholics to reserve a special adulation for clergy, many nearly venerated him. Doane pushed himself hard and at times needed to pull back, several times taking extended periods for recuperation at his physician's insistence. We again glimpse him at another homecoming from abroad, in 1879, when, as the *Advertiser* recorded, there was "an ovation such as has never been given to any man in Newark, and it testified most eloquently the warm affection and enthusiastic devotion with which the Very Rev. Vicar General is regarded by the Catholic population of the city. . . . Nor was the demonstration confined to Roman Catholics alone, for along the line of march flags were displayed from houses of Protestants, and well known Protestant ladies and gentleman stood on the stoops and balconies of houses waving hats and handkerchiefs as the procession passed, and in the throngs along the sidewalks were many Protestants who smiled and shouted welcome home Father Doane."[4]

The spring after this effusive greeting, at the close of the Pontifical Mass on Easter Day, Bishop Corrigan told the capacity crowd at Saint Patrick's that he had news that "will fill your hearts with joy."[5] A cable from Rome had arrived early on Easter morning with word that Father Doane had been named "an officer of the Roman Court and a prelate of the Pope's household." This honorific gave Doane the title of monsignor, a distinction far rarer than it later became. Corrigan commented that the "news spread like wildfire through the city, and by telegraph next day through the country, and created very general satisfaction." A month later, on Saint George's Day, his name saint's day, a hundred priests, his friends, former governor Marcus Ward, Newark's Civil War hero Theodore Runyon (with whom he served in the first months of fighting), the city's oligarchy, and a packed church watched George Hobart Doane vested for the first time in the colorful robes worn by those with the rank of monsignor.

EPISCOPAL EXPECTATIONS

A bishop's son and a bishop's brother (William became the first Episcopal bishop of Albany), Monsignor Doane might have hoped that he would one day have his own (Catholic) see. Others certainly did. Well known beyond Newark, Doane came to the attention of members of the American hierarchy by spearheading a campaign for the North American College in Rome, a training ground for the most promising seminarians. The young college's finances were foundering and, canvassing the American continent, Doane raised $100,000. It attracted notice.

Openings in the hierarchy were like tides in the affairs of promising clergy. When rumors mentioned Doane's name for dioceses in the west, Bishop Bayley bit his lip but said, "No one thinks more of him than I do. He is a most zealous and devoted Priest, but in my opinion he would not make a good Bishop."[6] Bayley's self-interest perhaps gets closer to his true feelings at this point: "But besides this it would not be right to take him away from me. As it is I am hardly able to work the ship . . . and without Father George's help I could with difficulty get along." When another assignment from the hierarchy threatened to take Doane away for an extended leave, Bayley pleaded, "There is not a person in the Diocese to whom I could trust the management of the temporal affairs of the Diocese except Father George." Ultimately, Bayley seems to have had his protégé in mind for Newark, acknowledging, maybe recommending, "if by and by he be thought fit for a Bishoprick it is here that he would do the most good."

As we have seen, however, New Jersey's new bishop in 1872 was not George H. Doane but young Michael Corrigan. Corrigan had cerebral gifts and the endorsement of Bernard McQuaid, who had left Newark in 1868 to become bishop of Rochester. And counter to McQuaid's advice, Corrigan made Doane his vicar general. A few years later, Corrigan was asked to identify priests under him fit for the episcopacy and named Doane and several others. When Corrigan himself left for New York in 1880, destined to become its archbishop, Doane was again on a list of possible bishops.[7] He was popular with many priests, especially the young, best, and brightest, and no one—clergy or not, Catholic or otherwise—enjoyed more esteem in the community. Other priests, however, never liked his Brahmin manner and envied his easy entry into the inner circle wherever he moved. And there were those who treated convert priests, not cradle Catholics, as somehow provisional churchmen. Doane and the cagey, forceful Bernard McQuaid were almost congenital antagonists.[8] Polar opposites in every social and personal category, the elder cleric pointedly rejected the idea of Doane's advancement. Putting aside the matter of personal fitness, Doane no longer fit the altered profile of an American bishop. New appointments started to be representative of the high number of Irish Americans in the priesthood's ranks, as well as a pronounced wish to have more German American bishops. It was a wistful day for many in 1881 when word spread that Doane, having administered the diocese during the vacancy between bishops, was passed over. Disappointed, he also wholly accepted what he believed to be God's will.

The new bishop of Newark, Winand Wigger, to be sure, was a quixotic choice. When Wigger was sent as pastor to Saint John's in Orange during its financial troubles, he held on for nine months, when his pleas to be released were heard. When this quiet, frail man heard that he was being considered for the episcopacy (and without a hint of the disingenuousness of many in that position), he demurely said, "I intend to escape the miter, if possible."[9] And though there was pressure to appoint more German American bishops, stateside Church leaders were shocked when word came from Rome that Wigger had been chosen for Newark.[10] In any event, Wigger did not escape the miter. He wore it uneasily. His twenty-one years as bishop had many moments (among the first was passing over Doane for a leadership or advisory role) that suggested that his reluctance in the face of advancement might better have been respected.[11]

A protracted problem during Wigger's episcopacy stemmed from feuds with an obstreperous Hoboken priest over various policies and practices.[12] These embroilments, aired in the press and bringing threats of action in ecclesiastical courts and tribunals, became woeful distractions for Wigger and those around him—and among the reasons why Wigger and the diocese took so long to return to the cathedral project.

Life Force

Under his new superior, Doane found himself at a remove. Being a Doane, he did not spend his life in restricted, quiet labors. His appreciation for architecture was one facet of a vibrant intellectual and cultural life. A modest inheritance derived from his mother's wealth allowed him to collect books, drawings, and etchings. He avidly followed the contemporary art scene. A pillar of the Newark Public Library, he helped initiate an exhibition program when Newark did not yet have an art museum and, as a trustee, persevered with others until the city financed an elegant new Beaux Arts movement library building.

Strong as such interests were, Doane was no unworldly aesthete. A voluble, informed conversationalist, his interest in nature and the arts endeared him to women, and a grasp of enterprise and politics, science and medicine put him on even footing with Newark's leading men. He moved easily within and beyond the parish borders, always a favored dinner and house guest. And he was a regular spectator at sporting events involving the parish youth, particularly the popular boat races and regattas on the Passaic River. Like his father, Doane instinctively wrote to sharpen his thoughts and give them currency. He published talks delivered at the Newark Public Library and a travel diary based on a trip to Oberammergau, Germany, to attend a popular play about Christ's Passion. For years he contributed a column or letter on diverse themes published in the *Newark Sunday Call*. These literate, warm pieces, written quickly and lightly edited, gained an ecumenical following. Doane wrote often about his spiritual, civic, and cultural interests. Always, he championed Newark. In a typical submission, he called attention to examples of the city's recent development:

> At the last meeting of the Wednesday Club some idea could be formed of the progress Newark is making, as views were given of the beautiful Public Library, with its exquisite details; the wonderful Prudential group of buildings, great oak grown from a little acorn planted less than thirty years ago; the new Court house, City Hall. . . . In this connection I might ask another question. Reader, have you ever been inside the Public Library and seen its beauty and its convenient arrangement? I ask the question because I often meet persons who, though they constantly pass it, have never taken the trouble to cross its threshold, go up the marble stairs, admire the columns and arches, enter the distribution room and the reading room and the children's rooms, all of them as fine as anything of the kind on the face of the earth.[13]

Nor did Doane back away from challenging subjects: he reported on visits to hospital wards for those with incurable diseases, prisons, and workhouses. These conveyed a disquieting immediacy that brought his readers into contact with lives often sharply, sadly different from their own. Doane accompanied an English jail chaplain on a visit to prisoners. Watching the punishing turn of the treadmill, he told his readers, "There were one hundred and thirty men upon them the day I saw them. They work in sets of three, ten minutes on and five minutes off. I certainly never saw a more humiliating or painful spectacle."[14]

His readers watched him prod Newark officials about anything he thought might improve the city, though he never seemed like a cleric shooting arrows over the wall between church and state. While on the cathedral planning tour in 1870 he wrote a letter for publication in the *Advertiser* that gave his view of Newark's roads: "The paving of Paris is magnificent. . . .

the streets are macadamized. The result is a splendid roadway and a pavement at half the cost that we are paying. . . . After we have spent fortunes in the various systems of paving, that are now being tried with us, we shall fall back upon what we should have long ago adopted, the macadamized road. Orange has done it, why not Newark?"[15] And a later appeal, from 1904, about the still abysmal streets in Newark: "Many are very dirty and full of holes and broken pavement and systematic examination should be made and steps taken to correct these evils, which are a great drawback not only to looks but also to convenience. All which is recommended to the Board of Works and Common Council of our good and fair city of Newark. The Parks Commissioners have set the standard, and everything about the city and country should be in keeping with that."[16]

Sometimes Doane delivered secular sermons in print that warned of Gilded Age materialism and promoted an appreciation of reading, art, music, and especially nature—irrespective of one's wealth or position. He cajoled:

> People do not know it, they are so busy with shopping and calling, and all the comparatively little things of life, busy about nothing very often, but Newark is surrounded with good roads and beautiful drives. I have mentioned some of them, but where would you find a more beautiful one than up one side of the river to Belleville, where the view from the bridge is lovely, and down the other, especially since the roadway on the east side has been so much improved, or out Washington avenue to where it ends down to the river and south along the west bank to the Satterthwaite place, where there is a fine old house and rows of elm trees better than which you would have to go England to see.[17]

This was typical of many of his *Sunday Call* letters, for he loved to comment on his outings in Newark and around the country, where he observed the world with a Transcendentalist's wonder. He gloried in the Eden-like displays of the new Branch Brook Park, near the cathedral site. After one of his customary drives around Newark (and in the autumn of his own life) he drew attention to another park in the county system in a *Sunday Call* letter, titling it "The Last Rose of Summer":

> The parks are at their autumnal best just now, with their divine October air. They are sources not only of pleasure, but of health to all who have the good

> fortune to enter them. Weequachic Park is well worth a visit to see what progress has been made in clearing the lake of reeds and bulrushes. The lower half is almost entirely clear. When the other, upper half, is clear, it will be a beautiful sheet of water, blue as the heavens above, and a superb place in winter for skating; in summer for boating and aquatic sports. . . . Regattas can be held there to great advantage as the water, unlike that of the Passaic, is clear as crystal. The water has been raised and some few of the trees have been submerged and sacrificed, like Philae, by the waters of the Nile. You can not have everything in this world, and the lake was worth the sacrifice . . . there are plenty of trees left.[18]

Orthodox in the pulpit, Doane's *Sunday Call* pieces flow from a humanistic teacher's heart and pen. He wanted to help people to see and to hear, and most of all to feel. In later years, especially, his writing more evoked his father's old friend William Wordsworth than his own early hero John Henry Newman.

William Croswell Doane and Cathedral Building in the Episcopal Church

At George's conversion, the paths of the Doane brothers diverged. But their interests and activities continued to run parallel. William succeeded their father as rector of Saint Mary's Church in Burlington and later was elected the first Episcopal bishop of Albany.[19] Like his brother in Newark, William championed the creation of church-affiliated educational and charitable institutions, but nothing enthralled him more than a dream to create a great cathedral. He wanted his Albany cathedral not only to look like its English models but to function like them, with a dean, canons, and a men and boys' choir to sing the choral services. The building he planned was the first in the Episcopal Church that approached the scale and role of its English cathedral models.

In general, Episcopalians' desire to raise great cathedral structures took hold more slowly. But why did they build cathedrals in the first place? Anglicanism's origins in the Roman Catholic Church determined its institutional structure, which included diocesan jurisdictions, bishops to lead them, and hence a purpose for cathedral churches; the essence of this was preserved when American Anglicans reorganized themselves as the Protestant Episcopal Church, following the American Revolution. (Thus, strictly speaking, among American denominations, only Catholics and

Episcopalians have an ecclesiastical need for cathedrals.) Because a royalist cast clung to them long after the Revolution, Episcopalians tended to tamp down the trappings of Anglicanism. And Episcopalians, as Catholics had done here, for the most part first used an existing parish church as a diocesan cathedral and less frequently created a purpose-built structure.[20] But by the middle of the nineteenth century, owing to the influence of people like George Washington Doane, some Episcopalians became both committed to and comfortable with more elaborate liturgical practices and church buildings, including cathedral churches. And in the Gilded Age, wealthy and socially prominent Episcopalians brought cachet and resources to their church- and cathedral-building ventures. Bishop Doane of Albany was in this vanguard. In the 1870s, he held a competition for a new cathedral in Albany, pitting the most gifted American architect of the day, Henry Hobson Richardson, against an Englishman, Robert W. Gibson. The bishop issued a clear requirement: the cathedral had to be Gothic. The architectural profession closely watched the selection when Richardson, willfully submitting a design in his signature Romanesque style, failed to persuade Bishop Doane, who went with Gibson's Gothic plans. Gibson and the Albany cathedral project have faded from memory, but Ralph Adams Cram believed that in the Episcopal Church, Doane was the bishop "primarily responsible for the introduction into the Church in America of the true cathedral idea."[21]

Although William Doane only partially realized Albany's Cathedral of All Saints, its elegant choir was completed, thanks to the generosity of Doane's admirer J. P. Morgan, the legendary financier and philanthropist. William's friendship with Morgan was one of many with illustrious figures, among them Harvard president Charles Eliot, with whom the bishop founded the elite Maine summer colony of Northeast Harbor. The University of Pennsylvania, Columbia University, and the Universities of Dublin, Oxford, and Cambridge awarded him honorary degrees. William's prominence showed the foresight (and poignancy) of George's realization, made shortly after his break from the Episcopal Church when his motives for converting were questioned and he provided this extraordinary testimony, "What had I to gain, humanly speaking? I had to leave a denomination composed of the most influential, learned and wealthy portion of the community, to attach myself to a church despised, persecuted, and trodden upon."[22]

George never became a bishop, but another honorific was awarded to him. A decade after being named a monsignor he was made a prothonotary apostolic, which granted him the privilege of wearing a miter and ring and pectoral cross at ceremonial occasions. This only drove home what had been anticipated in some quarters a decade before: He already had an episcopal ring and a pectoral cross, which had been given to him when, he said, "it was thought I could use them"—almost certainly by James Roosevelt Bayley.[23]

10

Stilled Project, Ceaseless Change

THREE FACTORS STILLED THE Newark cathedral project for more than two decades, from 1875 to 1897. Oscillating economic conditions made it difficult to make long-range plans. Leadership troubles plagued and distracted the bishop of Newark. And an onslaught of new immigrants sorely stretched the resources of the diocese. The zigzagging trajectory of the Newark cathedral project cannot be followed without appreciating the administrative issues associated with these matters, especially immigration.

The second wave of European émigrés arriving in the United States in this era transformed northern New Jersey, which is adjacent to New York City, the nation's largest port of entry for immigrants. Frequently, new immigrant groups succeeded earlier ones in the least expensive (and least desirable) city neighborhoods, as the former gained economic footing and could afford the better housing that their improving circumstances made possible.

Statistics convey the challenge for the region and the Catholic Church. In 1850, New Jersey's population was about half a million, and one in ten residents was born abroad. By the end of the century, the population approached 1.9 million, and the foreign-born ratio was about one in three, with the state's northeastern region responsible for most of the shift. Even though the Diocese of Newark shed the southern portion of New Jersey in the 1881 reorganization that created a new diocese centered in Trenton, Newark's membership more than doubled after the division and approached three hundred thousand by 1900. The number of churches also almost doubled in those two decades.

A Complex Catholic Culture

For the Church, serving the new immigrants, mostly Catholics, brought special challenges. Language differences raised high communication barriers. From dissimilar European lands and cultures, each group spoke separate languages, and these were sometimes subdivided into dialects. Although Catholic rituals were universally conducted in Latin, sermons and some sacraments were intended to be in a congregation's vernacular, as were social ministries. This meant training or bringing in priests able to speak with the new members in their native tongue. The Church's outreach became sharp-eyed and at times defensive: bishops and priests understood that other denominations stood poised to lure away Catholic newcomers struggling in a strange land, putting immigrants' attachment to their traditional faith at risk.

All this represented a new order in American Catholicism. First- and second-generation Irish and Germans had predominated in the Newark diocese since its founding. The Famine-era Irish had posed severe challenges that were partially mitigated because they were English-speaking. Few German Catholic immigrants arrived speaking English, but many German clergy came alongside them; young German Americans later entered the priesthood and joined in serving their coreligionists. Thus, for about three decades the diocese was essentially bilingual: English- and German-speaking. It fast became polyglot. Whereas in 1881, it administered seven national (or language) parishes, all German, by the turn of the century, it had thirty-five language parishes: thirteen German, nine Italian, four Polish, three Slovak, two Greek rite, single Hungarian, Lithuanian, and French parishes, and a joint French-Italian parish. The territorial parish (often called "the Irish parish" in these years) frequently first attended to non-English-speaking immigrant groups, often turning over its church basement to them; but the goal was usually to establish a parish specifically to serve their needs. And, as had been true for German Catholic immigrants, the national parish was a critical means for assuring that these new Americans preserved their old faith, language, and culture, which became passionate aims for most of them. Compounding the diocese's challenge, the new arrivals also brought religious practices and customs less monolithic than the Catholic way of life that Irish and German Americans shaped.

New immigrants from the first-wave countries slowed in number but did not cease. Through much of the second half of the century, ongoing political and religious oppression drove Catholics out of Germany. They continued to come to New Jersey, which had a German American culture that was now well rooted. As with earlier Germans, they tended to have more vocational skills than most immigrants. In the Newark diocese, as elsewhere, German American Catholics remained deeply invested in their language churches and parish schools.

Newark remained a popular destination for Irish émigrés, who also found an existing ethno-religious culture, but the number of new Irish never again reached the levels of the Famine years. Nonetheless, the prior rush and ongoing arrival of new immigrants from Ireland assured their dominance among ethnic groups for decades. As elsewhere in the United States, Irish clergy remained in the majority in Newark and also controlled the hierarchy.[1] Faster than other immigrant groups, the Irish also gained ground in the political realm, becoming party leaders and operatives, and holding elected and appointed government positions.

The largest second-wave immigration came from Italy. When the Newark diocese was founded, there were only about a hundred Italian Americans in all of New Jersey. But a variety of circumstances propelled mass Italian emigration. In 1900, there were more than thirty-two thousand Italians in the Newark diocese, which now administered nine Italian-language parishes.[2] The influx severely tested the immigrants themselves, American society, and especially the Church. Most Italians who came to New Jersey left behind an agricultural life and found themselves in an urban industrial region. A fraction worked as carpenters, masons, tailors, bakers, shoemakers, and the like, but most did menial labor for low wages. They were often looked upon by others, including some only a generation past immigration, as prone to disease and crime. (Even the state's earliest Italian immigrants, such as the skilled textile workers drafted by the Paterson silk industry, disdained the newcomers who nevertheless shared their language and faith.)

The Church contended with knotty problems. Though Catholic in name, many Italians were disinclined to attend mass, likely to regard religious practice as the province of women and children, and unlikely to contribute monetarily to the Church. A diocesan report on Catholics in Paterson in 1885 noted that of the about eight thousand Italians there, only one in four practiced their religion.[3] Also, and unlike other ethnic groups, many Italian men arrived in the United States alone and did not plan to stay; they came to gain financial stability and return home. Further complicating the challenge was that Italian-speaking immigrants came from diverse regions with distinctive religious practices and customs and wanted these accommodated and preserved here. The latter produced trials for a denomination in which centralized control and prescribed rites were the ideals.

In resisting the norms of the Church in the United States and often holding anticlerical attitudes, Italians were, in fact, stiffening at the conformist religious culture of Irish Americans, who had a near instinctual loyalty to the clergy and the Church. This sparked friction between the groups. The situation is conjured by the experience of an Irish American priest serving in an Italian parish in Newark in 1892. Writing to the bishop to plead for a transfer, he admitted: "I have a sort of dread of the Italians. . . . I have spent days plucking up courage to call on families that were being perverted from the faith, [but] time and again I . . . have walked past their houses for the want of courage to enter."[4] Overall, however, the Church's success in rising to the challenge presented by massive Italian immigration was a turning point in its destiny in America. In the first thirty years of the twentieth century, the number of Italian national parishes in the Newark diocese grew from nine to four times that. And for generations their Old World rites, devotions to particular saints, pageants, and festivals richly animated Newark and other city neighborhoods in the diocese.[5]

Polish people represented the highest number of Slavic immigrants to come to the Diocese of Newark, though in relative terms their numbers were about half of those of Italian origin. Most Poles had been rural peasants who came for survival and opportunity. In New Jersey, their major point of entry was Jersey City, where the diocese founded its first Polish national parish, Saint Anthony of Padua, in 1884. Polish immigrants poured into Jersey City at such a rate that by 1902 they made up the largest ethnic group in that overwhelmingly ethnic city. Its shipyards relied on manual labor to move freight, and many Polish Americans supplied it. But they also spread throughout northern New Jersey to work in mills and factories and the like, concentrating especially in Newark, Bayonne, and Passaic.

By 1900, the Newark diocese had four Polish parishes, and it established thirteen more over several decades. Poles arrived with deep attachment to Catholicism and assiduously built churches, schools, and affiliated organizations. There were complications, however. The diocese at first had difficulty in supplying Polish-speaking priests to serve them. Also, Polish American Catholics, in certain respects reacting to centuries of oppression in the old country, inclined toward autonomy, wanting control over the appointment of clergy to their churches and management of financial affairs. They sometimes strongly resisted the Church's controlling arm. The most charged battles in the Newark diocese over the bishop's authority involved Polish parishes. And, as with Italians, Poles resented how few of their own had been made bishops. One of the sharpest fractures in U.S. Catholic history occurred with the organization of the Polish National Church in 1897, the type of schism the hierarchy had desperately tried to head off. But predominantly, Polish Catholic parishes were places of intense religiosity and the principal means by which their people passed on their faith and traditions.

Other groups from the Austro-Hungarian and Russian empires, and new German-speaking immigrants from the former, who settled in northern New Jersey presented still more challenges. These heterogeneous peoples often looked to the Church to provide a foothold in a land that felt intensely foreign. An appeal to the diocese from Slovaks and Bohemians living in Bayonne made the point that the sole nearby church had a pastor who spoke English only and consequently could not provide for their spiritual or temporal needs. They said that to find a priest who "speaks and understands our mother tongue we have to make long and laborious journeys, while in sickness, sorrow, and destitution. We are without that consolation that our Holy Church bestows: and again, being without the watchful eye and guiding hand of a leading shepherd, to go astray is only a too natural danger amid the unrestrained temptation besetting on all sides, where vice and immortality are left to go rampant."[6]

The Church, while hardly deaf to such petitions, could rarely mobilize a response immediately. But it understood that the stakes were high and did much to respect the individuality of ethnic groups. It was easiest when priests were among the new immigrant groups, but many times they had to be trained or brought in. In due course, the Newark diocese established languages parishes for Slovakians, Hungarians, Lithuanians, and other Catholics from eastern Europe. Finally, Newark Catholic leaders had to administer to those under Roman Catholic authority but who used non-Roman liturgical rites (largely Byzantine and Greek rite) and whose culture was sharply different from other Catholics in the region. The amazing diversity of new Catholics within its jurisdiction pressed the Diocese of Newark's resources. Nevertheless, it managed to nearly double the number of its churches in two decades.[7]

Church Institutions, Religious Women, and the Parochial School

The parish, nucleus of Catholic life, extended charity at a local level, but institutions that reached beyond parish boundaries were also established in this period. All of these institutions and agencies required close attention and substantial support. Indeed, the expansion of services that they represent helps further explain the diocese's resistance to taking up the cathedral project. Bricks and mortar for parishes and institutions trumped cathedral building.

The evidence that the Church cared for its own and, in many cases, for non-Catholics in an era of exploding numbers is charted in the growth of new ancillary organizations. By 1872, the diocese sponsored four hospitals and twice as many in 1901, by which time it had organized seven orphanages, an almshouse for the poor, two homes for the elderly, and a residence for the blind. The diocese also opened the House of the Good Shepherd for girls and young women, and a Protectory for boys. Both offered stability to those marginalized by social or personal difficulties, who some labeled "unfortunate" and "wayward." In an era when government, national or local, did little for such individuals, these places harbored and taught them workplace skills for when they moved on.

The Church's organization building and provision of services during this time was extraordinary. How was it achieved? Two resources—one financial, the other human—principally made it possible. Effective, persistent fund-raising initiatives supported organizations. And religious women made most of them function. The first sisters came to the diocese to care for orphans in Newark. In 1859, the Sisters of Charity established the first religious community, also in Newark. The Sisters of the Poor of Saint Francis helped with several of the early hospitals, and in the ensuing years numerous other religious orders came to work as teachers in parish schools and to provide other services. By the turn of the century, there were 1,172 religious sisters in the diocese, and in less than four decades their numbers nearly quadrupled, including a sizable group from Italy and Poland who served in many language-parish schools.

Religious women have been called the Church's "foot soldiers," "handmaidens," "servants"—expressions that convey degrees of respect and recognition but also locate them hierarchically. The institutional Church is traditionally characterized as a male, priest-centered culture, but in terms of workers, women were its biggest human asset. Although religious women's caste in the Church's organizational life was a largely subservient one, this was an era when elsewhere women scarcely had more opportunities for professional advancement, and single-sex religious orders provided the chance for talented women to make extraordinary contributions and gain leadership roles. For generations, parochial schools, almost all managed and staffed by religious women, were factories for Catholic values, and the religious orders' fervent, systematic approach to education exerted a potent influence on students and the American Catholic Church's future. Bishop Bernard McQuaid, formerly of Newark, while speaking to an assembly attended by many Sisters of Charity, after praising the executive accomplishments of their superior, Mother Mary Xavier Mehegan, made this point: "The noblest fruit in this magnificent Church of America, the greatest work that is going on [throughout] the whole of America over, is the very work in which your teachers, the Sisters, are engaged."[8] And this work paid a variety of dividends. A tangible one was that, when the Church over the years turned to its laity for financial support of large capital projects such as educational and social institutions—and, indeed, cathedral building—its success was a by-product of the long-term contributions, direct and indirect, that religious women made.

American Cathedral Building in the Last Quarter of the Nineteenth Century

In the final quarter of the nineteenth century, westward expansion and population growth in general produced many new dioceses nationally. However, improved communication and transportation systems somewhat diminished the need for new dioceses because the latter facilitated oversight of larger geographical areas. Also, the ancillary educational and service structures that each diocese usually called for (a seminary, colleges, hospitals, and the like) made each see an expensive proposition. New dioceses in the West were more likely to spread over a large territory, also affecting the role their cathedrals played: Catholics in the Diocese of Newark or Archdiocese of Boston, for instance, were more likely to have the opportunity to visit and worship in their cathedral than one in the sprawling western dioceses.

The new dioceses, as earlier, tended to use large parish churches as their cathedral churches, and when they raised new purpose-built cathedral projects, for the most part they reflected more modest aspirations. Still, significant cathedrals were completed or emerged in this era, especially after the economic woes of the 1870s ebbed. And the first great wave of Catholic immigrants, increasingly established in America and gaining a stronger economic footing, were in a better position to fund major projects.

Following Chicago's great fire of 1871, Patrick Keely planned the new Holy Name Cathedral there. Raised quickly, Keely made aggressive economies in design and materials. When it opened in 1875 for a reported sum of only $25,000, its 210 foot spire was the highest in Chicago. In the next several decades exponentially more than that was spent on Holy Name to improve and embellish it.[9] Keely's early dominance of the Catholic market and continued reputation for both economy and a cooperative working style brought him the other major Catholic commissions in this period, in Boston, Hartford, and Providence.

Both the City of Boston and the number of Catholics there grew vigorously in the post–Civil War period. Church officials started buying land in 1860 for a new cathedral in the city's South End, an area seeing rapid growth after its marshlands were filled in; like many Bostonians, they believed this district was destined to become the most fashionable in the city. Keely's Cathedral of the Holy Cross is enormous, 364 feet long and 90 feet wide at the nave. The archbishop wanted virtually unobstructed views from everywhere in the building, which seated more than three thousand, and Keely specified thin columns of iron to carry the wooden roof. Good sight-lines were achieved, but the architectural consequences made pundits sneer.[10] When the Gothic-style cathedral opened for dedication in 1875, it had cost $1.5 million, but not all expectations were realized. Economic conditions meant foregoing the spires, including one intended to rise three hundred feet. Nor did the South End emerge as a choice Boston neighborhood. Across town, the Back Bay area had also been transformed by a massive landfill project, and it gained the upper hand socially. This nonetheless had an upside. The cathedral's environs became a magnet for immigrants, most of whom were Catholic, assuring that the cathedral had a large, local congregation for generations. And in a less-we-forget gesture, the arch between the narthex and nave was constructed with bricks from the Ursuline convent burned in 1834 by an anti-Catholic mob.

The year after the Boston cathedral opened, the Diocese of Hartford started a new cathedral, also to plans by Keely. The brownstone exterior of the Cathedral of Saint Joseph was undistinguished, but inside it had highly elaborate woodwork and trusses, and rich sculptural and mural programs, some painted by the German-trained Wilhelm Lamprecht, muralist of choice in many Catholic circles. It took more than a dozen years to finish, but when it was consecrated in 1892, the diocese had supported it with $500,000 and had assumed no long-term debt. With seating for more than two thousand people and two 150-foot towers topped by 100-foot spires, the cathedral made an imposing presence in a stylish part of Hartford.

Keely's Cathedral of Saints Peter and Paul in Providence, begun in 1878, derived from his Hartford scheme and, reflecting a trend, introduced more Ruskin-inspired touches. Though always intended to be smaller than the Hartford cathedral, Providence's bishop told Keely to build the finest church he could conceive, and he would find the support. Reports at the project's inception said the cost would be $250,000, but by the time of its consecration in 1889, stained glass imported from Austria and sumptuous furnishings helped lift that figure to $400,000. It, too, bore no debt.

Monsignor Doane's Brother and the Cathedral of Saint John the Divine

As we have seen, Monsignor Doane's brother drove the admired project for an Episcopal cathedral in Albany. He was also associated with what would become one of the truly great cathedral projects in the United States: New York City's Cathedral of Saint John the Divine. The commission for a new cathedral for the Episcopal Diocese of New York had stirred broad interest since 1888, when its trustees announced a competition for a monumental building in the northwest corner of the city. The project's leaders envisioned a building that would serve the Episcopal Church and also be a venue for diverse religious, civic, and cultural events. (In this, the Episcopalians directing the construction of Saint John the Divine were very different from Catholic cathedral-building clergy. Catholics at the time did not imagine interdenominational or civic roles for their cathedrals, functions misaligned with their understanding of its sacramental purpose and dilutive of its potency as a symbol of sectarian pride.)

The trustees for Saint John the Divine first asked for designs from fourteen architects but then opened the doors to a full competition. Narrowing the field to four firms, they conducted another competition, ultimately choosing Heins and LaFarge's eclectic scheme over those of many well-known professionals. Despite his purer Gothic predilections, Bishop Doane was the principal preacher at the 1892 cornerstone ceremony. In another instance of the challenges and snares of cathedral building, the project hit trouble in the first years of construction. To its planners' dismay, the majestic site in Morningside Heights disguised the nature of the bedrock below and the amount of excavation required to put the cathedral on a sure foundation. Slow, costly site preparation taxed the resources of even the richest denomination in the nation's wealthiest city, though a large gift from J. P. Morgan saw the project through the problem-filled phase of excavating for, and constructing, the foundations.

A Near-Cathedral: O'Rourke's Scheme for Saint Paul the Apostle in Manhattan

In this period, Jeremiah O'Rourke had the opportunity to design a church that was as large as many cathedrals in the nation. In the depths of the depression of the 1870s, he was given his biggest break when the order known as the Paulist Fathers commissioned him for their new church in New York. After Saint Patrick's Cathedral, the Church of Saint Paul the Apostle would be the largest church in Manhattan. The order's superior, Father Isaac Hecker, had seen O'Rourke's Saint John's in Orange when he preached at its dedication, and the priest then in charge of decision making about the new church was a friend of Monsignor Doane's.[11]

O'Rourke provided the Paulists with an immense, cathedralesque scheme that evoked several of the large churches in England and Ireland that he had seen with Father Doane, especially those by George Goldie and also Edward W. Pugin and George Ashlin's partnership and that bore the French Gothic inflections (rose windows, apsidal east end, gargoyles) that had come into vogue for large English and Irish Catholic churches. O'Rourke's rose window appears to derive from those in Pugin and Ashlin's Saint Colman's Cathedral in Queenstown (later Cobh), Ireland, one of the best-known Gothic Revival buildings in Ireland, begun in the late 1860s. Rising over Cork Harbor, Ireland's principal port for travel to and from America, it is the first or last great building O'Rourke would see on his Irish journeys. Saint Paul the Apostle's external length was to be 285 feet, and it had massive towers and spires reaching 320 feet. Even the *American Architect and Building News*, which passed over most Catholic architecture in this period, provided a detailed account: "Mr. Jeremiah O'Rourke has here designed on a grand scale the most spacious church edifice in the city certainly, and perhaps in the country. . . . The position of the church is an elevated one; and with the towers of this height exceeding anything now erected, the new church will be a conspicuous object in the city's landscape."[12]

Grand as it was, the commission started to unravel not long after construction began. The sinking economy scared the Paulists, who rightly paused in the face of the estimated $500,000 it would take to build O'Rourke's scheme. Also, Father Hecker returned from an extended stay in Europe with evolving ideas about liturgical practice and a fresh conviction that the church, being Roman Catholic, should be in an Italianate style. The Paulists had O'Rourke make heavy design revisions, and it became a classic case of a client with a conflicted or shifting vision. Questions were also posed about the design's engineering, but it appears that they arose mostly as the result of opposing stylistic preferences. Nonetheless, work was started under O'Rourke, though he was soon unsatisfied with the quality of construction on the foundations, insisting that the Paulists fire the workers and replace them with more skilled contractors.[13] Eventually, O'Rourke was distanced and finally removed from the project, and a Paulist priest, a former structural engineer in the U.S. military, took over as manager and designer.[14] He eliminated virtually every graceful external feature. Revision after revision resulted in a building exterior that made no one particularly happy, although in the end, the interior would come to hold outstanding examples of American decorative arts.[15] O'Rourke later had the chance to call upon some of the features he intended for the church of Saint Paul the Apostle in two different schemes, including Newark's future cathedral.[16]

PART III
Sacred Heart Cathedral

11

Newark's Rise and the Project's Revival

At one point in the aftermath of ill-fated 1870s cathedral project, the Diocese of Newark considered selling the cathedral property. Monsignor Doane rallied with others to protect it. Guarded interest in resuscitating the plans occurred in the late 1880s. This was accompanied by doubt of another kind. Despite the picturesque effects that the site promised for architecture, it begged a practical question: Were there enough Catholics near it to justify the services of a new parish? So the diocese repeated a first step of the generation before and put up a small church, designed by O'Rourke, to test the location's utility.

Much had changed since the first cathedral chapel was built in 1870. Newark had become a modern city, with a population of a quarter of million. New industries, especially jewelry, foundry, and machine operations broadened an already wide business base. In the city's rising skyline were the headquarters of some of the country's largest insurance companies, one of which occupied Newark's tallest building, twelve stories high. Grand department stores—Plaut's Bee Hive, Bamberger's, and Hahne's—enlivened a busy commercial culture. New technologies changed the rhythms and tempo of everyday life, and many were obvious everywhere: the city was festooned in thickets of electric and telegraph and telephone wires. Trolleys plied all the major streets and fostered additional suburban communities around Newark. The latter added to the appeal of the new cathedral site because the trolley system's crosstown line passed it, giving ready access to all east-west routes.

"SACRED HEART": REFLECTING CHANGE AND DIVERSITY

When the diocese opened the small church meant to test the viability of the location in 1891, it placed the church under the patronage of the Sacred Heart. As it turned out, this established the cathedral's dedication.[1] Devotion to the Sacred Heart was at fever pitch at the time, a phenomenon of piety that had been building for two centuries. Its main themes were Christ's love for humanity, His suffering to redeem it, and the continuing sorrows hostile or indifferent men and women inflicted on Him. Aspects of this preoccupation with suffering seem understandable in America, where most Catholics had experienced wretched years: first, troubles in their homeland, the wrenching decision to leave it, and then the degradations of immigrant life.[2] A popular hymn of the time assured: "All ye who seek a comfort sure in trouble and distress / Whatsoever sorrows vex the mind or guilt the soul oppress / Jesus who gave himself for you upon the cross to die / Opens to you his Sacred Heart; oh to that Heart draw nigh."[3]

Images of the Sacred Heart were ubiquitous. In churches, they appeared as statues and in murals and stained-glass windows. Catholic households with virtually no other decoration often had a print or chromolithographic image of the Sacred Heart.[4] In the early 1870s, the dedication "Our Lady and Saint Patrick," had made sense, given Irish dominance in the diocese. "Sacred Heart," not referential to the patron saint of any one country or faction, was a prudently universal dedication for a cathedral meant to serve a place as multicultural as Newark had become. And in fact the district just around the cathedral site became a predominantly Italian neighborhood.

HESITATIONS

Strong interest in starting to build the cathedral itself arose again in the reviving economy of the late 1890s. Deliberations were held in an advisory body to the bishop, who stepped back from his earlier stance that he would not build a cathedral until every diocesan church was debt-free. When he aired the cathedral project with his clergy, it met a mixed response. Many had witnessed economic cycles that ended with ferocious busts. Just a few years before, the Panic of 1893 and its tail of depression raised the specter that doomed Newark's former hopes, and some priests felt that fund-raising prospects remained poor. Others thought the venture would bleed resources needed for parishes, schools, hospitals, and other institutions. Formidable Father McNulty of Saint John's in Paterson, expressing a view that others furtively harbored, believed the money could be better spent, though his fellow clergy recalled that when he planned the church over which he still presided, he built what the ecclesiologists would have described as an "urban minster," which his sometimes nemesis Bishop Wigger called "too big, impossible to preach in, and a monument to McNulty's vanity."[5] For his part, the bishop pointed to the twin-spired $300,000 church recently erected for Saint Patrick's in Elizabeth. If a single parish could support such a venture, the bishop prodded, surely diocesan churches together could sustain a $1 million campaign.

Not that Wigger threw caution to the wind. In part, no doubt, because of his submersion in the financial cauldron of Saint John's Church in Orange, he opposed borrowing to build the cathedral. He told Monsignor Doane, "I do not propose to go into debt at all for the cathedral, paying twice or more the price of the same by having to meet interest on money borrowed."[6] Instead, he thought they could raise $1 million over ten years to support a phased construction plan that would leave the cathedral entirely finished—and without a penny owed.

Doane was skeptical. In a role reversal with his bishop from the days of the 1870 project, he feared it was unrealistic to expect to raise $100,000 each year for a decade and said Newark should scale back, tactfully cautioning Wigger:

> No one is better pleased that you are about to utilize the magnificent site on Sixth Avenue or more ready to cooperate with you than I. I cannot help however thinking that it would be better to build a less expensive building than the one you propose—say, half a million rather than a million. It would be I think feasible to raise $50,000 a year, but I do not see how it would possible to raise $100,000 a year for ten years. We have very few rich Catholics, and many of the churches, notably those in Jersey City, are heavily burdened with debt. I thought I would write this to you rather than raise the question in the meeting next Tuesday. I want to see you succeed in this great undertaking, but to do so it is most important that all should feel that the undertaking can be carried through. With the best will in the world failure would be sure to come, if priests and people feel that they are called upon to do what is out of their power. I hear probably more than you do on the subject, and there seems to be a general consensus of opinion like the one I have expressed. If any body could do what you propose I believe you could, but I fear that this is even beyond your powers.
>
> P.S. I should be sorry to see the Brooklyn experience repeated here.[7]

Doane's postscript referred to the Diocese of Brooklyn's failed $1 million cathedral, begun in 1868 and another prey of the Depression of the 1870s after only a chapel and parts of other walls were built. (Doane presumably thought Newark failed less in those hard times, because construction on the Cathedral of Our Lady and Saint Patrick never actually began, while decaying foundations still mocked the Brooklyn diocese's grand plans.)

GOING FORWARD

Bishop Wigger and his advisers nonetheless thought they could raise $1 million through ten years of annual gifts and complete the cathedral in the same period. It was a sanguine view. In the United States to date, only the New York and Boston sees had raised more than a million in nominal and relative dollars for cathedrals, and it took longer than a decade for most of the major American cathedrals to be usable. And although the Catholic cathedrals in Albany, Buffalo, and Chicago had been raised and made usable swiftly (if not entirely completed), other sizable structures had not, with their construction times ranging from nine years (Boston) to nineteen years (New York's second Saint Patrick's Cathedral). The great medieval cathedrals, by contrast, took at least a quarter of a century for some portion of them to be usable, usually longer.[8]

Wigger felt that he could tap three revenue sources: the clergy, the parishes, and wealthy Catholics. He proposed that pastors make yearly gifts of $150 and assistant pastors $100. Pressure from the chancery would make these a virtual obligation, a substantial tax on meager compensation; after a delicate back-and-forth, the amounts for the clergy's gifts were reduced. Every parish in the diocese was assessed for 8 percent of its annual revenues, in aggregate expected to bring in about half the projected $100,000 of yearly construction expenses. The bishop hoped that a personal approach to lay people of means would yield about a third of the annual goal. Doane was considered indispensable to the latter appeals. Able to move in affluent circles, adroit, resolute, he had all the qualities that are essential in capital fund-raising campaigns. He put aside his doubts that Newark could sustain round after round of canvassing at all economic tiers within the diocese. But during the first year of fund-raising the stream from major donors trickled into a total pool of $8,200, a fraction of what Wigger anticipated.

On the other end of the spectrum, priests working at smaller outposts felt challenged in being asked to raise money for a distant cathedral. One at Franklin, in Sussex County, wrote to Wigger expressing his frustration and also said it was hard to host fund-raising events in places with no sidewalks and no electricity, conditions found in many of the diocese's rural parishes.

Whose Commission?

Monsignor Doane thought that the cathedral commission belonged to O'Rourke, saying that he had been integral to the project from the start and that, twenty-five years later, and despite shifting architectural preferences, the 1870s design for the Newark Cathedral remained distinctive. He wrote to the bishop: "With regard to the plans I think it should be remembered that the English ones made by Mr. Goldie, one of the first Catholic architects of the day, were adopted by Archbishop Bayley, and that it was understood that Mr. O'Rourke who went to England with me was to have charge here. One advantage about them is that they are entirely different from everything we have here—and so many of the Cathedrals are simply replicas of each other—if the building would not be large enough the dimensions could be increased."[9]

But Wigger regarded the current project, at least the design itself, as a new start and chose to run a limited competition. This approach, eliciting different plans from which to choose would, ideally, also convey that the selection was made by an open, fair process. In addition to O'Rourke, who entered as "J. O'Rourke & Sons, Architects," three firms were invited to submit designs: Audsley Brothers, O'Connor and Metcalf, and Schickel and Ditmars.[10] They were all small professional practices that had done work for New Jersey Catholic parishes. If the others speculated that O'Rourke had an insider's advantage in the competition, they were not deterred from entering it as contenders playing to win.

William Schickel was the architect of the large church in Elizabeth to which Wigger referred in the discussion about the expense of the cathedral project. It made an impressive appearance on the horizon south of Newark, with its facade and towers that descended from the design of Cologne cathedral. Schickel had also, encroaching on O'Rourke's territory, designed Alumni Hall at Seton Hall, a fine Gothic-style building opened in 1884. Born in Germany, he came in 1870 to New York City, where he began his career in the office of William Morris Hunt, the first American graduate of the École des Beaux Arts. Prior to the Newark competition, Schickel had designed a large seminary building for the Archdiocese of New York, parish churches in Manhattan and Brooklyn, as well as commercial and institutional buildings.[11] Near the time of the Newark competition, he and his partner, Isaac E. Ditmars (who will come to the fore later), planned a grand Italian Baroque church for the Jesuit parish of Saint Ignatius Loyola on upper Park Avenue in Manhattan.

Also based in New York, Lawrence J. O'Connor, O'Rourke's exact contemporary, had a big practice working for Catholic parishes around Manhattan. He made inroads into New Jersey in the 1870s, with commissions in South Amboy, Newton, Bayonne, and Morristown.[12] O'Connor usually worked in brick, a factor that helped him compete on cost. Shortly before the competition, he brought in a young partner, Fred L. Metcalf, a Plainfield, New Jersey, architect, a circumstance that, if they won, would blunt the edge of the persistent anti–New York bias.

The most remarkable entrant had produced the fewest buildings. George Ashdown Audsley and his brother William were natives of Scotland who had practiced architecture in Britain for a quarter century. William came to this country in the mid-1880s, and George eventually followed him and settled in North Plainfield, New Jersey, where he had family. George and William renewed their partnership. Two years before the Newark cathedral competition, they designed the Bowling Green Offices, the largest office building yet to be erected in New York City. Audsley, of all the competitors, was the most knowledgeable about architectural history and design.[13] A rigorous historicist, he objected to using iron or steel in Gothic design, believing it defied the style's principles. George loudly faulted much Gothic-style architecture in this country, especially Catholic churches. Though the Audsleys were not Catholics (George, in fact, took a skeptical view of religion), they came into the ken of Newark diocesan officials through their decorative scheme for the interior of the enormous Church of Our Lady of Grace in Hoboken and a parish school in Bayonne. They submitted to the competition under the name "Audsley Brothers."[14]

Awarding the Commission

The four competitors were interviewed and asked for a preliminary proposal and drawings. At these sessions, each of the heads of the firms presented in accents and inflections that spoke of their birth abroad: Schickel in Germany; Audsley in Scotland; and O'Connor and O'Rourke in Ireland. Shelving the 1870 plans, O'Rourke prepared an entirely new scheme. Wigger organized a building committee of priests who had experience with construction projects and who were "good financiers."[15] After studying the entries, the committee requested that the architects develop their designs and submit a ground plan, front and side elevations (what the cathedral would look like), and a description of the design, with its dimensions and building materials indicated—typical requirements for a limited competition.[16] The firms were also asked to comment on how they would represent the diocese in the construction process. In a letter accompanying the O'Rourke firm's entry, Jeremiah noted that it was largely on his recommendation that the cathedral site had been purchased almost thirty years before and that he "went on a professional tour of Europe, at heavy personal expense and, in connection with George Goldie, the most prominent English Catholic architect of the time, developed in London a complete set of plans for a cathedral for the Diocese of Newark."[17]

During four days in November 1897, the committee considered the submissions, a day dedicated to each. The deliberations were held behind closed doors, and no record of them appears to have been made. But when the morning mail was delivered to O'Rourke's office at 765 Broad Street on Thursday, November 18, it held a letter from the bishop informing him that his firm had been selected.

It was front-page news later in the afternoon, and the next day the *Newark Evening News* carried a drawing of the facade as rendered by the newspaper's artist. The accompanying article announced that the plans were being exhibited at Seton Hall. On the weekend, the *Sunday Call* gave a telegraphic description of the design:

> It will . . . have two imposing towers. The total length of the building will be 309 ft. and its breadth 150 ft. The floor area will be 25,000 sq. ft. and there will be seating room for 2,000 with standing room for 2,500 more. The height of the nave ceilings will be 96 ft. and of the aisle ceilings 40 ft. Two towers will be of stone and the spires will be of different height. . . . The Gesu Tower will have a spire reaching 350′; the B[lessed] V[irgin] M[ary] tower 250 ft. Modern steel construction is to be used in the building. Walls will be of stone. The nave columns will be of polished red granite with carved marble caps and bases of unpolished granite; quartered oak, white marble floor, roof of red tile, main doors of bronze. Nave to Chancel 258 feet long; width of nave and aisles 86 feet; Transept width 142 feet. Tiled vestibule 20 feet × 80 feet. Cost $1 million.[18]

The disappointed entrants had the consolation that they were mentioned in the press as competitors, at least getting a bit of publicity.[19] And much as O'Rourke thought that he deserved the commission, he was pleased and proud, calling it a "labor of love and not of profits," and contracted with the diocese for the discounted fee of 3.5 percent, 30 percent lower than the standard 5 percent commission.[20]

12

The Cathedral of the Sacred Heart

Accounts of O'Rourke's winning design were clear about the cathedral's style. One called it "thirteenth-century Gothic Style" and another, more precisely, "continental Gothic of the thirteenth century." The composition owed much to the High Gothic masterpieces of Chartres, Notre Dame, Rheims, and Amiens, but it equally called upon the Gothic of Pugin and his followers. It reflected Jeremiah's forty-year career steeped in a mode that in later years was informed by new scholarship on medieval architecture and photography of original specimens. In overall proportions, Sacred Heart is closest to Chartres and Amiens, though its nave has only five bays, fewer than its principal models. Its abundant Gothic detailing also blended historic antecedents and O'Rourke's personal manner. Arched window openings were filled with Gothic tracery from the period of its medieval models. The Rayonnant-style rose windows were set in arched rather than in circular openings, and they were placed over a row of lancets. The rose windows' composition itself suggested a synthesis of the outstanding west windows of Chartres and Rheims. This French-derived arrangement also appeared in his plans for the Church of Saint Paul the Apostle in New York, influenced by Pugin and Ashlin's Saint Colman's Cathedral in Ireland. High in the main gable, O'Rourke placed a niche for a patronal statue, a favorite Pugin touch that he admired.

At the design's particularly inventive east-end, five chapels radiated from the chancel, with a deep Lady Chapel on the central axis to which a small cloister was attached that led to the bishop's sacristy. The early newspaper accounts mentioned a red tile roof, though the 1906 rendering has a raised-seam metal roof.[1] A flèche marked the crossing, and the roof ridges over the chancel and the Lady Chapel were crowned with iron cresting; their eastern ends terminated in small metal statues. These were restrained embellishments in a conservative design about which the architect said, "no expensive ornamentation has been indulged in other than is necessary to carry out the style selected."[2]

O'Rourke's construction plans included a limited use of steel, which in the last quarter of the nineteenth century was supplanting iron. He used it conservatively, in the flooring throughout and for the roof. Otherwise, Sacred Heart was a masonry structure whose vertical, load-bearing elements—walls and columns, for instance—were designed according to the established standards that had guided O'Rourke in the past—ones that he had articulated at a meeting of the American Institute of Architects the year before: "My practice is to construct the walls as if I had not steel or iron in them. Every building designed under my supervision in Washington, for the government, or in my private practice, will be found to stand that test, the walls when built show neither steel nor iron construction; this construction is added for additional rigidity and strength, but in case every post rusted out, the building will stand just the same, with a reduced but still sufficient factor of safety."[3]

TOWERS

Turrets at the corners of the transepts and pinnacles rising from nave buttresses, in the Anglo-Irish manner of the nineteenth century, created a vertical thrust that visually prepared for a pair of towers and spires of immense height. Given the dedications "Gesu" and the "Blessed Virgin Mary," O'Rourke, in a gender-laden description, said that the taller Gesu tower "is distinguished by strength and dignity in treatment, the square plan developing into the octagon at the fifth stage," and the smaller Mary tower, "is treated in a more elegant and graceful manner—the square plan developing into the octagon at the fourth stage." The towers and spires, replete with tabernacles for statues and crocketing, were the design's most unreserved gesture. They are traceable back to Pugin's Saint Giles Church and to which O'Rourke looked when he designed Saint John's Church in Orange.

When Sacred Heart was started in 1898, the nationwide race to raise ever higher buildings was under way, yet Newark's tallest structure stood at twelve stories. Sacred Heart's spires, the tallest being the equivalent of about a thirty-five-story building, would pierce the city's skyline spectacularly. More than a matter of mere height, the towers and their diagonal placement is the cathedral design's defining feature. Where did the idea for this placement come from? Although the building's French Gothic elements can be found in many Gothic and Gothic Revival models, the facade had both a particular Continental, and a more local, forerunner.

The Abbey Church of Saint Ouen at Rouen, in northeastern France, erected for the Benedictine monastery there, was one of the last large-scale building projects of the Middle Ages. Its protracted construction extended from the early fourteenth until the sixteenth century, when the towers were about the height of the nave roof and construction ceased. Drawings and a nineteenth-century lithograph show this configuration and the unfinished towers. During the 1840s, however, Saint Ouen was altered in a fashion that became controversial. In the nineteenth century, the French, no less than the English and Germans, rediscovered their medieval past, building again in the Gothic style and restoring and renovating old churches and cathedrals; the Saint Ouen project was one of many in France. The diagonal towers were torn down and replaced by a new facade and towers with a conventional plan.[4] Europe's ascendant architectural profession screamed that it was the act of vandals. This proto-preservation crisis conveyed a sense of avoidable loss that resulted, like some later ones, in heightened respect for historic construction. Largely forgotten today, the contretemps over Saint Ouen's rebuilt facade was nearly as well known in the nineteenth century as the one in the United States that was ignited by the demolition of New York's Pennsylvania Station in the following century.

Saint Ouen was celebrated, and its original facade arrangement mourned, in the most popular architectural history text of the nineteenth century, James Fergusson's *History of Architecture in All Countries*. Fergusson wrote: "The church of Saint Ouen, at Rouen, was beyond comparison the most beautiful and perfect of the abbey edifices in France. . . . Nothing indeed can exceed the beauty of proportion of this most elegant church, and except that it wants the depth and earnestness of the earlier examples, it may be considered as the most beautiful of its kind in Europe."[5] About the rebuilding of Saint Ouen's facade, he opined: "the western spires as rebuilt within the last few years, are incongruous and inappropriate, . . . had the original design been carried out according to the drawings that still exist, it would have been one of the most beautiful facades anywhere."[6] Reading Fergusson (and it will soon be clear that he must have), O'Rourke would have noted the architectural historian's assertion about the angled towers: "Had the idea occurred earlier, few western towers would have been placed otherwise; but the invention came too late, and within the last few years we have seen all traces of the arrangement ruthlessly obliterated."[7]

An Unbuilt Model

Patrick Keely used this unusual plan for the Brooklyn cathedral that he designed in the late 1860s and elsewhere.[8] O'Rourke himself turned the belfry of Saint Paul's in Princeton at an angle to the facade, though he and Keely were by no means the only architects to play with this device.[9] Contemporary accounts of Keely's design for Brooklyn suggested no connection with Saint Ouen, but in the 1890s, the successor to the bishop who planned it was aware of an association with the French abbey, writing from Rouen: "I have come to look at the Cathedral and at the Church of Ouen. There is some similarity between the lines of the latter and the general outline of the New Brooklyn cathedral."[10]

Still another trail leads back to Fergusson. Passages in the press describing Sacred Heart's design, almost certainly scripted in O'Rourke's office, are cribbed from the *History of Architecture in All Countries,* revealing the French abbey church as an influence on—or at the least, an after-the-fact rationale for—the design. Where Fergusson wrote, "The diagonal position of the towers met most happily the difficulty of giving breadth to the façade . . . and at the same time gave a variety to the perspective which must have had the most pleasing effect";[11] the *Newark Evening News* account offered, "The diagonal position of the towers gives great breadth and effectiveness to the façade and variety and beauty to the perspective effect when erected."[12]

O'Rourke explained in another passage that the towers were of different heights because "of an old Catholic custom." This notion about varied dimensions follows from Pugin's preferences for parish church design more than from medieval cathedral design conception. The latter by no means excluded matching towers and spires, though the numerous building campaigns, separated by decades or centuries, that were required to build most cathedrals often resulted in multiple guises and asymmetrical schemes, with Chartres the prime example.

Interior Architectural Features

Although Sacred Heart's interior scheme was not yet fully worked out, its characteristics were decided. O'Rourke manipulated the relative dimensions of the interior elevations so that the arcade was proportionally shorter and the triforium and clerestory higher than was typical in High Gothic structures. It meant that the open expanse above the columns would appear more soaring, compensating for the short nave. The short, stout columns of the nave arcade were also reminiscent of those sometimes used by Pugin, and the intended polished red granite for the columns was traceable back to the Cathedral of Our Lady and Saint Patrick scheme. The alternating round and octagonal columns of the arcades, a relatively rare treatment, had precedent in Chartres, in the choir of Canterbury Cathedral, and in many churches in the east of England. Among the latter is Saint Michael's Church in Longstanton, the direct model for Saint James the Less in Philadelphia, which both became critical models in the American ecclesiological movement.[13] O'Rourke employed the alternating columns forms for the Church of Saint Paul the Apostle in New York and the Church of the Holy Cross in Harrison. The large granite band in the middle of Sacred Heart's columns is a device that O'Rourke saw with Father Doane at the Englishman Goldie's Saint Wilfrid's Church in York.[14]

O'Rourke's boldest design stroke carried the triforium gallery across the mouths of the transepts. Though it ran counter to the High Gothic aim of "voiding the wall," this unusual arrangement would have produced an elongated, uninterrupted horizontal band of arches down the nave, emphasizing its axial thrust and sharpening the focus on the east end and high altar. Setting off Sacred Heart's substantial transepts with a screen of masonry would also have made for unexpected spatial and lighting features, the type of episodic surprise that the High Victorians liked. It was one of the "original touches" of the Goldie-O'Rourke design that Monsignor Doane thought made it distinctive.

Where did this idea come from? George Goldie employed it for a cathedral in Sligo, Ireland, and also for his firm's design for Saint James Church in Spanish Place, in London. (The plan of the latter, published in the *English Builder*, clearly shows this device.) Edward W. Pugin and his Irish partner George C. Ashlin used it in the Church of Saint Peter and Saint Paul in Cork City, built between 1859 and 1866. Saint Colman's Cathedral, mentioned earlier, was another source; one can also see this building's general influence on the Newark scheme.[15] Though O'Rourke's use of this treatment at Newark may seem unusual, it had precedents admired in his own time.[16] O'Rourke had previously looked to details of Saint Colman's for his scheme for Saint Paul the Apostle in New York in the 1870s.

Newarkers, of course, were little aware of these matters of architectural design and history. It satisfied most, and enchanted many, when they read in the *Newark Daily Advertiser* that the new cathedral would "compare with many noted cathedrals of the 'Old World.'"[17] Some people in and around Newark would have seen one of the legendary cathedrals abroad before leaving their homelands, but the vast majority of Newarkers—the working class, immigrants, or first- and second-generation Americans—probably had not; moreover, they had a slim chance of ever seeing one in their circumscribed futures. But they now looked forward to having a great cathedral in Newark. The *Advertiser* article also claimed that the new cathedral would "take its place among the greatest productions of architectural art on this continent." If the latter came from O'Rourke's promotional material, the newspaper was not embarrassed to use it. It only sounded more brassy chords for Newark: "It is a matter of pride too that the plans of a Newark architect should have proved superior to others offered and that the cathedral will be erected under the auspices of local talent."

Branch Brook Park: A Sanctuary outside the Cathedral

Simultaneous with the cathedral project, another form of design and construction began to transform Newark. Public funding and private donations made possible an extraordinary county park system, Newark's glorious response to the nationwide City Beautiful movement. Its proponents, taking cues from Europe, believed that civic life and the spaces where it was enacted should be planned with more discipline and imagination and that the government should direct and systematize these efforts. Some of this impulse also spread, as did a taste for classical architecture, from the 1893 Columbian Exposition. Though O'Rourke was doubtful about the Columbian Exposition's effect on architectural preferences, Monsignor Doane became the City Beautiful movement's local apostle. In public statements and in his *Sunday Call* letters (and always knowing with whom to have a quiet word), he joined with other persuasive voices on behalf of Newark's efforts to build a new post office, police station, city hall, and public library, all in various classical styles (and none designed by O'Rourke), as well as the county park system. When locals spawned the latter and voters assured its success with a $2.5 million bond bill, it had the distinction of being the first county park system in the country. After praising the seven parks making up the Essex County Park system in one of his *Sunday Call* letters, Doane used an inquiring, friendly rhetorical device that he always favored:

Cathedral Chapel of Our Lady and Saint Patrick. Dedicated in 1870, it was erected on the second of three sites eventually purchased for the Newark cathedral. *Courtesy of Seton Hall University Archives & Special Collections Center.*

Jeremiah O'Rourke; his wife, Elizabeth Dunn O'Rourke; and two children, probably William and Joseph, about 1864. *Author's collection and courtesy of Helen O'Rourke Denig.*

George Hobart Doane. *Center*: Father Doane about 1870, when he traveled abroad to study cathedrals. *Upper left*: Monsignor Doane, about 1889. *Lower right*: Saint Patrick's Pro-Cathedral, where Doane was pastor. *From a program hosted by the Young Men's Catholic Association in 1889; courtesy of Seton Hall University Archives & Special Collections Center.*

Christ Church (Episcopal) Newark. With ties to the Doane family, it served as a model for Jeremiah O'Rourke. *Photograph (1948); courtesy of the Newark Public Library.*

Chapel of the Immaculate Conception, Seton Hall, South Orange, New Jersey. This small Gothic gem was designed by Jeremiah O'Rourke. Father Doane preached at its dedication. The photograph predates later additions. *From a postcard (about 1900); courtesy of Seton Hall University Archives & Special Collections Center.*

Saint John's Church, Orange, New Jersey. Its fine spire also suggests those O'Rourke intended for Sacred Heart Cathedral. *Photograph (2011) by the author.*

Pugin's Saint Giles Church, Cheadle, England. Splendid in every way, it became very influential. *Courtesy of Rex Harris.*

Design for Saint James Church, Spanish Place, London, by Goldie, Child, and Goldie. The scheme conveys English architect George Goldie's manner and design features of Newark's unbuilt Cathedral of Our Lady & Saint Patrick. Published in *Building News*, 1885. *Author's collection.*

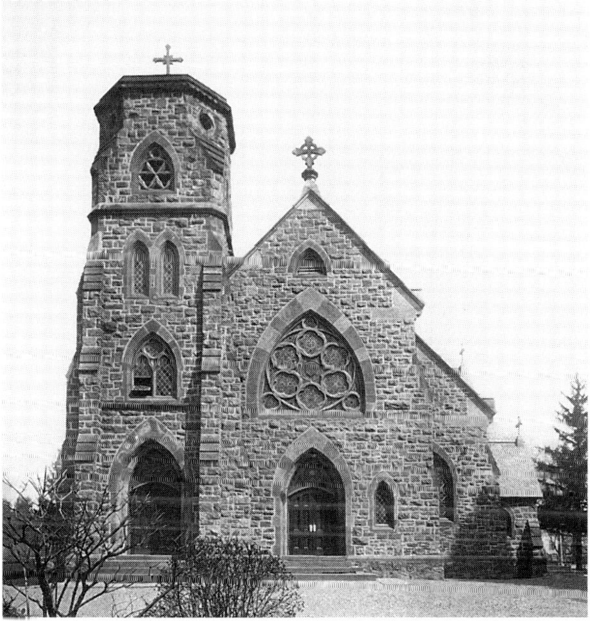

Saint Mary's Church, Dover, New Jersey. Another of O'Rourke's Pugin-influenced works, its spireless tower is a reminder of the Panic of 1873 and the economic aftermath that extinguished Newark's original plans for a new cathedral. *Photograph (about 1901); courtesy of the Archives of Saint Mary's Church, Dover, New Jersey.*

Saint Colman's Cathedral, Cobh, Ireland. Begun in the late 1860s, this project influenced later large churches in Britain and the United States, including O'Rourke's. The cathedral's prominent siting is also like that of Sacred Heart in Newark. Its spire was not built until the early twentieth century. *From a stereoscope photograph (before 1911); author's collection.*

O'Rourke's scheme for the Church of Saint Paul the Apostle in New York, 1874. *From John Gilmary Shea, ed.,* Catholic Churches of New York City; *author's collection.*

The O'Rourke firm's scheme for Sacred Heart Cathedral. The watercolor rendering was published with other detailed drawings in *American Architect and Building News*, 1905. *Courtesy of Avery Architectural and Fine Arts Library, Columbia University.*

Abbey Church of Saint Ouen, Rouen, France. The angled towers, later replaced, became a model for Sacred Heart. *From D. Ramée,* Le moyen-âge monumental et archéologique *(Paris: A. Hauser, 1843); author's collection.*

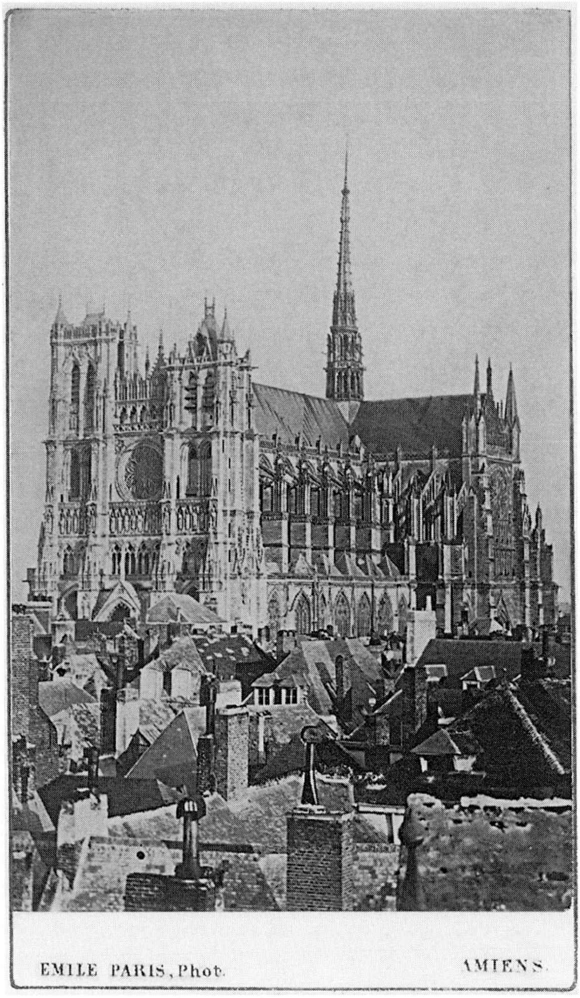

Amiens Cathedral. Isaac Ditmars drew upon some of its features when altering Sacred Heart's scheme beginning in 1910. *From a* carte de visite *of Father Doane from the 1870 trip abroad to study cathedrals; courtesy of Seton Hall University Archives & Special Collections Center.*

Rheims cathedral capital. Isaac Ditmars copied the mounded leaf in the upper center as a repeated device for Sacred Heart's capitals. *Photograph (detail) from Paul Vitry,* La cathedrale de Rheims: Architecture et sculpture *(Paris: Librarie Centrale des Beaux-Arts, 1919); courtesy of the Morgan Library & Museum.*

Edward M. Waldron. His construction firm built Sacred Heart from 1899 through its exterior completion in the 1920s. *From C. Albert Gasser,* Men of Newark *(Newark: Shultz & Gasser, 1904); author's collection.*

Workers and supervisors at the Sacred Heart construction site, circa 1910. The workforce that raised Sacred Heart, like Newark itself, was ethnically and racially diverse. Architect Isaac Ditmars is in the first row standing, second from left, wearing a vest. *Courtesy of the Newark Public Library.*

Sacred Heart Cathedral, unfinished exterior, from the north, 1920. The boldly articulated composition of the apse side was part of O'Rourke's conception. *Courtesy of the Archdiocese of Newark.*

Sacred Heart Cathedral, unfinished interior, 1933. *Courtesy of Newark Public Library.*

Sacred Heart Cathedral, 1954. *Courtesy of Seton Hall University Archives & Special Collections Center.*

Adalbert Mayer, Bernward Mayer, Gonippo Raggi, Oscar Zettler, and Louis Raggi. The Raggis were in Europe to coordinate with teams of artisans, including leaders here of the firm that produced Sacred Heart's stained glass. *Courtesy of the Zettler family through Bernard Flanagan.*

Architect Paul C. Reilly. He joined Isaac Ditmars on the Sacred Heart Cathedral commission in 1926 and was architect for the cathedral's completion a generation later. *Photograph (mid-1950s); courtesy of the Reilly family.*

Sacred Heart Cathedral, 1954. Completed interior. *Courtesy of Seton Hall University Archives & Special Collections Center.*

Sacred Heart Cathedral, 1954. Completed sanctuary, showing (*left to right*) the cathedra, altar and baldachin, and pulpit. *Courtesy of Seton Hall University Archives & Special Collections Center.*

Sacred Heart Cathedral, facing the narthex screen and nave rose window and before the gallery organ casework was installed, 1954. *Courtesy of Seton Hall University Archives & Special Collections Center.*

Sacred Heart Cathedral, interior north transept portal. Newark's cathedral-building bishops are among the subjects sculpted in the screen: Bayley, Corrigan, Wigger, and O'Connor, as well as Archbishops Walsh and Boland. Bishop McNulty, who supervised completion, is also depicted. *Photograph (2009); courtesy of Robert Kozlarek.*

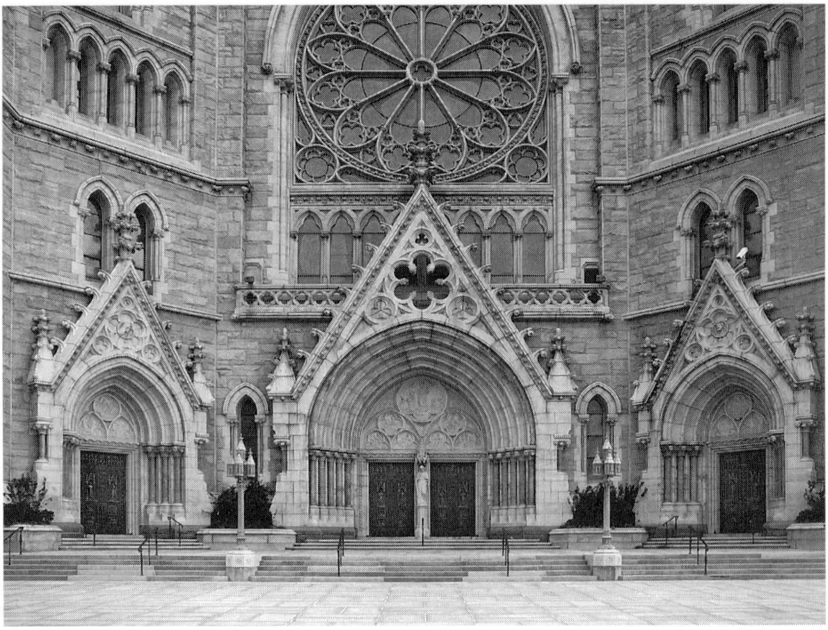

Sacred Heart's main portal. The angled towers create a broad, dramatic façade. The exceptional bronze doors were modeled and produced in Rome. *Photograph (2006); courtesy of Michael G. Soriano, AIA.*

Sacred Heart Cathedral, from near the Broad Street Station, Newark. *Photograph (2008); courtesy of Oren Levin.*

"Reader, do you know their names? Eastside, Westside, Weequahic Reservation, Branch Brook, Orange, Eagle Rock Reservation and South Mountain Reservation."[18]

The system's crown jewel was to be Branch Brook Park, adjacent to the cathedral site. Branch Brook's nucleus was sixty acres that had held a city reservoir. But the park's footprint of the mid-1890s soon expanded north, first to Bloomfield Avenue, then encompassing a long swath of marshland known as the Blue Jay Swamp. When a rumor spread that the park commissioners wanted to annex part of the cathedral property, Doane went straight to his friends on the commission and received assurance that the diocese had nothing to worry about.[19] By the time construction on Sacred Heart started, 278 acres of the new park wrapped the west side of the site and extended almost a mile and a half beyond it, well into north Newark.

The Olmsted Brothers, a leading landscape design firm, realized the park commission's plans. In the first decade of the century, as new greenswards and flowerbeds were spread out like carpets, and ornamental shrubs and specimen trees blossomed, Branch Brook Park (and the other parks, too) became a favorite destination for Newarkers' leisure hours. Doane declared:

> As the spring is coming on, I try to go to Branch Brook Park once a week to watch the grass as it throws off its brown and takes on its emerald hue, the trees as the leaves begin to appear, the plants and bushes as they grow green and all the marvelous changes which nature, with her two enchanter's wands, the sun and the rain, works every year before our eyes as she weaves her magic spell. . . . [T]he parks as they are and the parks as they were . . . are perfect transformation scenes. Who could believe that the old depository for rubbish should now be the southern division of the Branch Brook Park; the old Blue Jay swamp, with its tangled undergrowth and stagnant water, should now be its northern division? There is not greater difference between black and white, and night and day than between them. The same may be said of Orange Park, as it was and as it is.[20]

In summer, band concerts and a wading pool for bathers drew crowds to Branch Brook. In winter, the ice skating was perfect. Doane thought the frozen waters made the park "Holland over again," and seeing the young skaters made him wish he were "a boy once more."[21]

The Olmsted firm had designed the Columbian Exposition's amazing water features, and they brought their skill for these to Newark, where they were aided in creating them by the high water table of the old Morris Canal, whose former course ran along one side of the park. The Olmstead scheme for Branch Brook included a spectacular fountain in a former city reservoir a little southwest of the cathedral site.[22] Doane informed his *Sunday Call* readers that its discharge was "greater than that of any other fountain in the world," waxing, "How the watery diamonds sparkle and play as the sun shines upon them and the wind drives and tosses them about!"[23] A new craze for sending postcards had taken hold, and several scenes depicting the cathedral under construction, with this aquatic marvel in the foreground, were sent around the world by the thousands.

Several years after starting work, the park commission sought another $1 million in public funds to complete a number of features and assure adequate maintenance for the parks. They faced some resistance. Doane aided their case in a March 1902 *Sunday Call* piece titled "Essex County Parks":

> A thousand and one things remain to be done, the finishing touches have to be put, and that million will do as much in its way as the four that have gone before it. Fortunately, that bill passed the Legislature, as well as two other bills making provision for the maintenance of the parks. I admire the wisdom with which they were drawn. They certainly are sure of the Governor's signature. Two of the bills are to be referred to the popular vote next November, and can we doubt the result? The time has gone by for arguing in favor of the parks. When they were in the abstract, the question might be asked, why? But now that they are in the concrete, they speak in their beauty, their convenience, their utility, for themselves.[24]

Monsignor Doane foresaw that the future cathedral and the new park promised a symbiosis of building and nature and that the vistas of Sacred Heart as viewed from the park would call to mind the cathedral settings of Amiens in France and Durham and Salisbury in England. He, like others, also expected Newark's continuous growth, a dense urban reach pushing outward, especially around and beyond the cathedral site and Branch Brook Park. What then seemed somewhat remote, they thought, would in the future be part of a greater downtown district. "I think you are wise," Doane advised Bishop Wigger about starting cathedral construction, "to begin as soon as the Park is finished—that part of town will be built up, and ten years will make a vast difference."[25] Doane, it will be seen, was not infallible. Over time the splendid park would force Newark's Catholic leaders to contend with the disadvantage of Branch Brook's virtue. Its protected land prohibited residential development in a large precinct around the cathedral, and hence the number of regular church-goers living close by. This, in turn, forever altered the role that the cathedral would play in the daily life of the city.

Still, Doane and others were persuasive enthusiasts about Branch Brook's transformative effect on the Newark they loved: "There is no more beautiful pleasure ground in the world than Branch Brook Park, even as it is at present, with its roads, turf, flowers, trees, shrubbery, lake and waterways, and the Orange Mountains in the distance. They always remind me of the Alban and the Sabine hills as seen across the Campagna at Rome. What will it not be when the improvements now about to be commenced are completed?"[26]

13

Progress and Setbacks

SIMULTANEOUS WITH the grand-scale landscaping work in Branch Brook Park, contractors began readying the cathedral site in early 1898. In late spring, a firm led by Peter Boyle, from a family of well-regarded builders in nearby Kearny, constructed the foundations, subsurface bearing walls, and the underground footings for the cathedral's structural columns. An earlier press notice, almost certainly produced by O'Rourke, told Newarkers what was intended: "The substratum of the site will be of gray sandstone, and foundation walls and piers will be level in solid rock."[1]

Early the next year, Boyle's laborers added to the foundation walls of brownstone, bringing them to the height of the water table. The record of this early phase suggests that work moved ahead with quiet efficiency. The *Sunday Call* soon claimed confidently, "The foundation has been carefully and substantially laid."[2]

Laying of the Cornerstone

The time had come for the ceremonial laying of the cornerstone. It was scheduled for Sunday, June 11, 1899, and was to be preceded by a citywide parade. Early on that afternoon, and by the train-car-full, marchers and spectators arrived from Essex, Bergen, Union, Passaic, Morris, and Sussex counties, representatives from virtually every parish in the diocese. As special trains from Hudson County arrived at the Centre Street Station, they were greeted by the bells of Saint John's Church, chiming national airs and the sturdy tune of the unofficial American Catholic anthem, "Holy God, We Praise Thy Name." Vying with each other in turnout and deportment and led by the colorful banners of their allegiances came contingents of the Knights of Columbus, the Ancient Order of Hibernians, the German Parochial Association, the Catholic Benevolent League, Saint Patrick's Alliance, the Sons of Italy, and exuberant youth groups. Some were dressed in uniforms, many donned sashes and badges, all were in their Sunday best

More than a dozen bands marched—Beck's, McLaughlin's, Holding's, Saint Alfonso's, Drake's Elizabeth, Clementis, Washington, Larrett's Military, Alessio's Twenty-second Regiment, the American Fife and Drum Corps, the Imperial Fife and Drum Corps, and the Italian National. They played favorite marches and national airs, which in turn-of-the-century Newark meant American, Irish, German, and Italian melodies. Fifty, even twenty-five years earlier, such a demonstration would have disgruntled many Newarkers, but those bothered by the prospect of congested streets, packed trolleys. and noisy band music—all for the gratification of Catholics—held their tongues.

The line of march, more than fifteen thousand men—and they were all men (as in virtually every aspect of this history of building a cathedral in Newark, women were spectators)—was watched and cheered along a gently rising route of the city's wide streets and ended at the construction site, where the shoulder-high granite walls foretold the enormous scale of the future cathedral.[3] There, a vast crowd swarmed over the entire site. Estimated by some to be one hundred thousand people, by others twenty-five thousand, the police estimate of fifty thousand was probably the most accurate. Even this populist turnout had a privileged class, and it was seated on 350 chairs upon a covered platform erected over the future apse: priests and monsignors; bishops; mothers superior from the orders serving diocesan schools and institutions, wearing their veils and wimples and scapulars; and the local civic and Catholic elite. Across Ridge Street, spectators found their way into a new high school building, known as Barringer High, and watched from atop the roof and windows facing the site. Nickols's full band, the city's best, struck up arrangements of a march from *Tannhauser*, movements from Mozart's "Twelfth Mass," Mendelssohn's "Priest's March" from *Athalia*, and Haydn's "The Heavens Are Telling," interspersed with Bach and Rossini.

When the bell of the little Church of the Sacred Heart rang three times, signaling the start of the ceremony, a procession emerged from it: cross-bearer, robed acolytes carrying a vessels filled with holy water and incense, surpliced priests, prelates wearing pectoral crosses, and, finally, with miter and crosier, diminutive Bishop Wigger. An advance guard of police on horseback forged a path for the cortege through the dense crowd. As the throng joined in "Holy God, We Praise Thy Name," the bishop blessed the cornerstone, inscribed in Arabic and English, and in which was set two pieces of marble from Bethlehem and Jerusalem. Then he and a small entourage of clergy tried, as the rubrics instructed, to bless the entire cruciform perimeter of the partially built granite walls. But the faithful and the curious, pressing in for a closer look at such a rare ritual, formed an impenetrable human wall. After repeated attempts to push through it, the bishop and attendants concluded that the expedient course was to consider all the walls blessed and to move ahead with the remainder of the ceremony.

Bishop Bernard McQuaid, now in his late seventies, came from Rochester to preach the sermon. Some on the platform must have held their breath when he proclaimed, "I do not believe in monumental churches as a rule."[4] But he retreated from this precipice, saying, "when we have Greater Newark, and this magnificent city expands, this cathedral will stand in the center of it and will be a fitting monument to the faith. . . . Such will be the growth in this section that the cathedral will not be too large for the people."

He gave an off-the-cuff history of the Catholic Church in New Jersey. Reminding some, informing others in the crowd, McQuaid spoke of Bayley's arrival in Newark a half century before, of the hard times, and of the dark years among the Know-Nothings, "a low, mean contemptible organization . . . seeking to destroy the Church" and who "shot down innocent men and women." Not one to forget an offense, McQuaid felt "their crimes have not been atoned" and that time could not "wipe out the memory of these atrocities." Gaunt and stooped, his voice muted by age and hoarseness, McQuaid was yet the old warrior. Loath to release an enmity of fifty years, he said more about those atrocities and of Bayley's pacific approach to conflict. McQuaid's extemporization bowed to religious sentiments, and, as always, he made a plug for parochial education, but mostly he blew upon the horns of triumph in adversity, of pride in what had been accomplished, of what Catholics would do in the future. His appreciative listeners interrupted with clapping and cheers. Whether they (or he) realized it, most of McQuaid's themes about the Church's trajectory in Newark also described his own remarkable life story.

There was one sign, at least, that length of years might have mellowed McQuaid just a bit: he singled out Monsignor Doane for the contributions he made to the cathedral project. When the old bishop's voice gave out, he regretted that he had “more in his head to tell them than he could express with his throat” and turned the service over to Archbishop Corrigan, a son of Newark, to deliver the final blessing. Corrigan commanded the entire throng, and many instinctively fell to their knees on the bare ground and prayed with him.

It was by then early evening—a warm, lovely evening—and the crowd, after it joined in singing “America,” descended in a slow, orderly dispersal from the hill, making their way home by foot and carriage, on trolley and train. They took away souvenirs, a leaflet with the words to the hymns, and half-dollar-size pins showing a drawing of the cathedral. The perfect weather, the crowds, and the sense of expectation, gave the events a pulsing energy—an aura of a rite of spring—that stirred at least one young couple to become engaged that day.[5] Down the hill from the cathedral site, at the O’Rourke house on Burnett Street, night fell on a day that had been long anticipated. Jeremiah well knew that to design a cathedral—as enduring as anything in an ephemeral world—was an extraordinary opportunity, the fulfillment of a lifetime. And in the past few days he had the assurance of hearing and reading what none other than the bishop had said: “nothing shall be allowed to modify” his design.[6] At length, the capstone of the architect’s career, no less than the cornerstone of Sacred Heart Cathedral, had been set in place on that blessed, sun-kissed June day.

Construction Progress

Construction of the cathedral walls began again in early fall 1899 by E. M. Waldron & Company. The diocese had given a two-year, $200,000 agreement to Waldron following competitive bidding for the work of general contractor, meaning that the firm would supply all labor and the building materials.[7] Edward Waldron founded the firm that bore his name with his two brothers a decade before. Born in Ireland, he came at age sixteen to Newark, where he apprenticed as a bricklayer, eventually becoming a journeyman mason and forming a partnership with James Moran, an established builder whose daughter he married. (Moran’s firm constructed the Seton Hall Chapel and Saint John’s Church in Orange.)

Waldron aggressively built his operation into one of the largest in the region for commercial and institutional work, including the admired Essex County Park Commission administration building. The firm’s previous ecclesiastical contracts included Our Lady Help of Christians in East Orange, designed by O’Connor and Metcalf, competitors for the cathedral commission. Shrewd, ruggedly handsome, and increasingly well-off, Waldron took uncomplicated pleasure in the good life. Born in a cottage of no more than 150 square feet and shared with ten siblings, he resided in America in large, comfortable homes, first in Newark and, later, in a well-to-do South Orange neighborhood, and enjoyed big-ticket luxuries forever out of reach of all but the rarest first-generation Americans.[8] One was a pipe organ installed to entertain house guests, who frequently included the laborers he employed, binding their loyalty to him and his company. Like O'Rourke, Waldron was interested in Democratic Party politics; beginning in 1895, he served two terms as a Newark alderman. In 1908, he bucked his party leadership and ran for mayor, but lost the election and, for several years, the goodwill of the local Democratic establishment. His independent streak nonetheless well served his business interests.

For the cathedral's principal building material, O'Rourke and his clients considered marble, limestone, and granite, ultimately choosing granite. In planning the 1870 cathedral, Newark held to the Puginian preference for local stone, but different forces, especially those stemming from the 1893 Columbian Exposition, pushed prevailing taste toward light-colored building materials. O'Rourke's recommendation, to be supplied from quarries in Fitzwilliam, New Hampshire, that were controlled by Norcross Brothers, based in Worcester, Massachusetts, is formally categorized as a white granite.[9] But it has hues of light pastels that ultimately gave the cathedral a warmth absent in structures built of the snowy stones popular around that time.

A harsh winter and the stone supplier's dilatory shipments were drags on construction during the first year. The diocese and O'Rourke were frustrated by the pace, but O'Rourke nonetheless commented approvingly on Waldron's construction methods and, on the whole, the architect's and builder's early working relationship was productive and amiable. There was general satisfaction when this phase was finished in April 1902. O'Rourke took several opportunities to complement Waldron's work in letters to the bishop, saying at one point that his firm's work was "highly creditable to them as reputable building contractors, all the more so as, comparing the amount of their contract with the quantities and character of the works executed the margin of profit must, if any be small indeed."[10]

In this period, the Waldron firm was given a separate contract to build the foundations to carry the steel framing for the floors of the cathedral's apse end. As Waldron's workers built the concrete supports, they had, in some places, to dig eight feet beneath the basement level to find bedrock, an indication that it was both uneven and unusually deep across the northern end of the cathedral site.

The next construction phase called for erecting the interior piers (or columns), completing the exterior walls and the clerestory, and roofing the whole structure. One hundred thirty feet would also be added to the towers, bringing them to 180 feet, not quite twice as high as the walls. When the work of this phase was finished, scheduled in the contract for January 1, 1907, the cathedral's scale and design would be apparent. As O'Rourke prepared new construction documents, he also, at Bishop O'Connor's behest, worked out cost-reducing changes to the plans and specifications; the most significant was the decision to substitute a comparable but cheaper granite.

In August 1902, the diocese again awarded the work to the Waldron firm, but this time it made a "cost plus" arrangement, in which the contractor would be paid for all material and labor costs, plus an agreed-upon percentage, in this case 5 percent. Such terms assure the builder's profit margin. From the client's perspective, however, it is potentially worrisome, because the contractor has little incentive to contain expenses, which are reimbursed and then topped up with an assured profit. In this equation, the builder's earnings also rise as reimbursable expenses increase. In a "cost-plus" contract, the client must rely on the builder's cost-consciousness and integrity and the architect's diligence in examining and approving expenses.

By April 1903, thirteen workers at the site were preparing the stone from the Emerson (Troy) Granite Company, which O'Rourke had chosen in place of the former, more costly granite supplier. This and other quarries in Fitzwilliam, New Hampshire, ultimately were the source of the granite most visible in the cathedral. Fitzwilliam granite was admired in this period for its uniform color and, because of a low iron content, little discoloration.

Waldron wrote to the bishop of the work under way: "We have arranged that when ten car loads are delivered at the site, to start one gang of stone cutters, which is thirteen men with foreman and blacksmith and two helpers. We have to start with a small gang until everything is working as we want it to, and then if it be your wish we can easily add one or two gangs more. We call them gangs because of the rules of the union which require a blacksmith to sharpen tools for each gang of thirteen men."[11] He suggested, "We will be pleased to have you call and examine the stone and see for yourself that we have given the color and quality that we promised you in the way of matching the Norcross Brothers' stone [the previous source for the granite]. We have even been able to please Mr. O'Rourke who examined the stone on Saturday."

In late winter of the following year, construction moved quickly, with marked progress on the towers and the main facade. However, in the face of escalating expenses and overruns, the diocese expressed concern to Waldron and O'Rourke about the fiscal controls of the cost-plus system. Waldron was put out by the suggestion that his firm was in any way responsible for renegade expenses. O'Rourke thought that, while the arrangement burdened his office with examining and approving expenses (a task it had been doing with exacting care), it served the diocese well. He thought, however, that a change might help allay persistent complaints about the project's high expenses.

The diocese looked most seriously at the merits of a lump-sum contract, by which the client agrees to pay a fixed amount for specified work, and which is appealing because building costs are known in advance. For the contractor, his profitability is determined by how astutely he bids and then manages costs. O'Rourke warned of perils, and to be sure this arrangement creates an inherent incentive for the contractor to reduce expenses in order to boost profits—cost-cutting that can sacrifice the quality of materials and workmanship. It also means that the architect must be hawkish in protecting his client's interests.

After hand-wringing, the diocese finally decided on a lump-sum (or fixed) contract, and the bishop instructed O'Rourke to create new bidding documents. Eight construction firms were asked to make submissions. At the same time, O'Rourke revised construction documents, providing more detailed drawings. He altered as well the construction schedule, dividing this third phase of work into eight subsections of activity, a systematic program that would advance construction to the point, as the supplanted contract did, where the cathedral's superstructure would be finished except for the spires and decorative elements. Inflation had caused labor and material costs to spike, leading O'Rourke to advise the diocese to limit the new contract to only several of the eight subsections, in the hope that the construction market would cool and later subsections might be bought at lower prices. Entering a bid that was 10 percent below any other firm, Waldron was again given the job, and a new agreement was signed shortly after New Year's 1905.[12] The completion date was set for January 1908, though the diocese reserved the right to accelerate it by one year, presumably if fund-raising could support a brisker schedule.

Death of Monsignor Doane

As the project crept forward, Monsignor Doane bowed under advancing years. He kept a heavy schedule of official and social activities and still traveled, yet with waning vigor. He was frustrated but philosophical. In candid moments with friends, he confided that he doubted that he would live to see the cathedral finished. After a trip was curtailed by illness, he wrote a *Sunday Call* piece that lifted the curtain on his thoughts about the encroachments of growing old and less well and concluded with a wistful salutation to Newark:

> As a rule I avoid the "personal equation," but there have been so many kind inquiries about my health since my return, a month sooner than I expected, that I take advantage of this opportunity to say a word on the subject. People ask me, how I am, and it is a hard question to answer. All I know is that "I am not myself at all." Pius IX of happy memory said to me once: "*Senectus ipse est morbus*" (old age is a disease of itself). He had found it out then; I have found it out now. I am suffering from one of the Protean symptoms of advancing years. It has been coming on a long time, and every day I feel less and less well, though there seems to be no organic trouble. My old friend, Father Fulton, when he was failing, used to say to people who asked him how he was, "No better, thank you." I can say the same. It may be the "gradual drawing of the dusky veil." I can still do more or less, but am cut off from much that I could do, and loved to do. Whether it will ever come back remains to be seen. . . . Whatever more I may see, I am proud and glad to have lived long enough to see Newark develop into the great city it has, and promising to advance still more in beauty and prosperity. *Floreant Novarce!* (May Newark flourish.)
>
> G. H. Doane, Newark, August 12, 1903[13]

Sixteen months after offering this meditation, and following an afternoon drive around Newark and dinner with his curates, George Hobart Doane died peacefully in his study in the cathedral rectory. As the news spread, it seemed as if all the bells of Newark tolled in succession. An outpouring of official and personal tributes filled the newspapers, beginning with the *Call*'s declaration that "Newark has lost one of its most useful citizens."[14] He died on a Friday, and the following Sunday in pulpits all over the region, priests (and many ministers) gave panegyrics. A leader of Newark's Jewish community joined in the outpouring, noting that Doane's, "charities and efforts were spent alike on every denomination. Jew and Gentile join in revering his memory and paying just tribute to his worth. With Shakespeare, we can truly say of him, 'The elements so mixed in him, that Nature might stand up, and say to all the world "This was a man!"'"

Among the most dozens of memorials published in Newark newspapers, the attorney Cortland Parker's stands out:

> The death of Monsignor Doane is an event which will distress a very large number of the citizens of Newark. I do not think of any one who was personally more popular than he. He was so affable, so kindly, so charitable, so good humored, so prudent as to all differences of opinion, so learned, so witty and properly gay, and withal so interested in everything literary or artistic, so evidently fond of Newark and desirous of her prosperity and good name, that all men respected, and multitudes cherished a near approach to affection for him.
>
> The general good will which he obtained is remarkable, because his religious opinions and early departure from the Church of which his father in his life time, and his brother now are such great ornaments, naturally were obstacles to general favor in a city where religious sentiment hostile to those which he adopted were all but universal at the time he came among us. It is beyond question that his prudent life had done very much to generate charitable ideas toward the church he adopted and so earnestly served, and perhaps to increase the amount and the sway of Christian charity generally. Peace to his memory! He was a rare good man. Would that more such were found everywhere.[15]

Newark was small enough for Doane's passing to be felt genuinely and widely; it was large enough that the obsequies were played out on a heroic scale. A pageant of mourning commenced on the Sunday afternoon after his death, the likes of which the city had never seen. Nearly eight thousand people gathered around Saint Patrick's rectory to watch the transfer of his remains to the cathedral. A reporter felt that "an awe-inspired silence fell over" them as the rectory doors opened and the coffin was taken out. A cross bearer and thirty acolytes in surplices and purple cassocks processed toward the church, parting the mute crowd without a command, followed by eight men who carried the casket shoulder high. In the church, where black and purple bunting draped columns and capitals, altars and pulpit, priests chanted in Latin as the body was brought down the aisle. Children trebled Newman's "Lead Kindly Light" as the casket was arranged on the inclined catafalque. Then the coffin lid was lifted and, resting in violet plush, was Monsignor Doane, dead. The congregation gasped. Old women whimpered; young women sobbed; grown men cried. Over the next two days and nights, Doane's wake brought a stream of mourners through the cathedral at the rate of two thousand an hour.

Before the start of the Solemn High Requiem mass for Monsignor Doane, the honorary pallbearers filed in. Jeremiah O'Rourke was first among them, followed by Newark's leading professionals—Dr. Charles Zeh, Dr. James Eliot, Dr. John Richmond, jurists Michael Ledwith and Cortland Parker, Colonel Edward Wright, Michael Walsh, Hugh Smith, Hugh Murray, Timothy Ryan, and others of Newark's old and newer gentry. The deceased monsignor's brother, the Episcopal bishop of Albany, William C. Doane, led the family party and other prominent mourners given seats of honor: former governor Franklin Murphy, Senator James Smith, and numerous Shanleys, Kinneys, and Condits.

As the bishop began the rites, Seton Hall seminarians sang a Gregorian setting of the *Benedictus*, adding modal harmony that set a shiver through the church. As the bishop gave the final commendation to the soul of George Hobart Doane, the three hundred priests in the church held lighted candles, and after prayers, Joseph M. Byrne, a moneyed Newark insurance executive with a good voice, "with much feeling" sang the Victorian potboiler "Calvary." This musical touch, after the Gregorian chant, somber pieces on the large Erben pipe organ in the loft, and psalms and hymns, was characteristic of Doane, integrating, as it did, high style and popular appeal that the great and confident can mix with integrity.

Later in the afternoon, several thousand braved temperatures in the teens and wind-driven snow to attend the burial in Holy Sepulcher Cemetery. As the cortege moved along Newark's streets, the bells of the churches along the route tolled. At Saint Michael's Hospital, which Doane had done much to create and support, doctors, nurses, and patients watched from every window in silent tribute. When the hearse, pulled by four jet-black horses, approached the Central Bridge, several hundred schoolchildren assembled there sang out "Nearer My God to Thee" and "Calvary" and "Jerusalem."

Doane's sense of liturgical protocols was observed to the end: his three assistants at the cathedral parish officiated at the burial. Seeing that many men and women were on their knees on the snowy, wet ground and shivering, one of them encouraged the mourners to keep their hats on. In choked whispers they said the concluding three Hail Mary's and the Our Father, joined in the latter, a reporter noted, by the many Protestants at the graveside. The lowering of the casket and watching the ceremonial first shovels of earth brought more tears. The *Advertiser* reported that the mourning was "the most extraordinary demonstration ever witnessed in city and State."[16]

The new cathedral remained close to Monsignor Doane's heart to the last; letters asking for support that he had just drafted were found on his desk after his death. Many such letters remained to be written by others, but Doane made an irreducible contribution to the project. A movement to memorialize him started immediately, and O'Rourke played a leading role. Some, including John Cotton Dana, thought the funds raised in Doane's name should establish some form of educational endowment. Yet the inclination for a statue erected in a prominent location prevailed. A full-length bronze statue of Doane, in the robes of a monsignor, was put up, ironically or at least provocatively, in Rector Park, adjacent to Trinity Church, the oldest Episcopal church in Newark. Dana thought the result "a quite inferior bronze sculpture by a rather inferior sculptor."[17] Be that as it may, those erecting the monument concluded that no list of accomplishments or virtues, no dates, no epitaph or Homeric epithet needed to be inscribed on the statue's base. Two words, they believed, would bring to every Newarker's mind a legendary life, and two words only: "Monsignor Doane."

Doane left legacies, possible because of his own inheritance, to many Newark charities. He left money to build a stone wall around the cloistered Dominican convent and a bequest that helped fund a new rectory for Saint Patrick's.[18]

Other Perils of Cathedral Building

Other protagonists in the lengthening saga to build the cathedral had also fallen away. A few years before, and shortly into the first phase of construction, Bishop Wigger's poor health failed for the final time. Wigger was succeeded by Father John J. O'Connor. Son of a Newark building contractor, O'Connor was educated in Rome, and at the time of his elevation was vicar general of the diocese (assuring an easy leadership transition) and pastor of Saint Joseph's in Newark, a large church designed by O'Rourke on West Market Street.

The bishop who preceded Wigger and O'Connor in Newark, Michael Corrigan, ultimately paid a horrible price for cathedral building, albeit in

New York City. When Corrigan left Newark in 1880 to become archbishop of New York, he raised the funds to finish the spires of Saint Patrick's Cathedral on Fifth Avenue. Later in his years as archbishop, in 1902, a Lady Chapel was being added to Saint Patrick's apse. It was under construction when, on a winter evening, Corrigan went into the cathedral to pray. He had no reason to suspect that negligence had set a trap. In wrapping up their work in late afternoon, laborers failed to cover or rope off a gaping hole in the floor. As he made his way alone through the dim area under construction, Corrigan plunged into the opening. Viscerally extending his arms, he caught himself from falling through. Dangling in the half dark, the archbishop, never an athletic man, held on, and after desperate exertion, extracted himself. He emerged cut up, strained, and badly shaken. He never recovered. When he died a few months later, his doctors, including his physician brother, put the blame on conditions caused by the accident in the cathedral on the fateful night four months before.[19]

Growing Problems at the Site

In late winter and spring 1905, the construction site was humming. Masons sized, cut, and chiseled the New Hampshire granite. Workman successively erected and repositioned derricks and scaffolds as the masons and their assistants made progress on the walls. Construction was so efficient that by late May the towers had risen to almost 85 feet, within 12 feet of the goal for the immediate scope of work. Whereas the work site was visibly active, another matter related to the cathedral was not, nor meant to be.

The Waldron firm awarded a subcontract for the granite columns that would form the chancel and nave arcade to H. L. Brown and Co., which was among the construction firms that had bid unsuccessfully for the 1904 contract. Waldron and Brown, it appears, had friendly relations. The former neither told O'Rourke that he had signed the agreement with Brown nor that it called for a different granite than that indicated in his contract with the diocese. That contract stipulated that O'Rourke, as the architect and designated representative of the diocese, must approve all subcontractors before Waldron signed any agreements with them, and it also required that the architect ratify any substitutions or changes in the specifications. Such provisions, intended to assure the quality of building materials and construction standards, were, and remain, typical.

When Waldron's sub-rosa deal surfaced, O'Rourke cried foul. He had seen such a possibility lurking in the fixed-cost arrangement—and it came out of the shadows in the form of what he regarded as inferior granite. He asserted that by agreeing to Brown's choice rather than the specified granite from Hallowell, Maine, Waldron's profits increased by between $5,000 and $10,000.[20] The architect called it flagrantly dishonest. When Waldron delivered his next bill, for $12,000, O'Rourke would not approve it, on the grounds that the contractor had no right to payment for materials that he and his clients had not chosen. With O'Rourke's blank refusal, Waldron went to Bishop O'Connor, who soon asked O'Rourke to meet with the builder to discuss their differences. They found a patch of common ground, but not enough to satisfy O'Rourke, who told the bishop not to pay Waldron until he had met all of the contract's terms. On the Fourth of July, 1905, O'Rourke wrote the bishop: "My conference with E. M. Waldron & Co. yesterday afternoon was not all that I could have wished, still some progress was made. The details of the matters at issue with them are strictly business in their nature and connect solely with the proper performance of their contract on the new Cathedral. There is nothing whatever personal in the issues. . . . I hope to arrange them all satisfactorily by a little time and patience, for I have a sincere desire for W. & Co.'s success as all my acts and letters to them abundantly prove."[21]

Construction advanced little as the contractor and architect haggled. Waldron continued to press for payment, but O'Rourke told Bishop O'Connor, "there is, strictly speaking, no payment due them because of their persistent violations and attempted violations . . . of contract."[22] And the architect warned about capitulating: "Your leniency will make it harder for me to make them comply with the contract terms." O'Rourke wrote more to the bishop on the subject, "I have from the first favored Waldron & Co. and incline that way still, but the present issues are so plain as to leave no room for doubt in regard to them, notwithstanding the adroit and deceptive arguments used by Waldron & Co. to cloud and confuse them."[23] But, through negotiation, architect and builder arrived at a compromise they could live with. The substituted granite would be accepted on two conditions: that, as restitution, Waldron would polish the chancel and transept columns without charge and promise that in the future he would adhere to all of the contract's terms. In turn, O'Rourke authorized the outstanding $12,000 invoice and payment for additional work completed since the contested bill was submitted. When Waldron was slow to return the signed agreement, however, O'Rourke became more and more disgusted, telling the bishop that the real reason for delay was that Waldron and the subcontractor had not been able to agree on what part of the additional cost (Waldron called it a loss) each should bear. O'Rourke wrote to the bishop, "This so called loss is in reality nothing but the serious reduction of anticipated saving (graft) by the proposed substitution of granites, if successful, but it has all the effects on them of a real substantial loss. *O Tempora, O Mores.*"[24]

"O tempora, O mores O'Rourke" this time had good reason for his finger-wagging. Payment in hand, Waldron showed little evidence of reform or cooperation. Within weeks, O'Rourke enumerated eleven charges of delinquency. Beating on the drum of dereliction, he repeated the former complaints about subcontractors and inferior granite. Meeting with O'Rourke on the first day of September, Waldron gave his word that all shortcomings would be addressed. But when the architect met with both Waldron brothers a week later, O'Rourke found them "very unreasonable and obstinate" and took away only their concession to give "due consideration" to his grievances.[25]

Using the leverage of payment, O'Rourke refused to approve a new Waldron invoice. When a month had passed since Waldron had assured O'Rourke that his firm would remedy all its delinquencies and there were no substantive improvements, O'Rourke moved aggressively. After advising Bishop O'Connor, he acted on a clause in the contract that permitted him to inform the contractor to comply with the stipulations that they had agreed upon within three days or other laborers would be hired and the expense deducted from Waldron's fees. O'Rourke simultaneously dispatched this "three days' notice" to Waldron, the bishop, and the financial firm that assured Waldron's bond with the diocese. (Bonding protected the diocese in the event of the contractor's financial failure.)

Bishop O'Connor and His Vicar General: Monsignor Sheppard

The notice to Waldron provoked action. He and O'Rourke were called to a meeting at Saint Michael's Church in Jersey City, whose pastor, Monsignor John A. Sheppard, was also vicar general of the diocese. Bishop O'Connor had delegated direct oversight of the cathedral project to Sheppard. Pleasant and bookish, O'Connor was more inclined to scholarly interests than management, and he knew that running diocesan affairs was unlikely to engage his full attention. With self-awareness, he chose a vicar general with a high tolerance for the details of administration. His appointee was also someone with an appreciation for its frequent by-product: control.

John Sheppard was born in Ireland and early came to live in Paterson. He entered the seminary at Seton Hall and, as a new priest, served for seven years at Saint Patrick's Cathedral parish under Doane—where, of course, O'Rourke was a prominent parishioner. An astute operator, he became an early mentor and lifelong confidant of Jersey City's legendary powerbroker, Mayor Frank Hague. When he was made a monsignor, Sheppard arranged an operatically choreographed service at Saint Michael's Church at which a special choir broke into the repeated "Hallelujahs!" from Handel's famous "Messiah" chorus as Sheppard emerged from the sacristy to receive the symbols of his elevated station.[26] After the ceremonies, Delmonico's catered a dinner reception, serving sherry and champagne, a French repast of multiple courses (including *medallions de bass aux crabes d'huitres* and *ris de veau aux champignons frais*), and a thirty-year-old Bordeaux.[27] From his capacious rectory overlooking Hamilton Park in Jersey City, Sheppard presided with a firm hand on ecclesiastical affairs and an eye open to further advancement.

In Sheppard's presence, the exchange between O'Rourke and Waldron was productive, leading to specific understandings, most of which placed the onus on Waldron. The builder agreed not to deviate from the plans and specifications, change drawings, or sign subcontracts without O'Rourke's assent. Waldron also consented, under pressure from O'Rourke, to clean up the cathedral construction site and maintain it better in the future. Finally, Waldron agreed to rehire the project's former general foreman, whom he had dismissed. O'Rourke apparently felt that the poor progress made during the good working conditions of the warm months could be attributed to the new foreman's failings. Inserting himself in the rehiring process, O'Rourke also wanted to interview the earlier foreman before Waldron officially brought him back. It was another play for control in an escalating contest of wills.

Soon after the former foreman was rehired, O'Rourke asked for a meeting with the Waldrons. The builders thought it was unnecessary and dragged their feet, but a month later they agreed to meet. The session, without obstruction or edginess, brought forth good feelings. Shortly before Christmas, O'Rourke certified another Waldron payment. Their relations stabilized, for the time being.

14

The Great Foundation Controversy

IN THE WINTER OF 1905–1906, workers made preparations to build the cathedral's arcade. Waldron's men constructed the bases for the columns and then started the difficult task of raising the heavy granite columns upon them. O'Rourke suddenly asked Waldron to halt work, sending two letters in as many days about it. Here the record, though more sketchy than it had been or would be later, discloses trouble of a new kind. O'Rourke's first letter is missing, but Waldron's single response provides an understanding of O'Rourke's concern.[1] The architect saw that not all of the columns were perfectly vertical and questioned whether there were inconsistencies in the lengths of the shafts or in the amount of mortar used to join them. Waldron fired back that he measured the columns and found they varied by only one-half to one inch of each other. Such a variance was a permissible tolerance, a margin of error between the dimensions prescribed by the architect and actual construction, which fell in an acceptable zone of safety and appearance. In making his claim, Waldron was on good ground, but it was an early indication that the columns may not have been.

Other problems vexed them. Waldron repeatedly had to reject portions of the stone delivered by the subcontractor, H. L. Brown, who served as a local distributor for the stone quarry in New Hampshire. O'Rourke pushed Waldron to fire Brown and recommended others to take his place. Pushing from the other side, Brown complained formally to the diocese about Waldron, who countered the grievances. Waldron chided Brown in a testy, revealing letter, stating that all his (Waldron's) troubles with O'Rourke were because of their—Waldron's and Brown's—friendship. It was, of course, the covertly made contract with Brown that first enraged O'Rourke. Attempting independent contact with the supplier, Waldron sent his foreman to their New Hampshire quarries. But he found neither satisfaction nor evidence of any work on the stone for Newark. Whatever his shortcomings may have been, Brown was handicapped by his supplier's inaction. Eventually, it began to ship acceptable stone, and these problems abated.

As the episode wound down, Bishop O'Connor, whose father, it should be remembered, was a Newark builder, did not side with Waldron, saying O'Rourke and the diocese had merely demanded from the firm what it had contracted to do. He affirmed O'Rourke's position in unequivocal language: "Waldron . . . should perform, as every contractor does, subject to the architect."[2] It was a pointed charge that O'Rourke took seriously long after forces eroded it.

BUILDER'S MANEUVERS

The construction schedule lagged through the rest of 1906 and all of the next year. In late 1907, Waldron played at least twice under the table. Doing another end-run around O'Rourke, he demanded $12,000 directly from the bishop, saying he would take legal action if not paid promptly. The diocese, for whatever reason, quickly disbursed $12,000, widening the back-channel from builder to client.

Waldron also again made a substitution of building materials for another important architectural feature. Details of this new difficulty are murky but convey the mounting intensity of the troubles between architect and builder. Two years before, O'Rourke had decided to change the type of stone initially specified for the capitals of the interior columns, preferring a white Alabama marble. He had concluded that this marble was both more handsome and could be more readily sculpted. Bishop O'Connor concurred with the change, and O'Rourke notified Waldron. (It is not unusual for architects to revise the type or source of construction materials, making financial adjustments as necessary with the builder.) Whether this change was formally made in the specifications is not clear, but as the time approached when the stone for the capitals would be needed, Waldron bought neither marble nor the type of granite originally called for.[3] The diocese, or O'Rourke acting for it, had every right to reject it. In a later statement, the subcontractor asserted that O'Rourke had agreed to the substitution if it passed a specific engineering test. According to the subcontractor, it met that test, and he had sent the results to O'Rourke, notifying him that the substitution was being ordered. O'Rourke appears to have ignored the notice but later wrote to Waldron, repeating his assertion that the granite did not meet specification and later characterized Waldron's higher income on this cost-cutting scheme as "illegitimate profit."[4] The record of this new struggle, though imperfect, once more demonstrates Waldron's capacity to disregard specified materials.

Standard practice, formalized in the contract, gave O'Rourke authority to select and monitor materials. He always selected materials with concern for quality and appearance, and when (as was often the case) a tight budget meant cutting back, he carefully chose alternatives. We know, too, from the planning in the 1870s, the pains that O'Rourke and Doane took to search out superior materials and craftsmanship. Now, after years of waiting, a cathedral was finally being built but not exactly to specification. It galled O'Rourke that the diocese was coerced by Waldron's ploys (timed so that rejecting the substitutions would mean construction delays) into accepting substitutions. There was also every reason to believe that unless resisted, the switching game would continue.[5]

In May 1908, Waldron sent another bill. O'Rourke refused approval, contacting Bishop O'Connor immediately. It surfaced then that Waldron's previous bill had been paid. Enraged, O'Rourke said it was an overpayment that gave the builders more illegitimate profit. He also reminded the bishop that the contract had a completion date that was less than a month away and yet more than half of the work for that phase remained unfinished.[6] He pleaded with O'Connor to make no more payments without his consent. Yet Waldron had bills to pay and a payroll to meet and was contending, like everyone, with the business decline precipitated by the Panic of 1907. He needed cash for the work that had been done and through his attorney gave the diocese an ultimatum: Pay the new bill or be sued for breach of contract. Without telling O'Rourke, the diocese paid Waldron again. Learning about this months later, Jeremiah castigated Waldron for circumventing him "in manifest violation of contract and of law, and by deceiving Bishop O'Connor and Monsignor Sheppard."[7]

Though the wrangling between architect and builder slowed construction, the Waldron firm completed the apse and nave columns and was thus able to begin erecting structural elements that would carry the clerestory. As this was under way, at least one of the columns appeared to have shifted or settled under the weight of the additional load. At this juncture it is unclear how serious the problem was and whether it indicated systemic troubles with all of the columns.

Behind this worrying development were several years of progressively hostile clashes between O'Rourke and Waldron, unreconciled grievances, and a residue of mistrust. O'Rourke's desire for control and insistence on following the protocol that ordered and bounded the responsibilities of architects, owners, and contractors had deeply frustrated the Waldrons. For their part, they often tested accepted boundaries, and their most arrogant maneuvers violated them, leaving the diocese little sensible choice than to see the cathedral built with materials it had not at first preferred. The Waldrons' modus operandi also, as O'Rourke kept saying, left them with higher profits, and the architect countered with the best weapon he had: control of payments. It was also deep in O'Rourke's nature to lash out at perceived moral or ethical failing. Moreover, he now felt it was his professional duty to protect the cathedral project from what he considered to be Waldron's deceitful, undermining maneuvers. Weighing the legitimacy of their grievances up to this point, the scales tip in the architect's favor. But in the face of this potentially grave problem with the columns, each now seized upon it for his own purposes.

Confused over the conflicting words of O'Rourke and Waldron, displeased by how the acrimony between them was retarding the project, and sore at being threatened by lawyers, Monsignor Sheppard wanted disinterested advice. He sought out Isaac Ditmars, whose firm, Schickel and Ditmars, competed unsuccessfully for the cathedral work in 1897. Ditmars had remained familiar, as the architect for other projects in the diocese.[8] Thoroughly professional, he resisted becoming entwined in a dispute that involved another architect and a situation rife with possible ethical conflicts. In these discussions, however, Ditmars at one point said to Monsignor Sheppard that the bishop "should not stand for" Waldron's maneuvers.[9] But for the most part, he kept his distance and instead offered to suggest three other architects who might help the diocese evaluate the disquieting situation.

Arbitration

After considering Ditmars's suggestion and other options, the diocese resorted to arbitration as a means to resolve the most serious points of contention: the quality of the stone Waldron substituted and the stability of the erected columns. The arbitration process became irregular, however. There were to be three arbitrators, one chosen by the diocese, one by the architect, and one by the builder. O'Rourke refused to appoint one and gave his position in a memorandum.[10] Given the charged circumstances, the choice of the two arbitrators was provocative. Waldron selected Fred L. Metcalf. Monsignor Sheppard, on behalf of the diocese, reached out again to Isaac Ditmars, Sheppard helping to soften Ditmars's earlier scruple about meddling in a professional colleague's business. (Sheppard had earlier worked with Ditmars's deceased partner, William Schickel, on a large church in Passaic.) It is perplexing why the diocese consented to have arbitrators who were partners in two firms that competed unsuccessfully against O'Rourke for the Sacred Heart commission. Perhaps Monsignor Sheppard and others felt that they did not know many architects, though that would have constituted an absence of the will to seek them. Whatever the reason, it belied a circumscribed perspective. O'Rourke resisted entering into arbitration to the last, telling Sheppard that the process was an "attempt of the contractor to mislead the diocese."[11] Even so, he felt compelled to cooperate, even offering the arbitrators use of his architectural office for their task.

Ditmars and Metcalf quickly took up their assignment and had Waldron's workers take down a chancel column and partially demolish the pier below it, and also excavate around another chancel and one nave pier. By mid-March 1909, they had begun to draw unhappy conclusions. Their instinct at this point was to determine if the bases could be fortified by remedial action, thereby sparing the cost of taking down the nave columns and pulling up and replacing the bases.

On Saint Patrick's Day, 1909, Ditmars telephoned Monsignor Sheppard with news that would not have filled O'Rourke with Irish pride. Off the record, Ditmars said that "affairs at the new cathedral are in a deplorable condition," and reported that he and Fred Metcalf had a stormy session with O'Rourke. O'Rourke and Metcalf, he said, "nearly came to blows," and when they went together to the construction site, the two "exchanged some very fine language."[12] A few days later, Ditmars also stated that the foundations were faulty, owing to "the manner in which the concrete was placed," and that O'Rourke had improperly calculated the load that the columns needed to carry, leading to design inadequacies.[13] The two arbitrators more slowly addressed the question of the substituted stone, saying it would probably pass but they had yet to reach a decision.

Based on Ditmars's preliminary assessment—major points of which Ditmars himself would soon reverse—Monsignor Sheppard attacked O'Rourke for the foundation construction and the accuracy of his plans. "It was a serious fault upon the part of O'Rourke to overlook such work," noted Sheppard. To these judgments, not yet supported by firm evidence, he also mentioned two earlier church commissions that he thought O'Rourke's incompetence had "spoiled."[14]

Sheppard's denunciation of O'Rourke for the previous builders' work raised a matter that vexes architects: How accountable are they for the performance of contractors? In practical terms, they are not continuously at the building site, so much work is done beyond their view and control. In later years, and with the maturation of professional standards, architects addressed the ambiguity by contractually delineating the limits of their responsibility for construction and liabilities that might arise. But O'Rourke's contract left him largely unshielded from Sheppard's accusation, quite apart from whether or not the cathedral's foundations were truly faulty.

Vicar General Sheppard knew of O'Rourke's role in buildings he "spoiled" only through hearsay, but his journal holds entries of someone who had made up his mind. He pitched these accusations at O'Rourke, who snapped back with facts that exonerated him about ruining anyone's church as well as denigrating the arbitrators' analysis. But O'Rourke should have sensed by now that Sheppard was prepared to believe the worst about him.

ARBITRATION REPORT

In the first week of April, the diocese received Ditmars and Metcalf's typewritten, eleven-page arbitration report. "O'Rourke stands condemned for the foundation of piers both nave and sanctuary," Sheppard wrote after seeing it, "also for his figures on weight to be carried."[15] His judgment was swift and harsh and his language loaded: "Three experts to date have condemned him." They had condemned not the architect's work or performance, but him—O'Rourke himself. We know what Sheppard concluded: "He ought to resign." Sheppard, however, did not record what the arbitrators actually said: the nave and chancel columns "as constructed were not of sufficient strength to bear the weight that would rest upon them." Further, that "our disapproval is based solely upon the defective materials and workmanship which we find in the piers as erected" and that the foundations and columns were "properly designed."[16]

Sheppard's strongest criticisms of O'Rourke were unsubstantiated, and inaccurate, but spectacular building collapses in the previous two decades were well known. These catastrophes were caused largely by a failure to understand fully and effectively integrate emerging new building materials and systems (which were not being used for Sacred Heart), though the public saw only the symptoms and not the cause.[17] As we saw, there were also problems at the cathedrals in Albany and Pittsburgh. As the Albany project unfolded, Patrick Keely reduced the height of the spires because of uncertainty about the subsurface conditions. In Pittsburgh, both design and construction failures required aggressive and costly measures. And, of course, the collapse of the enormous nave of the cathedral in Beauvais, in northern France, was rueful evidence that great religious buildings were not protected from engineering failures.

In fact, the Ditmars and Metcalf document was an arbitration report only in part. It evaluated the eight points of contention in which the Waldron firm claimed that O'Rourke had made changes in the plans and specifications so that it therefore had a right to additional compensation. They concluded that the granite Waldron contracted for was an acceptable substitute for the marble O'Rourke had stipulated. Indeed, in most but not all of the points of contention they sided with Waldron, and, in any case, concluded that, in net terms, the builder had not been overpaid.

In their report's second part, Ditmars and Metcalf said that they were serving, not as arbitrators but as "advisors to the Diocese of Newark," meaning that their findings were recommendations and not binding, as they would be in formal arbitration. Here they made two main points. The two piers and triforium gallery that they supported at the crossing were not necessary for the building's structural integrity. They thought that these should be eliminated and that the loads on the remaining columns and the lateral thrust this would create should be secured with the addition of a steel girder running horizontally through the entire structure at the triforium level. This measure, they thought, would strengthen the building's overall stability. Ditmars and Metcalf also sounded an alarm about the foundations under the towers. They said that their investigation "has given rise in our minds to a grave question with respect to the strength of the present foundation wall of the towers of the building. We understand that the stone of which these tower foundations walls are built is from the same source as the stone of the clerestory piers; and if the foundations of the towers be no stronger per unit of area that we consider the piers to be, we are satisfied from our calculation that it would be unwise to rely upon them to bear safely a loading materially greater than they now carry.[18]

A few days after filing their arbitration report, Ditmars and Metcalf submitted an additional memorandum expanding on the methodology used for their analysis and augmenting their technical findings. They particularly focused on the integrity of what they called the piers, the stone and concrete upon which the columns stood. They noted what they saw as an insufficient leveling of the bedrock and the quality of the concrete used to achieve a level and uniform surface, saying, "properly leveled surfaces have not been excavated for the piers. Leveling up for the masonry of these piers has been done with concrete. We find this concrete to be of varying thickness, and to be not sufficiently homogenous in composition."[19] They also faulted the mortar in which the pier's stonework was set.

They called attention to the cracking of stone in the piers they examined. What is more, they believed it did not occur at or around the time the piers were constructed, but well after. Such evidence could suggest that the cracking occurred as the piers were subjected to heavier loads when the columns and superstructure were added. Still, Ditmars and Metcalf acknowledged the inherently subjective nature of their findings:

> Any opinion which we or others may express as to the actual present strength of these piers must be very largely a matter of personal judgment and experience. With respect to the safe loading, even [of] sound, well-built masonry, authorities differ considerably, and in the case of materials and workmanship exhibiting such marked defects as we find in these piers no individual or committee of experts can say with authority how far short of recognized standard of strength the work may fall. We believe our estimates of the strength of the work to be as liberal as the facts permit; and we counsel on the part of the Church authorities a greater degree of conservatism rather than the assumption of greater risk.
>
> One fact of serious menace is proven: and this is that the stone of the exposed piers has cracked extensively since setting. This occurrence indicates, to our view, that the stone of which these piers are built is structurally weak to a degree the ultimate consequences of which it is not possible to foresee. The stone may still be in the process of cracking and to what extent disintegration may progress in the future is a question which we believe is beyond the possibility of answering.[20]

Sheppard, however, formulated possible answers to the immediate circumstances: He said Jeremiah should resign, accept an associate architect for the project, or stop work until he and Waldron agreed on what was to be done. O'Rourke fired back, refuting the arbitrators and saying, essentially, that he knew better than they. The diocese concluded that it had no choice but to take down all the columns and start over, and ordered O'Rourke to provide plans and specifications for Waldron to follow. O'Rourke's response sent a mixed signal. He agreed to revise the plans, indicating that he thought something should be done to fortify the primary load-bearing elements; he also said that he was working on a formal renunciation of the findings. In the meantime, he barraged the bishop with angry letters, refuting Ditmars and Metcalf and lambasting Waldron as a conniver and profiteer and as a deleterious influence on the diocese. Nonetheless, O'Rourke's office provided revised drawings, and Sheppard pushed to gather bids from contractors, though only a few braved the circumstances. When Waldron went to O'Rourke's office to pick up the new documents so that he himself might bid, they had another testy encounter. The builder said that it was only after the diocese (in the person of Monsignor Sheppard) repeatedly appealed to him that he agreed to bid. O'Rourke and Waldron, once respectful of each other, were now bitter antagonists.

In the summer, Sheppard began talking about bringing Ditmars onto the architectural team. O'Rourke was predictably hostile to the mere idea of it. Sheppard was finally able to arrange a meeting with the two architects at his Jersey City rectory. His record of this effort evinces the inimical feelings then charging the crisis: "In about ten minutes the usual war. O'Rourke accusing Ditmars of being unprofessional and of having in collusion with Waldron and Metcalf condemned his work. Ditmars immediately wanted to leave. I prevailed on him to wait and talk matters over, he did wait but no progress was made. O'Rourke when asked if he would consent to have him act as Associate Architect, said he would take him as Clerk of Board of Works, another insult. We then had to listen to the old man tell us of his expertise, education, etc. In fact, he was, in his own estimation a giant among architects and Ditmars a mere pygmy, etc., etc."[21]

When Ditmars left, O'Rourke stayed back but could not hold back. Sheppard moaned that he had "to listen to all sorts of things about the dishonesty and vulgarity of the Waldrons."[22] Jeremiah ranted that "E. M. was Michael, S. P. was Patrick. What was to be expected of men who changed their good old Hibernian names?" They were lines that might have been lifted from an Irish American farce, were they not so obviously the ravings of an anguished mind.

(Several times during this contentious period, O'Rourke made it clear that he did not regard Isaac Ditmars as his professional equal, implying that he felt that he had reached the heights of his profession, and Ditmars had not. His turn at supervising architect, though blustery, gave him certain bragging rights—and he exercised them shamelessly. Yet O'Rourke and Ditmars had in common early training in the offices of established architects, and by now both men were fellows of the American Institute of Architects. Ditmars was also president of the institute's Brooklyn chapter and partner in a firm that did very reputable work, even if, perhaps, he himself was a somewhat less imaginative designer than O'Rourke.)

As O'Rourke tried to discredit their findings, Ditmars and Metcalf buttressed them. They had a firm from New York with the self-evident titular, the Foundation Company, inspect an excavated area in the future apse. The new adviser agreed that shoddy workmanship had caused construction deficiencies and described the problems. The failings stemmed from the work of Peter Boyle's firm, the first contractor. But Boyle was dead, and there was no hope of recovery. The Foundation Company also thought that the original contractor had not sufficiently leveled the rock substratum upon which the nave piers rested. Furthermore, it said that O'Rourke's transept columns were insufficiently wide (they were, in fact, designed to be more attenuated) and thought as well that placing steel beams in the higher reaches of the cathedral's structure would help resolve any weakness in the building's structural integrity.

Despite the dead certainties of the participants, the diocese seemed not to know what to believe. At one point, Sheppard wrote in his journal, "[I] hope the Bishop will request Ditmars to act whether O'Rourke likes it or not and then we will have peace. Either this or quit work entirely on the Cathedral and let time "*Edax rerum*" [Time, the devourer of all things] settle the difficulty."[23] And at another moment, Sheppard admitted, with uncharacteristic hesitation, "Ditmars asserts emphatically today that if the building is constructed as proposed, it will fall, O'Rourke as confident that it will not."[24]

Associate Architect

The day after admitting perplexity, Monsignor Sheppard, talking with Bishop O'Connor, concluded that Ditmars should be pressed into accepting an appointment as associate architect. Ditmars at first said that he would not come on board unless O'Rourke was completely off, though a few days later agreed to terms that would give him oversight of the architectural documents and work, for which he would be paid 3 percent on the cost of construction, which would rise to 5 percent if O'Rourke resigned.

They could not truly have believed that O'Rourke would do so voluntarily: Sheppard was concurrently busy with lawyers attempting to insulate the diocese, Ditmars, and Waldron from possible legal action by O'Rourke.

Sheppard developed, in consultation with an attorney, what he called propositions. The first called for the diocese to give Ditmars architectural control, making Waldron's work subject to Ditmars's judgment, not O'Rourke's. The second was to fire O'Rourke outright; the third to quit work on the cathedral, but only if this would not result in Waldron suing them for violating his contract.

Firing O'Rourke appealed to Sheppard. "I personally am heartily sick of meeting and talk, something ought to be done," he said.[25] But this proposition had risk. Once dismissed, O'Rourke could sue to "recover," meaning it was possible, perhaps probable, that the diocese would need to prove him incompetent in court. Although it was conceivable that aspects of the design and the foundation work would support such a claim, this was not certain. O'Rourke could, of course, point to fifty years of professional practice and a sizable number of commissions from the Newark diocese. The bishop and his vicar general could not have been encouraged by the prospect of a legal proceeding in which some of the diocese's finest buildings were offered as evidence for the plaintiff.

Sheppard resorted to the clarifying exercise of list-making in his journal:

> There is one of the following things for us to do under the circumstances when all is weighed up:
>
> A. What will O'Rourke take to quit.
>
> B. Tell him he is incompetent and demand resignation then he can sue to defend himself. In this way we will save his percentage and cost of plans etc.
>
> C. Keep him on the payroll and have Ditmars as final judge representing owners.
>
> D. Or pay Waldron for what stone is on the ground and so settle with him without finishing his Contract and then stop work as long as we wish.
>
> E. Or remain in status quo and let Waldron sue to be permitted to continue his work and show how the Architect has constantly hampered him or oblige the Roman Catholic Diocese to settle with him.[26]

O'Rourke now chose to address Bishop O'Connor directly, telling him in no uncertain terms that he was deceived by "unscrupulous architects and commercial lawyers," who were in it only for the money.[27] He enclosed a copy of the letter he had written to Bishop Wigger that set out his credentials and qualifications when he had sought the cathedral commission ten years before. In July, at O'Connor's suggestion (or at least with the bishop's consent), Sheppard wrote to O'Rourke asking what he would accept to resign. O'Rourke shot back that he should not have to commit "professional suicide," and, as Shepard also recorded in his journal, "to suffer handing up the fine drawings he has made to irresponsible architects and contractors."[28] To this entry Sheppard penned, "etc. etc." Exasperated by O'Rourke for a long time, the vicar general was now dismissive.

O'Rourke next heard that Waldron had been given the contract for reworking the foundations and columns. Reflexively imputing dark motives, he bemoaned the builder's "rascality" to Sheppard, who soon hammered out yet another scheme. In this one, O'Rourke would continue to draw plans and specifications, but Ditmars, with the title of advisory architect, would superintend the work and adjudicate conflicts that might arise. Given the circumstances, it was an arrangement that had merits, and it must have seemed to the clergymen involved, in high summer of 1909, that some light was breaking.

If they were optimistic, it was not for long. This time, Waldron "was not quite satisfied" and said that he would not perform on the new contract if O'Rourke were to supervise construction.[29] In the first week of September, Sheppard met with Ditmars and an attorney and drafted a contract between Ditmars and the diocese and sent it for Bishop O'Connor's signature, along with a summary of the three courses of action that he believed were now open to them:

A) Get rid of O'Rourke,
B) Settle up with Waldron with unfinished contract and stop work on Cathedral, or
C) Take in Ditmars, or some-one else to supervise work.[30]

Trying to put the cathedral project back on track, the bishop signed the contract and sent it back. But it was not a ringing endorsement of their new architect: astonishingly, O'Connor was now "afraid that some troubles may exist with Ditmars."[31] Sheppard decided to hold the contract until he learned more about the bishop's concern. Waldron steamed about the delay and the diocese's handling of the whole affair. "So far as I can see Waldron is right," Sheppard penned in his journal, "but things don't move."[32]

But soon they did move. The diocese executed the contract with Ditmars in mid-September, at the same time demanding that O'Rourke provide new plans for the columns based on the findings of Ditmars and Metcalf, and engineering reports.[33] O'Rourke and Sheppard kept up a volley of ultimatums. When O'Rourke invited Sheppard to a meeting in his office, the monsignor noted that he replied, "plainly that I will not go and . . . that patience has ceased to be a virtue and that if he did not do as requested and as he promised, I will order Ditmars to prepare plans."[34] What Sheppard had not told O'Rourke, and did not tell him now, was that the diocese had already hired Ditmars for the newly conceived position of advisory architect. Not until the last week in October, more than six weeks after officially retaining Ditmars (on a day that O'Rourke had previously arranged to go to Jersey City to show Sheppard the revised plans) did the vicar general plan to bring the two architects together to inform them of their "respective positions." For reasons not precisely clear, O'Rourke ducked the meeting, sending his son Joseph in his place. Only then, as Sheppard read aloud to Joseph O'Rourke excerpts from Ditmars's contract, was the O'Rourke firm formally notified of the new arrangement.

Battle

The controversy over the foundations had remained a largely private affair, unreported in the press and unshaped by external pressures. Whether O'Rourke or Waldron tipped them off, or it was a matter of word finally leaking, Newark newspapers heard about it in the fall of 1909, and a dogged *Evening News* writer began an investigation in November. Pestered by the reporter and taking matters into his own hands, Waldron went directly to Bishop O'Connor for assent before talking freely to the journalist. When the evening paper hit the streets on November 13, the conflict became a public battle. The article, sloppily written, poorly edited, and a confusing summary of what it called a "strife," provided jumbled extracts from the Ditmars and Metcalf report, which, to Sheppard's chagrin, Waldron had proffered. Irritated that Waldron, having received the bishop's consent had not asked for *his* advice or permission, Sheppard declared that if the combatants chose to talk to the press, he and others from the diocese would not become embroiled. Sheppard told Waldron, "I thought he was foolish to air his troubles before the public and that if he did he and O'Rourke might fight it out alone as we should not interfere."[35] It was wishful thinking. Two days later, the public read what Joseph O'Rourke, Jeremiah's son, had heard in Jersey City. The *Evening News* front-page headline broadcast: "New

Architect for Cathedral: Ditmars Reported Named as Consulting Designer in Completion of Edifice—Was One of Arbitrators"[36]

A more coherent account of the dispute, it also touched on the financial impact of the problems—namely, that the diocese was raising money for a building that was perhaps dangerously constructed, being built with materials not specified by the owners, and subject to indeterminate cost overruns. It was a public relations disaster. And it became worse five days later, when the paper ran another story. This page-one article raised an eyebrow over the choice of Ditmars and Metcalf as arbitrators (as former competitors for the cathedral commission, their selection had always been susceptible to a cynical interpretation) and pointedly noted that both architects had offices in Manhattan. (New York's dominance still stuck in the craw of Newark pride, and the local press did not pass up an opportunity to snipe.) Moreover, many years later, a project insider felt it worthwhile to explain that, although Isaac was often a Jewish name, Isaac Ditmars "descended from an old pre-Revolutionary family and as a point of interest, Mr. Ditmars was not of the Jewish faith though his given name, Isaac, might indicate that he was."[37] In fact, Ditmars descended from some of the earliest Dutch settlers to North America, was Protestant, and lived in Brooklyn, where he was active in its cultural life.[38] And at least for now, all this gave the new architect on the scene the aura of an outsider among Newark Catholics.

In the midst of these worrying events, and after months of angry rebuttals, the O'Rourke camp became suddenly, inexplicably still. Monsignor Sheppard and Ditmars sent letters that were answered slowly or not at all. With this withdrawal, Ditmars began taking action, choosing Maine granite for the new foundation piers, preparing revised construction drawings for the new columns and other structural changes, and distributing them to contractors for bidding. It came as little surprise to some that the winning firm was E. M. Waldron & Company. Sheppard and Ditmars soon needed other drawings and importuned O'Rourke for weeks. Able to put off a meeting no longer, O'Rourke saw Ditmars two days before Christmas. Ditmars reported on the testy encounter to Sheppard, who recorded a present-tense version of the meeting: "Ditmars is treated like a schoolboy. He is asked in lordly fashion, 'In what capacity do you come here?'"[39] O'Rourke took the opportunity to tell Ditmars that he was an "interloper" and dismissed him without giving over the drawings. O'Rourke wrote to Sheppard immediately after this incident and rebuked him for bringing in another architect. It was the very first time O'Rourke criticized Sheppard directly, and it will soon be apparent what emboldened him.

An Estimable Defense

The diocese viewed O'Rourke's strange quiescence as obstructive. After checking with an attorney, Bishop O'Connor wrote to O'Rourke with an "ultimatum either to consult with Ditmars and resume work or resign."[40] His letter of reply oddly assured the bishop that he would work together with Ditmars. It also held two messages of serious consequence. Jeremiah took his grievance with Sheppard to the bishop and complained (ostensibly for the first time) about Sheppard's management of the project. The second was a bombshell. O'Rourke told the bishop that the chief engineer of the new Pennsylvania Station in New York had examined the cathedral foundations as they were designed and built, had said they were "correct," and that a report would be forthcoming.[41] This sent Sheppard running to his network of business contacts to uncover the identity of the engineer. Though they believed they had discovered who it was, the intelligence reports were wrong.

Through this lengthening ordeal, Bishop O'Connor maintained an executive posture. Calm and hopeful, he looked for a reconciliation that would preserve O'Rourke's role, give clemency to Waldron, and bring movement on the cathedral. Yet it appears that his vicar general, stiffening against O'Rourke's criticism, hereafter made decisions resolutely in opposition to Jeremiah. Waldron submitted an enormous bill along with a letter from his lawyer that put the diocese on notice to pay it. He also bluffly declared he wanted to quit. Though Sheppard called the charges "exorbitant" he blamed the O'Rourke debacle and not Waldron. The vicar general's journal entries attest to both his pique and his resolve: "I started to South Orange [where Bishop O'Connor resided] but returned as I was getting there late, and thought the Bishop might be out. In the evening I wrote him that I thought O'Rourke should be dealt with at once, that he was only procrastinating and playing his old game; that he had no more respect for him, the Bishop, than he had for me, since he still goes on with the same old protest, as though the Owner had no say as to whether he should have a consulting architect or not. How long more will he be permitted to preach?"[42] Sheppard also told the bishop that he thought "O'Rourke was making monkeys of us all."

O'Rourke, presumably buying time, made it difficult for the diocese to get the revised drawings. When they were at last ready, Ditmars sent junior staff to O'Rourke's Broad Street office to pick them up. The young pair related that O'Rourke interrogated them, wanting to be certain that they were not somehow agents for Waldron. Assured that they were not, he gave them the materials and, "at the same time a discourse on professional ethics."[43] It was O'Rourke at his worst—suspicious and sermonic.

About a week later, in an unexpected move, two of O'Rourke's sons went unbidden to meet with Bishop O'Connor to say that they would assume control of the project and work with Ditmars, if this would mean going forward.[44] They were also couriers for the report that Jeremiah had said was coming. And soon after Jeremiah's sons met with the bishop, yet another surprising turn occurred in the O'Rourke firm's office. Jeremiah met with Ditmars, and although it emerged that Jeremiah would not cede all control to his sons, as they had told the bishop, the meeting was the most pleasant and productive ever and signaled that the architects might be able to get along, or so it seemed to Ditmars when he told Sheppard about it. The vicar general was not swayed. It soon became clear that Jeremiah's sunny new face could be attributed to the report that the O'Rourke sons brought to the bishop.

To support his contentions about the cathedral's design and construction, O'Rourke surveyed the engineering profession for an undisputed expert. He seized upon Joseph H. O'Brien, a senior member of the engineering firm working on the Pennsylvania Railroad's new terminal building in Manhattan.[45] Designed by McKim Mead & White, the preeminent architectural firm in the country, Penn Station, as it would become known, was an immense and technologically complex project whose progress the building professions and the public had followed closely for the previous five years, and intensely at that moment. The behemoth was completed, and a publicity campaign had already been launched in advance of the official opening the following spring. Three times larger than any rail station previously built in the United States, it was one of the era's best-known construction projects and, pertinently, one that required innovative engineering. Joseph O'Brien, a member of the American Society of Civil Engineers, who had previously helped to design and supervise the construction of South Station in Boston and was now at the fore of the Penn Station project as resident engineer, was just the person O'Rourke was looking for: a respected professional in a high-profile position. The architect's dodging and ducking in recent months had given O'Brien time to conduct an investigation. The engineer studied the construction drawings and was stealthily brought into the gated site to examine the excavated foundations, piers, and bases.

O'Brien's report squarely countered Ditmars and Metcalf's. It said that the uncertified payments to Waldron violated the terms of the contract and were therefore illegal; the substitution of materials, because they were not in the contract's specifications, were similarly so. O'Brien faulted the arbitration method because it did not adhere to the one delineated in the contract. He dismissed the analysis and recommendations on the ground that they were not supported by a "structural expert or mathematician."[46] It endorsed O'Rourke's drawings, technical assumptions, and choice of materials as sound and likewise the foundations that had been constructed. O'Brien supported his findings with copious data and engineering calculations. The most troubling problem, in O'Brien's view, was that the illegality of the uncertified payments had invalidated the insurance bond, which meant that the diocese's financial protection was lost. He said that Waldron should return the payments that O'Rourke had not certified and then determine legally what the contractors were owed.

Digesting O'Brien's report, Monsignor Sheppard paled. "Theoretically it reads all right and is quite a disquisition."[47] Then he rationalized, "It defends Jeremiah's position, as of course it should, since O'Brien acts for him." Sheppard added knowingly, "It is not only the document of an engineer but also the document of a lawyer."

Final Gambit

As Waldron had done, O'Rourke now took his turn with the press. He gave a copy of O'Brien's report to the *Evening News*. The next day, a long, meticulous article appeared. Written for the most part from O'Rourke's perspective, it described O'Brien's report and his conclusion that the arbitration method adopted by the diocese was improper and the arbitrator's technical analysis flawed. It gave O'Brien's credentials and reported on his investigation, methodology, and assessment. It reprised the financial effects of Waldron's alleged overpayments, the delays, and the further run-up of expenses implied in adhering to Ditmars's recommendations. It also spotlighted legal and money matters: that payments to the contractor without certificates from the architect-of-record had invalidated the terms of the performance bond held by a financial firm in behalf of the diocese. The public was led to understand that, one way or another, the project had lost another $100,000, or 10 percent of what the cathedral was supposed to cost—a year's worth of fund-raising at the projected rate. The account remarked that O'Brien's findings "as given in the report, are said to be a refutation of all that was contained in that of the arbitrators" and "conditions at the building far the reverse to what the arbitrators found."[48]

The piece also recounted the meeting in O'Rourke's office the day before, about which Ditmars had reported sanguinely to Sheppard, but which in the newspaper, as interpreted by Jeremiah, sounds quite the opposite. Jeremiah's version lampooned the session, at Ditmars's expense: "Mr. Ditmars, it is said, simply informed Mr. O'Rourke that he had been sent by Bishop O'Connor to talk over the cathedral matters, and when called on to produce a copy of the agreement authorizing him as the bishop's advisor, showed an extract of the agreement containing a reference to the part Mr. Ditmars was to take in the completion of the building. Asked if he had any proposition to submit, the New Yorker is declared to have remarked that he was in a hurry to catch a train back to Manhattan and had not come prepared to enter into any extensive details."[49] The *Evening News* also noted that "there was some plain talk on the part of Mr. O'Rourke" about the ethics of the matter. O'Rourke, the newspaper commented, made it clear that he would vehemently protect his design from change, and would likely go to the courts if the cathedral was not built "in strict accordance with the original plans and specifications."

Finally, the article reviewed the history of expenses and overruns and calculated the funding deficit on the contract down to two decimal points and said that out in the parishes, clergy were raising an eyebrow. "The squabble is said to have led some priests in the diocese to try to calculate how near the estimate of $1,000,000 will be the cost of the cathedral."[50] The story further stated, "Based on what is relied upon as authentic information, it is declared that more than $600,000 has been paid on contracts thus far, with less than half the work on the building finished." The financial impact was worse, the newspaper mentioned conditionally, because "the bishop or whoever else was responsible failed to retain ten percent of the amount of the contract, as provided." "Whoever else" poked Sheppard in the eye. "All parties to the contract have refused to be interviewed since the outbreak of hostilities between the architects and contractors, but it is known that the O'Brien report has been the cause of no little concern in some quarters."

Concern was biggest in Jersey City. Whether because of negligence, confusion, or a desire to keep construction going, the diocese had not withheld the customary retainage on all invoices, a device that protects a project's owner because the builder is not given 100 percent of its contracted fees until the owner is entirely satisfied. Mentioning it cast doubt over the project leadership. More pointedly, in summarizing the problems, the paper said that because of them, the bishop, "through Monsignor John A. Sheppard, the vicar-general, who has entire charge of the cathedral matter ordered work on the cathedral stopped."[51] Having his name now publicly tied to the cathedral mess was a vein-popping outrage for the vicar general. Furious, he acted fast.

Endgame

The morning after the article appeared, Monsignor Sheppard dashed off a white-hot note and had it rushed to Seton Hall. Knowing that the bishop was scheduled to be presiding at a conference, Sheppard left no possibility of delay. The note was dispatched with instructions that it be handed to the bishop while the session was in progress. O'Connor opened it and knew the vicar general's position: "Procrastination does not pay."[52] Architect Ditmars hurried to see the bishop. "Disgusted" was how he described the prelate when he later telephoned Sheppard, who was summoned to a meeting at Seton Hall the next morning, when they quickly made a decision. They wrote a resolute letter, which Sheppard took with him to mail as he left (and whether he thought about it or not), passing in sight of Seton Hall's main building, chapel, and library, all designed by O'Rourke.

The next day, in a terse explanation over Bishop O'Connor's signature, O'Rourke read that he had been "retired" because work on the cathedral had stopped and he was unwilling to comply with the findings of the arbitration report. Stunned, Jeremiah told the bishop that he was misunderstood and pleaded for a meeting. "The old game," an unmoved Sheppard thought, "to my mind he is the best understood man in the country."[53] Waldron kept the heat on from his side by repeating his threat to pull out. A week later, the bishop signed a supplementary contract with Waldron and Ditmars, who was given sole architectural control.

O'Rourke was finished. He refused to believe what happened. He wrote to the bishop to suspend all work on the cathedral rather than continue "under such sinister auspices as confront us."[54] He also still regarded himself as responsible for the project and the diocese's interests, writing to the bishop that the new contract with Waldron was the "most insidious and serious attack yet made on the architectural, structural, and financial security of the cathedral."[55] He later wrote to Sheppard with a similar message, expressing regret over Sheppard's and the bishop's "inexperience."[56] He blasted Waldron in a letter that his actions and the new contract for the cathedral construction were "based on gross deception and imposition on the inexperience and credulity of Bishop O'Connor and Monsignor Sheppard by your firm and the so-called consultant Ditmars."[57] O'Rourke appealed more urgently as the day approached for Bishop O'Connor to sail for Europe. But discussions with the bishop and the vicar general were terminated. Sheppard had the diocesan attorney tell O'Rourke that during the bishop's absence all communication about the cathedral should be sent to a lawyer's office. O'Rourke, in turn, wrote to this attorney inviting him to a meeting to discuss "the ways designing men have of robbing the Church."[58]

Through the spring and summer of 1910, Jeremiah went repeatedly to the cathedral grounds. Surrounded by a wood fence, the construction area was accessible only through secured doors, and Waldron, as the general contractor, controlled access. O'Rourke was turned away every time. On one attempt, he railed to the gatekeeper that he "would like to send Waldron to the Penitentiary."[59] In late July, Bishop O'Connor, escorted by Waldron, visited the enclosed site to see the remedial work. Intentionally or by chance, O'Rourke appeared and created a scene that made its way to the press. Under the headline "Nine Raps," Newarkers read:

> The architect halted first at a small gate opening into a corner of the property where the office of the contractors is located. After giving nine distinct raps in groups of three, Mr. O'Rourke continued walking along Sixth Avenue until he came to the main entrance. The first rapping had attracted the attention of Michael Mulvey, a special policeman who is employed as a watchman on the grounds. Mulvey had already started to the main gate and was standing there when Mr. O'Rourke came up. Without a word the architect repeated the nine raps on the picket gate while Mulvey stood by and smiled. "You can't get in here," was the reply of the special officer to the architect's rapping. "Whose automobile is standing there?" inquired Mr. O'Rourke pointing to a car in which Mr. Waldron and Bishop O'Connor had reached the grounds. Informed that the machine belonged to Mr. Waldron the architect demanded that he be permitted to enter the gate, but the watchman was insistent and pointed to a sign nailed to the fence to the right of the gate on which appeared the warning, "Danger! Keep outside this property. By order of E. M. Waldron & Co." Without paying any heed to the sign Mr. O'Rourke resumed walking

> and turned into Ridge Street at the west of the Cathedral property. There he rapped nine times on another gate which at the time was not more than fifteen feet away from where Bishop O'Connor and the contractor stood talking. . . . Mr. O'Rourke was ignored. As Mr. O'Rourke disappeared into Ridge Street, Mr. Mulvey the watchman stepped outside the main gate and was chuckling to himself when the architect reappeared on his way back to the main entrance. At sight of Mr. O'Rourke the watchman dodged inside the gate and quickly closed it. Mr. O'Rourke however, passed by and took up a position at the north east corner of Clifton and Sixth Avenues. Apparently enjoying the situation, Mulvey stuck his head out of the gateway so that he could keep Mr. O'Rourke under "surveillance." Bishop O'Connor and the contractor had concluded their examination of the work and were walking toward the main gate, when Mr. O'Rourke boarded a Clifton Avenue trolley going toward Bloomfield Avenue. The Bishop left and the contractor returned to the works.[60]

O'Rourke's histrionics and the buffoonery of the gateman made Jeremiah a figure of fun. He had lost his most important commission. This caricature now imperiled his personal dignity.

15

New Architect and New Era

FEAR THAT THE FOUNDATIONS might be compromised in places other than the piers that had been examined led Isaac Ditmars and the diocese to have all of them dismantled so that other possible deficiencies could be addressed. This radical measure permitted the remedy of deeper excavation in some places, further leveling of bedrock, and reconstruction of selected footings.[1] In the course of this work, contractors found at least one place where the men of the Boyle firm, contractors for the foundations, had left a large boulder in place (presumably because they thought it was too big to remove or was, in fact, bedrock) and built footings upon it. It is unclear how extensive these potential problems were. But the infinitesimal probability of structural failure was intolerable. Few could quarrel with the conservative course of removing and then reconstructing the foundation piers; but once the decision was made to rebuild them, there was an incentive to proclaim publicly that it was a dire necessity, which the new team did.[2]

Design Revision

At his dismissal, O'Rourke lost control of the cathedral design. He warned the diocese not to make a single change, but legally his firm's drawings were work-for-hire and his now-former client was free to use them as it wished. Responding to a further apprehension about the foundations under the towers, Ditmars reduced the load they would carry by eliminating plans for the florid spires and one stage of the towers, now designed to reach 232 feet. He retained both their asymmetry and gender symbolism: the projecting gables of the Gesu (east) tower are modestly higher and have pointed arches; those of the Mary (west) tower are in the more rounded form of the ogee arch. The ogee configuration belongs to a late Gothic phase, implying that, as in many medieval Gothic churches, the styles found in Sacred Heart's towers were the work of successive generations and architects. The treatment of these derived from the towers of Amiens cathedral, as did a new balustrade across the facade. All things considered, Ditmars's reworking of the tower profiles was an elegant solution to a design challenge. The flèche that Ditmars ultimately redesigned also owes most to the form and the dramatic visual effect created by the one on Amiens. Monsignor Doane once wrote that, among the great cathedrals, Amiens deserved "the plume."[3] So the citation of Amiens in some of Newark's features obliquely honored the sentiments of one of Sacred Heart's prime movers.

Ditmars's other substantive alteration was in the tracery of the rose windows, lifted in this instance from Rheims. In the interior, he revised the capitals for the arcade, also drawing on Rheims. He was very direct about this, proud even, telling the press that he copied the capitals from photographs made of Rheims's capitals before the First World War. German bombing during the war hideously damaged the cathedral at Rheims, but it had been extensively photographed in the preceding decades.[4] Prewar photographs of the nave capitals show at least one whose very similar lobed, mounded leaves are repeated in the foliage element at the top of Newark's columns. Taking this specific detail, Ditmars transposed it into the simple, repeated pattern seen, not at Rheims, but on capitals in Laon Cathedral. What is more, among medieval cathedrals, Laon's columns are close models for the proportions of those in Sacred Heart (as distinct from Pugin's influence, also evident).

These changes were significant but not a fundamental alteration of the O'Rourke firm's scheme for Sacred Heart, which would have been close to impossible, given how much had been built when Ditmars took over. Much of O'Rourke's conception survived the switch in architects. More telling of a new architectural philosophy, Ditmars named the models for his revisions. "The exterior was re-designed," he explained, "the good points of the historic Irish Gothic being maintained and blended ingeniously with the strong values of the French. Chartres, Laon, Saint-Lô, and Rheims, all yielded suggestions or motives and form to the grand composition."[5] (He curiously omitted the obvious Amiens antecedents.)

Ditmars further claimed that the O'Rourke scheme "came from Irish and English archeology" and that such a manner was a doubtful source to possess "the great qualities necessary for a cathedral of mammoth proportions."[6] Ditmars would have come closer to the truth if he had pointed to the Gothic Revival mode of Pugin and his followers in nineteenth-century England and Ireland rather than Irish and English archeology. (As it relates to "archeology" Ditmars uses it to mean the direct citation of historic architecture.) It was Ditmars who introduced truly archeological elements, though if he spent time in Europe studying High Gothic structures, he left no record of it.[7] Copying from or closely citing specific precedents was inimical to the way O'Rourke and many revivalists thought about Gothic, hoping as they did to take the Gothic style and ideals and make them their own. Ditmars's approach, particularly his willingness to cite specific historic models and name them, thus constituted a sea change in the design philosophy informing the cathedral project.

When construction began again after an almost four-year hiatus, the early stone shipments from the quarry led to the first of Ditmars's own quarrels with Waldron. There were serious problems with how the granite at the site had been cut and shaped. To make many stones usable for construction it was necessary to employ unacceptably large amounts of cement as filler. After testy finger-pointing, architect and contractor joined to discipline the stoneyard's output. Following this unpromising start, a well-functioning system was worked out. Isaac Ditmars appears in a photograph of supervisors and laborers at the construction site dating from this period; his tie is off, and the sleeves of his white shirt are turned back above his elbows.[8] It seems to suggest a roll-up-your-sleeves approach to architecture that may well have appealed to Newark Church officials at this juncture. In this phase, local sculptor Dominic A. Walsh was retained to model the Gothic detailing and features, including medallions of the four bishops involved in the cathedral project, which were to be placed near the transept entrances.[9] Over the next three years, scaffolding and derricks were transferred from the apse to the clerestory and transepts, as the granite walls steadily rose; the accidental death of two workers became a lamentable cost of progress.[10]

After the loss of the cathedral commission, Jeremiah continued in practice with his son Joseph.[11] (William had left the firm to become the Newark building superintendent and Louis to form his own partnership.) Not long after his eighty-second birthday, in 1915, Jeremiah's professional twilight went dark. Poor health ended his office routine, and six weeks later he died at home, in the care of his unmarried daughter. He had been a widower for thirty-six years. The medical examiner gave cerebral arteriosclerosis as the primary cause of death, with old age a contributing factor. Obituary writers described a distinguished career and credited him with designing Sacred Heart Cathedral. At his funeral in Saint Patrick's Pro-Cathedral, every seat was filled. His nephew, the Rev. John H. O'Rourke, a prominent Jesuit, officiated. Bishop O'Connor and a large group of priests were in the sanctuary; Vicar General Sheppard was not among them. In the pews reserved for the honorary pall bearers sat his fellow managers of the Howard Savings Bank, an ecumenical gathering of Newark's men of affairs, including A. Pennington Whitehead, Marcus Ward, and Frederick and George Frelinghuysen. Saint Patrick's pastor, Doane's successor, delivered a "brilliant eulogy on the character of Mr. O'Rourke," the *Star Ledger* thought.[12] The newspaper also regarded "the aged architect" as one of "Newark's foremost citizens." The terms of Jeremiah's will left his practice and architectural instruments, drawings, and books to Joseph, on the condition that he "use the same for the purpose of honorably conducting and carrying on such practice and business as my successor."[13] "Honorably conducting"—even from the grave, Jeremiah was adamant about professional ethics.

More Progress

By early 1915, construction teams worked efficiently on the main gable and the east tower, and a year later they had nearly completed the cathedral walls. In unperturbed succession, they raised the steel and iron structural system for the roof and slated it with gray tiles, crowing the ridge with cast-bronze cresting. The Gothic details of the stone trim around the wall openings then started to be carved from models by artisans at the New York studio of Rochette & Parzini, who supplanted Dominic Walsh.[14]

The Rochette & Parzini firm enjoyed a nationwide practice and a roster of blue-ribbon clients by helping artists and designers convert drawings and ideas for three-dimensional work into reality. Their behind-the-scenes, often anonymous, model-making had been critical to many important public- and private-sector buildings during the rise of the Beaux Arts style, beginning in the 1890s. Handling moist clay, Rochette & Parzini craftsmen worked up a model, either to scale or full-size, depending on the intricacy of the work. Ditmars typically reviewed these, and when he was satisfied, hot glue or a gelatinlike concoction was poured over the finished clay representation. When this hardened, it was peeled off, thus producing a rubbery model (a negative, as it were) into which gypsum or plaster of Paris was poured, sometimes reinforced with wood, fiber, or steel framing. The finished representation was then ready for the stone carvers. Some models served only once; those for repeated devices such as moldings and tracery forms were used many times over.

For the next decade and a half, Rochette & Parzini continued to execute models for figural and decorative elements whenever they were needed. It also fashioned the forms for much metal work—features such as the gargoyles, the copper statues at the crossing of the roof that were part of the flèche's composition, and the Christ-figure atop the apse roof, an O'Rourke touch that Ditmars retained. For one of Sacred Heart's finest symbolic effects, in the sculptural program of the superb flèche, its eight statues of the Doctors of the Church are placed so that those great thinkers of the Eastern Church face east and those of the Western Church face west.[15] It has reached skyward over Newark since its completion in 1919.

Newark and the Cathedral at the Time of the First World War

Bishop Wigger's approach to financing has been described as pay-as-you-go, meaning that phases of construction went forward as funds were raised. His successor found no reason to alter it. But in 1913, this method incurred an unexpected cost. City tax authorities sent a bill to the diocese for the assessed value of the property. It instigated a year of legal wrangling.[16] In the end, the diocese found protection with the help of schoolchildren. On May Day 1914, the nuns of Sacred Heart parish school shepherded their pupils over to the cathedral site. There, the church's pastor led them in the recitation of the rosary and the Litany of the Blessed Virgin. The priest told the students that they were certain to regard this first regular service there as a "treasure of a memory."[17] The diocesan attorney simultaneously prepared formal notice to the Newark tax office that such services would be held throughout May and that there would be similar services in June—and that the city's treasury would be lower by the amount of the disputed assessment. The prayers of obedient children resolved the tax flap.

In the autumn of 1916, the cathedral's exterior was at last finished, and the scaffolding was removed. A photographer was dispatched from the *Sunday Call*. It published a spread of "the first pictures of the city taken from what is now the highest point within the municipal limits."[18] The photos showed a place transformed since the cathedral site had been purchased more than four and a half decades earlier. Between the first cathedral project of 1870 and the laying of Sacred Heart's cornerstone in 1899, Newark's population had more than doubled, to almost a quarter of a million residents. During the first decade of its construction, new immigrants, drawn to employment in the city's widening manufacturing base, helped to add one hundred thousand residents to the census. Newark was now the nation's fourteenth-largest city. More than thirty trolley lines weaved through the city, and a thousand or so passenger trains served it daily. Both types of rail lines carried riders to and from the pulsing metropolitan center and spreading residential suburbs. By 1910, tunnels under the Hudson River provided train access to Manhattan.[19] Commercial and private financial transactions were conducted in the offices of nine national banks, eleven trust companies, and five savings banks. More than 250 savings and loan associations helped locals to buy homes, invest in real estate, and to save for their future. Newark's schools and its public library (under the genius of John Cotton Dana) were among the most progressive in America. A staggering seventeen thousand plants and commercial structures, many using cutting-edge technology and systems, sustained Newark's reputation for industrial prowess. The city had four daily newspapers.

The half-dozen years before the 1916 *Sunday Call* photographs were taken had seen a construction boom of multistoried office buildings downtown. The tallest, at sixteen floors, was the Fireman's Insurance Company, one of many firms in a business for which Newark was second only to Hartford as a center. About this time, Newark partisans invited the writer Walter Pritchard Easton to author a small book about the progress and virtues of their city. It was a vanity publication, and Easton found much to admire. Even so, he thought the high-rises in Newark were only "a pathetic imitation of New York," a pesky comparison that joined a march of unflattering comparisons to Manhattan. Despite Easton's swipe, and although vestiges of an earlier time still endured (at nightfall, gas lamps still lit more than a third of city streets), Newark had come of age as a modern city, with all the expected services and amenities. Newark was never or ever would be New York City, but it was not provincial.

The drumbeat of war in Europe reverberated worryingly in Newark during this period. A xenophobic isolationism spreading in the United States brought murmuring that the cathedral was built with foreign stone. The diocese let it be known in the press that Sacred Heart's walls were entirely of American stone. It had been sourced, newspaper articles instructed (or reminded), in the quarries of Massachusetts and New Hampshire and Maine, in towns that read like a patriotic paean to the geology of New England: Worcester and Fitzwilliam, Jonesport and Waldboro.

At the same time, the diocese acknowledged that, although there was to be Tennessee marble in the sanctuary, the altars being planned would be made of the finest Italian stone, that marble and French Caen stone would cover the walls, and that the floors would be laid with tiles of French flint. (Masonry from France and Italy—at least the diocese did not feel compelled, in the disturbed international climate, to have to interpret materials sourced from a hostile Germany.) The diocese understandably wanted to shape public perception in a perilous time and, totally within the bounds of fact, to correct misstatements. But one of its declarations would soon frustrate everyone. It pronounced the hope that the interior would be entirely finished and the cathedral ready for dedication in 1920, fifty years after the site was purchased. But as the United States was pulled into the Great War in Europe and local men departed as soldiers, labor shortages and a cloudy future took their toll. The bishop permitted the current scope of work to be completed. Then, leery of fund-raising, he idled the project.

16

Boom and Bust Again

NEWARK, LIKE OTHER AMERICAN CITIES, roared during 1920s, fueled by a zeitgeist of prosperity that grew stronger as the decade unfolded. Commercial plants multiplied and boomed. Retail operations, from the big department stores to store-front shops, grew unabated. It was an era when Newarkers came to have a choice of more than sixty live theaters and forty movie houses. In all, it evinced the materialism and secularism that had disquieted Monsignor Doane early in the century, which had increased unchecked.

Prosperity, Inflation, Clever Substitutions

The financial buoyancy of these years also restarted the cathedral project. This, in turn, brought fresh lessons about the complexity of economic forces: like everyone else, project leaders had to contend with war-induced inflation. Wincing on the part of both the clergy and laity at spiraling costs for cathedral construction prompted builder Edward Waldron to put them in perspective. He provided "then and now" statistics for the newspapers that any reader could grasp: When Sacred Heart was begun more than twenty years before, masons were paid 40 cents an hour but now demanded $1.25; a team of a horse and a man that cost $4 a day now was $12. At the start of construction, hoisting engineers had daily rates of $3.50, granite cutters $3, and granite setters $4. All commanded $10 now—for a work day that was two hours shorter (a shift attributable to changing societal norms and government laws born of the workers' rights movement).[1] The builder stressed that the problem was not only double and trebled labor costs. Portland cement that had been bought for eighty-eight cents a barrel now cost more than three times that. All these facts and figures buttressed the case for an upward revision in fund-raising goals.

Soon the cathedral facade's three portals were planned. In developing their sculptural program, the diocese sought advice from an American agent of the Mayer studios in Munich, which Monsignor Doane had visited in the 1870s and which was long famous for its ecclesiastical arts. Themes related to the Sacred Heart were provided for the iconographic scheme for the main portals. The tower portals' subject matter was treated as the towers themselves were named, one pertaining to Jesus and the other to Mary.[2] Regrettably, the fusion of architecture and sculpture inherent in Newark's High Gothic models was lost in these compositions. The under-scaled and shallow reliefs pointed to a waning artistic vision that was fore-shadowed by the decision to look outside for advice from abroad.

The planners also began to consider the windows. The carving of stone tracery, with its curves and lobes and intersecting forms, was never expected to be cheap for such an array of window openings. But when the preferred contractor proposed to supply window and doorway tracery for a little over $1 million, everyone stood back. Lower estimates were produced, but these too reflected labor costs that had spiked sharply and did not mitigate the need for still greater funds to fill the tracery with stained glass.

During discussions that left everyone dispirited, Ditmars brought an enticing alternative to the table. He suggested terra cotta be considered as a substitute for stone. Terra cotta, which means baked earth, is a clay-based material produced in molded forms and that is fired and glazed. In can closely approximate the color and texture of stone, and in the previous two decades, terra cotta's popularity had spread. The building professions admired its structural strength, appearance, apparent stability, and relative affordability. Because it is produced in molds, terra cotta was well suited to creating, in quantity, the geometric units that are assembled to form Gothic tracery.

Told that the necessary terra cotta could be produced for one-fifth the cost of stone, the diocese welcomed the substitution and turned again to craftsmen at Rochette & Parzini for the clay models from which molds would be fashioned.[3] The terra cotta was produced in a Woodbridge plant only fifteen miles south of Newark—a novel variation on Pugin's theme of building with local materials.

The increasingly complex project meant that Ditmars needed help in supervising offsite progress. In a move that raised no eyebrows, he hired

Fred Metcalf, his former fellow arbitrator of the O'Rourke-Waldron dispute, to help inspect the terra cotta prototypes and work with technicians at the Federal Terra Cotta Company to achieve a glazed finish that mimicked the granite used to date. After many iterations, a convincing imitation was achieved. When placed in Sacred Heart's wall openings, only a trained eye would have taken it for anything but quarried stone, finely cut. Metcalf was also dispatched on an inspection visit to Barre, Vermont, where the stone for the various jambs, sill pieces, lintels, and the like of the entrance portals were being quarried and cut for finishing in a subcontractor's stoneyard in Brooklyn.

Another Architect's Woes

The granite supply again became a source of woe. Labor agitation and a strike at the Vermont quarries created a domino effect on the project's coordination. Ditmars fell hardest. Terms in his contract, dating from when he succeeded O'Rourke, permitted him to earn fees based, not on his own output of drawings and specifications, but when they were realized as actual construction. Such terms mismatched architectural work and revenues earned; construction documents, naturally, had to precede building. It had been a burden, but for the most part, not onerous. It became painful as Ditmars's office had to produce drawings and yet various forces, set in motion by a hiccupping stone supply, led to spasmodic building progress. Ditmars's livelihood was now largely from the cathedral project, and the income squeeze strangled him. When Bishop O'Connor apparently tried to make light of his appeals, saying that Ditmars's demands would bankrupt him, the architect saw no humor. "Your reference to bankruptcy moves me to congratulate you, rather than commiserate with you, in that your situation is so fortunate that the dreaded state of insolvency can have for you personally only a more or less academic interest. Quite otherwise for the poor architect, to whom the prospect of such a catastrophe has an intensely real and intimate application."[4] He also told the bishop that he had replied in a letter to Monsignor Sheppard, "in response to a delightful telephone conversation in which he favored me with certain very frank comments on the manners of architects in general and of myself in particular."[5]

For the next several years, Ditmars made more urgent requests for payments. Sheppard droned the mantra of the contract's terms. Indeed, by this time, the monsignor brooked no argument: priests learned fast not to question him, and laymen presumed only to bow. His approach to management was simple and efficient: obey or be gone. In response to one vociferous plea from Ditmars, the vicar general (priests under Sheppard wagged that when he added "V.G." to his signature, it stood for "vinegar and gall") gave Ditmars a dose.[6] But cash-strapped and desperate, the architect turned around and gave Sheppard a piece of his mind in a letter, sending a copy with a cover note to the bishop. It read:

> Dear Monsignor Sheppard,
>
> Referring to our recent telephone conversation, you will recall that I accepted the work of the Cathedral of the Sacred Heart most reluctantly and only in response to your urgent solicitations. The architect's responsibility in the case of a structure of this type is very great, and the care and labor demanded of him are excessive in comparison with any return he can expect.
>
> I regret that your opposition to measures which I have regarded as essential to the successful prosecution of the work has at times increased the difficulty of my position, and your present objection to the proper completion of the crypt is a case in point. I am requesting Bishop O'Connor, in a letter of which I enclose a copy, to approve this work, and I trust that you will accept my judgment in the matter as worthy of full confidence.[7]

The project's architects were not the only ones to suffer. The builder now had his own headaches. The stuttering stone supply tangled Waldron's efforts to coordinate his squad of stone, terra cotta, and temporary window subcontractors in a rational use of derricks and scaffolding; these cascading problems retarded progress. Despite such agitations, in early summer 1924 the last work truck drove out of the cathedral interior, and the elaborate stone portals and temporary doors enclosed the great space for the first time.

Not long after reaching this signpost on the way to completion, Monsignor Sheppard died. Builder Edward Waldron and scores of Jersey City politicos, Mayor Hague first among them, were listed as public mourners; the architects with whom he worked were not.[8] Tributes extolled his administrative skills, commitment to Catholic organizations, and his easy congress with businessmen and politicians. He left his estate to a friend, a local doctor.

CREATIVE SOLUTIONS

The talented new vicar general who was handed the reins of the cathedral project, Monsignor John A. Duffy, infused it with fresh purpose. Persuading the bishop that the moment had come to rally everyone behind it, he had Ditmars and Waldron begin calculating the cost to finish the cathedral. But when the estimate came in at more than $3 million, the planners tactically withheld the news from the bishop as they turned over cheaper alternatives.

Their attention fixed on the possible materials for the interior walls, narrowing them to marble and limestone. It was not simply an aesthetic matter. The sheer amount of surface to be covered in stone meant that it would be the greatest single expense. Designer and client thought about cost-saving devices, such as limiting the finer masonry to a wainscoting course and covering the remaining wall surfaces with a less costly material. This reduction did not lower the projections sufficiently, and marble was knocked out as an option. Various American limestones were considered, with Waldron pushing for one from Indiana quarries, though Ditmars and the diocese pressed to compare it to French samples.

The forbidding estimates bred worry and doubt, but Duffy refused to be discouraged. With his ascension to the project leadership came an openness to new ideas. The best of these may have been reaching beyond the architectural team for help in developing an interior scheme that was beautiful and affordable. Duffy, more akin to Doane than Sheppard, asked for advice from Ralph Adams Cram, the unsurpassed Gothicist who had succeeded to the commission for the Cathedral of Saint John the Divine in New York. Within the Newark diocese, he had recently completed, between 1921 and 1924, Sacred Heart Church in the Greenville section of Jersey City, giving it a brilliant Spanish Gothic inflection. (The record is not at all clear that Duffy told Ditmars about his contact with Cram.)

Cram, like Pugin, had deeply probed Gothic's underlying principles, which freed him to offer Newark historically sound, artistic, and economical alternatives. He recommended that the sanctuary and choir walls be given a skin of French limestone and the naked granite of the nave and transepts be left unadorned. He asserted that his solution would produce an effect that was, in a characteristic Cram phrase, "acceptable, dignified and impressive." He thought the floor could be common granolithic, a composite of granite and concrete, painted "Navy gray." He also offered to make sketches for simple liturgical furniture that could serve indefinitely or until Newark could afford more elaborate pieces.[9] Duffy liked Cram's concept and wasted no time. He also reached out to a structural engineer whom Cram had suggested, discussing the type of limestone to be used. Cram's cohort weighed in for Saint Quentin, a French limestone, in part, it seems, because of Sacred Heart's French Gothic style and because it was warmer-looking than most American equivalents.

With his superior's consent, Duffy, in turn, went to his fellow priests and proposed that Bishop O'Connor's approaching twenty-fifth anniversary as bishop and fifty years in the priesthood be the goal to inspire finishing the building. An aura of broad prosperity and a levitating stock market played their part when Duffy made his fund-raising case at a special meeting of the clergy. When the priests gave their approval, of course, it was an agreement to be taxed, and Duffy took away the promise that pastors would make personal gifts of $300 and assistants $100. Parishes would also be expected to contribute an amount equal to the Christmas offering, the year's largest. The clerical levy and over-brimming collection baskets were expected to bring about three-quarters of a million dollars, barely shy of the cost Duffy was told would make the cathedral both attractive and suitable for use.

The Cram association was never formalized, nor is there evidence that this master had more discussions with the Newark authorities about Sacred Heart. And yet the cathedral's architectural team changed about this time. Isaac Ditmars, motivated either by the need to plan for a successor or because he perceived that his client wanted another design sensibility (or both), brought in Paul C. Reilly as a partner.

Reilly, much younger than Ditmars, was a New York native who had studied in Columbia University's fine architecture program. Like many emerging professionals, he had taken commissions for whatever building types came his way, including commercial structures and theaters, many of the latter done while working for Thomas W. Lamb, a firm noted for this work.[10] Churches eventually became a large segment of his practice. Ditmars had confidence in Reilly's abilities and his command of the historic Gothic style. Also, because Reilly was Catholic and an Irish American, Ditmars must have thought that this would be grist in their relations with Newark Catholic Church leaders, who largely had the same roots. Ditmars readily turned over a good deal of Sacred Heart's design work to Paul Reilly, while as senior partner he attended to the business side of the contract—just as he agreed eventually to turn over the firm, and the cathedral contract with it.[11]

O'Rourke versus Waldron Revisited?

Monsignor Duffy radiated optimism about completing the cathedral. But in no time, the first of several serious setbacks jolted him. In a telephone conversation with a representative from the stone supplier, Monsignor Duffy's ears pricked when the fellow let slip that his firm was paying a commission to get the contract. Appalled, Duffy stopped everything until he was able to convene the diocesan Board of Consultors, an advisory group appointed by the bishop, which now shared responsibility for the project. When Waldron heard about the session, he asked to be there in the event that his "reputation might be questioned."[12] The upshot was that concerned clergy reined in the builder and insisted that henceforward all such contracts be awarded after competitive, sealed bidding. (It may or may not be a coincidence that the new diocesan representative, Monsignor Duffy, uncovered such an irregularity so soon after taking over from Monsignor Sheppard, who had been in that position for two decades.)

The consultors also decided to join in judging the different stone samples for the interior, requesting they be set up for their review in the unfinished cathedral. They ultimately preferred limestone quarried in Indiana, where the sedimentary rock is found in abundance. And they conceded that in Sacred Heart it would be carried beyond the east end of the interior only as a 13-foot-high course, a masonry wainscoting. The diocese in the end also settled on terrazzo floors, with marble trim. Waldron submitted the lowest of three bids and secured the job.

When this supposedly final push was under way, and as if subject to some sinking, primordial force, architect and builder took up arms against each other. Waldron blamed Ditmars for slow delivery of the drawings he needed for construction. The architect countered that he could not finish them until Waldron's subcontractor (Rochette & Parzini) fashioned the models on which many architectural details were to be derived. Waldron circled back and said that Ditmars had created the problem, as the architect had insisted that he work with the very subcontractors who were hindering progress. As they hammered at each other, the vicar general toured the cathedral site in late June 1926. Alarmed that so little appeared to have been done, he upbraided Ditmars. The architect's calm, albeit ill-founded, reply was that things were in better shape than they seemed. Ditmars assured Duffy that all would be well. So the vicar general drove forward, orchestrating the opening rite and festivities and exultantly sent word to the Vatican's apostolic delegate in Washington to reserve an October date to be on hand for Newark's momentous day. But the tainted relations of architect and builder, mostly over coordination and areas of responsibility, poisoned progress, and the diocese ruefully unwound its plans.

VAULTING AND CRYPT

The essence of Gothic is a construction method and tectonic phenomenon from which the form of the Gothic style emerges: pointed arches, buttresses, traceries, and, most complex of all, Gothic stone vaults. Much Neo-Gothic work, as we have seen, no matter how visually persuasive, was hollowed by trickery of one sort or another. Stone vaults, in fact, had never been in Newark's plans. O'Rourke projected that they would be formed with a plaster that went by the trade of name of Keene's cement, an expedient of his day that dampened the ringing claim of "true Gothic construction."

But a novel system, called Guastivino vaulting, remarkably split the difference between imitation and authentic stone vaulting. It had been used as early as the 1880s, and by this point in the Newark project, it was well understood and appreciated for use in monumental structures—civic buildings, churches, rail stations, and the like. It was brought to America by Rafael Guastivino, an architect from Barcelona who mastered the technique of an ingenious practice known as timbrel vaulting that developed in various Mediterranean locales and was raised to an art form in Spain's Catalonian region. Guastivino perfected, patented, and commercialized the eponymous system. Made of masonry tiles and cement and layered into a thin, amazingly strong, and often very beautiful vault, it was also fireproof and could be treated with sound-absorbent materials, for acoustical control. The Newark cathedral team enthusiastically elected to install Guastivino vaulting in Sacred Heart. The warm color of the tiles chosen harmonizes with the limestone walls and ribs. But it does not attempt to match them or suggest that the tiles are actual stone. It effectively communicated the honesty or "truth" in the use of materials that Pugin espoused and Ruskin canonized in his *Seven Lamps of Architecture.*

In the summer of 1927, however, another beastly problem with the cathedral's structural integrity raised its head. Specialists preparing to install the Guastivino system concluded that the cathedral walls were not engineered to bear safely the weight and thrust of the tile and stone ribs of the vaulting. Those walls—redesigned by Ditmars, built by Waldron, approved by both—had embedded in them problems akin to the old O'Rourke-Waldron war over the foundations. Fundamental as this new worry was, however, it brought little finger-pointing and no dysfunction. Engineering consultants were engaged, and their advice, to reinforce the superstructure with concrete girders and steel rods, was accepted.[13] To mitigate similar concerns, buttresses were added out of sight under the triforium roof.

The collegiality occasioned by the vaulting challenge contrasted with work on the crypt. Waldron managed to dodge the architect and win Monsignor Duffy's authorization to purchase an altar for it from a church-goods purveyor (a stock item rather than one designed by the architects) and instead of consulting Ditmars when his men put down the crypt floor, simply installed the pattern of terrazzo used in the sanctuary.[14] These unilateral actions infuriated Ditmars. In another dustup, Waldron sent a letter to Ditmars that listed grievances about the firm's pace and negligence, and, generally, for not being forthcoming with information. In a quick follow-up missive demanding a response, Waldron threatened to take the matter to Monsignor Duffy. Ditmars wrote on it "Impudence—Moonshine—No Answer!?" before assuring the letter was seen in the chancery.

Part of the trouble over the crypt arose from the client's ambivalence about it. A logical sequence for interior construction required that the planners deal with the matter of a crypt or undercroft intended as the burial place for Newark's prelates. Bishop O'Connor, asked to address these plans, seemed to push them away, claiming that it would be hard to raise money for a space of such "doubtful necessity," noting that the diocese was then seventy years old and only one bishop was buried there.[15] The aging, ailing prelate's ambivalence—almost literally whistling past the graveyard—meant that, at his death less than three years later, workers scrambled madly to ready it for his coffin.[16] The fourth of Newark's bishops engaged in building the cathedral, O'Connor's remains were the first interred in its crypt.

Yet another confrontation echoed those between O'Rourke and Waldron. When several subcontractors had trouble getting payments from Waldron, they asked Ditmars to use his leverage, and he withheld money from the contractor. Waldron exploded and wrote to Monsignor Duffy, saying to pay him directly. Ditmars extirpated, "Bunk," penciling it in the margins of Waldron's letter, which he somehow saw.[17] Yet Duffy, stepping away from the pitfalls of his predecessors who violated payment protocols, sought resolution by other means. Fred Metcalf was summoned once more to mediate, and he sought and found middle ground.

Pride before the Fall: Bishop Walsh and the Depression

In this period, Ditmars received recognition that his profession coveted. *The Architectural Record* published an essay that he wrote about Sacred Heart, accompanied by photographs.[18] O'Rourke often provided journalists with useful (and promotional) statements about his architecture. Ditmars now offered a text that streamlined the cathedral's architectural history and celebrated his contributions. It was a moment of self-aggrandizement, rare for the reserved Isaac Ditmars, that few could begrudge him.

By the late 1920s, the incomplete cathedral was a fixture in the Newark cityscape, and the local press carried news of the project's progress or delays. The landmark also produced at least one veteran of its multiple building phases. By 1928, Frank Colucci had labored on or supervised Sacred Heart's masonry construction for twenty-eighty years, the *Star-Ledger* reporting that "three-fourths of all stonework passed his inspections."[19] At the time, he recalled, "Back in 1899, I attended the cornerstone laying ceremonies here. Bishop Wigger was in charge. Every Catholic church in the city and nearby cities was represented. It was grand sight." The long-serving Colucci observed, "The hardest job of all was the building of the walls. At times as many as forty men a day worked on them." He went on to reminisce about the two fatal falls from those walls in 1913 and 1914. Mostly, however, this Italian American Catholic conveyed enormous pride in having been associated with the long initiative to raise a great cathedral in Newark.

Like many of those who worked on Sacred Heart, Colucci had immigrant roots, and though a large number of other Italian Americans worked on the cathedral over the years, the laborers who built it were ultimately as ethnically and racially diverse as Newark itself. Most had been employed by Edward Waldron's company (by this time including a second generation of Waldrons), which offered opportunities without discrimination and rewarded hard work with good pay, especially recognizing loyal service.

The Diocese of Newark's new leader toured the cathedral site in the winter of 1928, soon after his appointment. Thomas Joseph Walsh, who had been the bishop of Trenton, was a seasoned leader. Quick and absolutely confident in his decision making, he apparently concluded then and there that his installation rite would be held in the unfinished structure. And when it was conducted two months later, prelates, priests, members of religious orders, and lay people—some four thousand in all—could see what more than $3 million and three decades had produced. Inside the largely complete exterior was an unfinished shell. Buff-colored Indiana limestone covered the sanctuary and ambulatory walls and formed a high wainscoting everywhere else, for which Rockport sea green granite formed a base molding; the flooring was a sturdy terrazzo. Otherwise, the project awaited fresh revenues, and Walsh calculated that gathering his new flock into the cathedral might be a grand overture to entice them into another round of contributions.

For the installation ceremony, banners and bunting were hung in the building, and Newark's fifth bishop sat in the splendid black walnut cathedra crafted for Newark's first bishop. The stark Gothic forms of the space made a powerful impression. So did the pomp and ceremony. As a young man, Bishop Walsh had pined to study in Rome, and when the opportunity came, he savored the city's infinitely beguiling culture and allurements. He carried home a triumphal Roman aura. No one who watched him that day, or at major ceremonies anytime, was likely to forget the experience. Preceded by papal knights in plumes and capes and fastidiously surpliced clergy, the short, intense Walsh walked in violet stockings and episcopal slippers. A purple train, falling from an ermine cape, was carried by young pages in starched collars and silk and velvet vestments. He liked ritual and music. The latter improved everywhere he went, owing to the programs he instituted to promote performance of Gregorian chant and polyphonic choral music. Like the procession that brought him into the cathedral, Walsh's era in Newark was disciplined, impressive, and supremely hierarchical.

Bishop Walsh told the architects to keep working on the interior scheme, and their efforts went toward developing designs for essential sanctuary furniture. They planned a cathedra capped by spires, terraced stalls in the sanctuary that ended in a final row crowned with elaborate gabled canopies, and an altar with a reredos of panels, carvings, and pinnacles that aspired to make it the focal point of the interior. They sought in Newark to avoid what Cram said about the then extent main altar in Saint Patrick's in New York: "trivial, and stamped with mark of the wedding confection."[20] They also planned a divided organ case in the western gallery to leave an unobstructed view of the rose window.

Although Bishop Walsh was an autocrat by instinct, he was surprisingly quick to reach out to specialists for advice. He appointed three of the best theologians from among his priests to a cathedral subcommittee and suggested that the diocese consider asking several architects and designers to review and comment on the drafts coming off the drawing boards of Ditmars and Reilly and their staff. This proposition had the potential to bring a clash of artistic sensibilities and egos. But lacking Monsignor Doane's taste (or Monsignor Sheppard's aesthetic indifference), they convened a panel of Catholic architects to evaluate the plans.[21]

The October 1929 stock market crash and immediate aftermath caused anxiety about the cathedral but did not derail Walsh's plans. The later descent into the Great Depression, however, began closing a curtain on what had been clearly in sight in 1926. Solicitations for the cathedral ostensibly stopped. That did not mean, however, that Bishop Walsh's relentless fund-raising ceased. The lean times merely forced him to order his priorities. In the bleak 1930s, he raised staggering sums for new construction. Pictures of Walsh frequently appeared in diocesan and local newspapers—working a shovel at ground-breakings, spade in hand at cornerstone ceremonies, sprinkling holy water at dedications. Churches, houses for religious orders, and all levels of educational institutions mushroomed in the most strapped years of the Depression. Walsh said that he preferred to lay the cornerstone of one Catholic school to those of ten Catholic churches. The suspended progress on the cathedral project, greatest of all the churches under him, proved he meant it. And however much Walsh dreamed that a procession of unexampled pomp would escort him down the aisle of the finished cathedral, his pastoral mission led him elsewhere. Not that he forsook all grand manners. He traveled around his see in royal style, in his own, chauffeur-driven automobiles—a Cadillac, a Packard, and, for special occasions, a Rolls-Royce.[22]

The fitful starting and stopping of this period took a toll on an anxious, octogenarian Isaac Ditmars. Once again, the architect was snared by the need to produce drawings and specifications but contractually unable to collect fees. He pled. His lawyer made claims. But the new diocesan leadership also interpreted his contract strictly. Only his death, in 1934, ended Ditmars's hope that he would be paid the fees that he believed were unfairly withheld. His family accepted a settlement for about half of the firm's outstanding invoices.[23] The sorrows emanating from Sacred Heart in Newark took many forms.

17

Regional Developments and Twentieth-Century Cathedral Building

UNFINISHED, SACRED HEART CATHEDRAL sat in still watch over a city that was transformed once again. In the boom years of the 1920s, a small metropolis of tall structures rose in downtown Newark. When the Military Park Building opened in 1926 at twenty-one stories, it was the tallest building in New Jersey. New Jersey Bell Telephone put up a twenty-story tower two years later. The completion of projects born before the 1929 stock market crash first brought the Lefcourt-Newark Building in 1930, which held the height record for one year, until the National Newark & Essex Building of thirty-five floors topped it by one story. These early-twentieth-century skyscrapers, trophies of a thriving Newark, were nearly a mile away from Sacred Heart and left unrivaled its 232-foot towers and the 260-foot crossing spire, projecting from a prominence in the city's northwest.

Newark's maturation in this period extended beyond commercial interests and in one instance brought a building that, as a source of cultural and spiritual enrichment, was the cathedral's cousin. In 1926, Louis Bamberger, one of the city's merchant princes, donated three-quarters of million dollars to build a new home for the Newark Museum, custodian of the art collection (first housed in the public library) that Monsignor Doane had nurtured.

ASSIMILATION, SUBURBANIZATION, AND A NEW KIND OF MIGRATION

Although the largest cities in the diocese—Newark, Paterson, Jersey City, Elizabeth—spawned suburbs early on, the increasing availability of the automobile, along with better roads (in the single decade of the 1920s, the number of New Jersey's paved roads doubled) and highway systems constructed with government funds, pushed development farther out from urban centers. The Church responded to newly settled or rapidly growing existing communities by starting parishes and missions in them.[1] Soon major bridges and tunnels also promoted business and residential development within the Newark diocese's bounds. In a burst of river-crossing projects in the five years starting in 1928, the Goethals and Bayonne bridges and the Outerbridge Crossing connected Staten Island to three different locations in New Jersey; the Pulaski Skyway tied Newark to Jersey City; and the Holland Tunnel and George Washington Bridge linked New Jersey to Manhattan.[2] All of these served the state's big industrial plants, a growing number of light manufacturing operations (especially producers of electronics, chemicals, and pharmaceuticals), and the new towns and bedroom communities where their employees lived; they further stimulated interstate commerce.

These new highways around Newark also altered the perception of Sacred Heart Cathedral in the cityscape. North and south, and also east (over the swampy meadows of Essex and Hudson counties), ribbons of roadways, many with long, elevated stretches, provided views across the lowlands to Newark and to Sacred Heart. From some vantages it looked colossal, from others like a metallic paperweight, a souvenir model from a vacation in the cultural capitals of Europe. In the same period, another phenomenon of the transportation revolution permitted even more extraordinary perspectives of the cathedral. An airport opened in Newark for commercial airplane travel in 1929. Within two years it was the nation's busiest, with many flight patterns offering a bird's-eye view of Sacred Heart's cruciform profile.

The 1910 census recorded the peak of New Jersey's foreign-born population; during and following World War I, fewer new immigrants arrived. And in the 1920s, the U.S. government imposed quotas on immigrants. As a consequence, the Diocese of Newark was increasingly constituted of second- and third-generation Americans. Another major shift occurred. Whereas global migrations had progressively altered Newark's makeup since the nineteenth century, a new one—from within the United States—changed it as thoroughly as any originating abroad. African Americans, largely from the rural South, began arriving about the time of World War I. Many of them found work in companies ramping up production to supply the Allied war machine and whose traditional labor pool was depleted as many workers departed for military service. African Americans kept coming to Newark after the war, and by about twenty years later, accounted for 8 percent of the city's population. New Jersey and its urban centers continued to receive part of the exodus of African Americans from the South and Southwest to cities during the twentieth century; known as the Great Migration, six million left for places in the North and West. Many of the later of these, especially, met an alien urban environment and scarce employment opportunities, as well as racial prejudice. In this era of segregation, the Diocese of Newark established two parishes specifically for African American congregations in 1930: Queen of Angels Church in Newark, and the Church of Christ the King in Jersey City, where African Americans also settled in significant numbers.

Near the same time, the diocese made its first efforts to serve the modest number of Spanish- and Portuguese-speaking Catholics then in the region. It remodeled a former Baptist church in Newark in 1928, naming it Saint Joseph's Church. In later years, these two language groups would make up a substantial percentage of Catholics in the region and strongly influence the Church's character and stewardship.

The 1920s also saw a recurrence of nativism in two of its historic manifestations: racism and anti-Catholicism. The Knights of the Ku Klux Klan gained members nationally, demonstrating their largely furtive presence by gathering at "klan-caves," marching through communities in hooded regalia, and with brazen cross-burnings. In New Jersey, Klan members in Paterson ignited three crosses high atop Garrett Mountain on a Friday night in spring 1922. The next year, they set ablaze thirteen crosses in the Newark region on a Saturday night, most but not all on empty lots. Elsewhere around the diocese in this era Klan members burned crosses on hills and mountainsides, positioned to be widely visible. They lit others on private property, including in the yards of Catholic families. For Catholics, these aggressions served as a reminder of a persistent undercurrent of prejudice based on religious affiliation. Klansmen were no moral abstraction: they were neighbors and coworkers. The region experienced little outright violence, but ugly rhetoric, threats, and fear-mongering stained community life in religiously and racially mixed places.

The Church, with its national (or language) parishes, played an essential role in preserving the distinct ethnic cultures that grew up vigorously in the era of immigration. Yet time brought a widening of individual and group identity, and softening of divisions. It was attributable to the natural transformation occurring over generations as descendants of immigrants grew more distant from their ancestors' origins, married into other ethnic or religious groups, and generally became acculturated. And the expanding suburbs, more heterogeneous than city neighborhoods, accelerated the change. These evolving conditions altered northern New Jersey and especially Newark itself. The city's expansion began to slow after the first decade of the twentieth century, as a growing share of employers and the population moved elsewhere.[3] The Depression flattened the City of Newark's arc of growth. It also affected Sacred Heart Cathedral unexpectedly. One of the government's remedies for the fiscal collapse, the Works Progress Administration, financed an extension of Branch Brook Park, further insulating the cathedral's northwest exposure. Buffered now by still more protected parkland and located in a district that failed to experience the growth that the cathedral founders foresaw, Sacred Heart stood remotely above a city in stasis.

Newark Becomes an Archdiocese

Although Newark proper stopped growing, the increase of Catholic numbers and vigorous development of the broader region and of diocesewide activities and services called for a further division of the Catholic Church's administrative units in New Jersey. In 1937, three northern counties were split off as a new diocese, with Paterson as the see city. Simultaneously, the Vatican made New Jersey an ecclesiastical province and made Newark a metropolitan archdiocese, meaning its leader had general oversight of other dioceses, in this case those in New Jersey. Some on the western side of the Hudson River thought they were at last released from the dominion of New York. An archdiocese meant there must be an archbishop. There was never doubt that he would be the sitting bishop of Newark. In the complex economies of the Church, Bishop Walsh, a brilliant executive, earned the appointment. As archbishop-elect, he set in motion the machinery for an installation ceremony of audacious pageantry. Sacred Heart was again made presentable, this time for an occasion grander by far than any before.

Nicola Montani was placed in charge of the music.[4] This maestro of American Catholic Church music assembled a large, all-male choir. The Wanamaker's department store in New York provided an Everett Orgatron, an imitative electronic instrument. This substitution did not in the least compromise the musical talent brought in for the occasion. Belgian-born organ virtuoso Dr. Charles Courboin was recruited, joined by brass players from the New Jersey Symphony orchestra.

The Solemn Pontifical Mass began with a procession that foreshadowed Franco Zeffirelli's staging of *Tosca*. Altar boys and seminarians were led in by a vanguard of the Knights of Columbus. The clergy followed, first the order priests, in their habits of black and white and brown, with the secular clergy after them. Trailing the priests were the provincials of the religious orders. The purple could be seen with the coming of the monsignorii, cued punctiliously by rank. Mitered abbots led the bishops, who preceded the more exalted archbishops. Still they came in. Papal knights, wealthy or accomplished laymen, with plumed hats, capes, and swords, signaled the arrival of the officiants. In this long train were chaplains of honor, book bearers, miter bearers, acolytes and thurifers, and bearers of arcane ceremonial instruments carefully named in the printed program—a visual crescendo that rose at the last with the archbishop-elect and, finally, in place of highest exaltation, the apostolic delegate, Archbishop Amleto Giovanni Cicognani, the pope's own representative to the United States.

Moving down the aisle, passing Newark and New Jersey civic and private-sector leaders, a sea of religious nuns and brothers, and a congregation of amazed lay people, the ecclesiastics in the service settled into their places and listened to the closing phrases of the bombastic anthem. The brass players and Dr. Courboin at the console of the amplified reed organ gave the strongest fortissimo they could manage. Loud as possible the choir sang "Ecce Sacerdos Magnus" ("Behold a Great Priest"). No one there doubted for a moment that Thomas Joseph Walsh, who had heard those heady words sung to him for two decades, believed them. And, by many measures, he was.

The raw interior, rather than detracting from the ceremony, brought it into relief. The medieval and Renaissance dress of the clerics and attendants looked all the more impressive set against the stark limestone walls of the apse and largely unsheathed nave. Following the breathtaking installation ceremony—it must have seemed a near coronation—the newly elevated Walsh flashed signals that he was gearing up to finish the cathedral. But when the United States entered the Second World War, talk and action ceased.

Through the Depression and the war years, Sacred Heart was occasionally opened for the consecration of Newark's auxiliary bishops or bishops in the region, but was usually locked up behind a chain-link fence. It was mysterious in the way that all shuttered buildings are; more sepulchral perhaps, because of the shadowy, hidden, and tucked away Gothic spaces and the entombed remains of Newark's fourth bishop in the crypt.

By the end of the Second World War, almost half a century had passed since construction started on Sacred Heart. In the intervening years, both Catholic and Episcopal dioceses undertook notable cathedral projects. Broader trends affected this activity. The architectural profession in the United States grew to maturity as architects were increasingly trained in academic programs. Although this did not guarantee creative work, with regard to church design it tended to show in more sophisticated and fully developed historical interpretations. Modernism also emerged as a vital aesthetic movement. A review of the most significant cathedral undertakings and the relevant developments in architecture between 1900 and 1945 will provide a context for looking at the midcentury completion of Newark's cathedral.

Developments in Church and Cathedral Building after 1900

Since the beginning of the twentieth century, numerous cathedral projects have been initiated by other Catholic dioceses; those in Pittsburgh, Richmond, St. Paul, Omaha, Toledo, St. Louis, Helena, and Seattle were among the most significant.

The Diocese of Pittsburgh replaced its Cathedral of Saint Paul, troubled by construction and financial woes in the nineteenth century, with a large, refined Decorated Gothic structure by the Chicago architectural firm of Egan and Prindeville that opened in 1906 and cost about $730,000 to construct.[5] About the same time, wealthy Catholics Thomas Fortune Ryan and Ida Barry Ryan donated half a million dollars for constructing a new cathedral for the Diocese of Richmond, Virginia. Built between 1903 and 1906, the Italian Renaissance Revival building was designed by New York architect Joseph H. McGuire. An even larger cathedral in that style was undertaken in St. Paul, Minnesota. Unmistakably influenced by the Beaux Arts, it was designed by a graduate of the Paris institution for which that style is named. Architect Emmanuel Louis Masqueray, chief designer of the 1904 St. Louis World's Fair, in partnership with the powerful archbishop of St. Paul, John Ireland, set out to make an architectural statement with the new Cathedral of Saint Paul.[6] They succeeded. Ready for use by 1915 after $1.6 million was spent on it, the eclectic granite monument is one of the Twin Cities' most prominent landmarks and seats three thousand people within its marble interior.[7] The Richmond and Minnesota cathedrals (and other major church projects) manifested the lessening popularity of the Gothic style as a model for ecclesiastical architecture in the twentieth century.

Thomas Rogers Kimball, a Nebraska architect with a national reputation, designed the Cathedral of Saint Cecilia in Omaha. Unusual for the time, Kimball rendered it in the manner of the Spanish Renaissance Revival, drawing on the conceit that Spain and Mexico were influences in the region's early history.[8] When it opened for regular use about a decade after it was started in 1905, it ranked among the ten largest cathedrals in the country. Stained-glass from the accomplished Boston-based Connick firm filled its windows. A new cathedral in Toledo, Ohio, also reflected awakening interest in Spain's historic architecture. William Perry designed the relatively compact 1,400-seat Cathedral of the Holy Rosary in a Spanish Revival style. Begun in 1925, after six years and $3.25 million in expenditures, Holy Rosary was sufficiently complete for use.[9] It earned accolades from architectural critics, including Ralph Adams Cram.

The sumptuous Cathedral of Saint Louis, in St. Louis, Missouri was in use six years after its cornerstone was laid in 1908. A synthesis of Byzantine and Romanesque styles, it replaced a modest 1831 structure that was nevertheless among the significant early cathedral projects west of the Mississippi. Architect George Barnet of a local firm gave the new cathedral a lavish mosaic interior. One of its important influences was the new Westminster Cathedral in London that was under way when it was designed. The British project, by architect John Francis Bentley, was inspired by early Christian monuments and won the admiring attention of Catholic clergy and lay people in Britain and abroad, as well as architectural professionals. By the time of the St. Louis cathedral's blessing in 1914, it had cost $1.3 million, and by 1931, an estimated $3 million had been spent on it.[10]

Contemporaneously with the Saint Louis Cathedral, the Diocese of Helena, Montana, modeled its large new cathedral on the Gothic Revival Votive Church in Vienna, Austria. The Helena diocese, given a choice of Romanesque or Gothic by its architect, A. O. von Herbulis, chose a strongly referential design that cost $645,000 to realize.[11] Completed in 1924 with twin 230 foot spires, the Cathedral of Saint Helena is assertively picturesque in its open-sky Montana setting.

In the first years of the twentieth century, the bishop of Seattle wanted a cathedral that would "surpass anything in the West" and, more or less, received what he asked for when he awarded the commission to Heins and LaFarge, the firm that won the competition for the Cathedral of Saint John the Divine in New York. The Italian Renaissance scheme for Saint James' Cathedral was quickly realized between 1905 and 1907, but less than a decade later, catastrophe struck. Under the weight of a heavy, wet snowfall, steel girders supporting the central dome gave way, and what was estimated to be four hundred tons of brick, terra cotta, steel, and copper plunged to the floor of the cathedral, mercifully empty at the moment of the disaster. This colossal failure embarrassed everyone involved and was hugely costly to remedy.

SIGNIFICANT EPISCOPAL CATHEDRAL BUILDING

Several of the most visible cathedrals nationally in this period were Protestant Episcopal projects. These included more work on Saint John the Divine in New York, Grace Cathedral in San Francisco, a Philadelphia undertaking, and one that was, literally, a National Cathedral.

The Episcopal Church long fostered a desire to have a major cathedral in Washington, D.C., a kind of Westminster Abbey in the capital of the United States. When the new Diocese of Washington was created in 1895, its first bishop, Henry Yates Saterlee, took up the cause with conviction. A decade-long battle over what architectural style was proper for a cathedral in Washington is a reminder that the debate over style never ends. Architect Ernest Flagg worked with Saterlee and produced both Renaissance Revival and Gothic schemes. Charged to make a recommendation, the architectural committee, which included influential classicists Charles McKim and Daniel Burnham, endorsed a Renaissance-style building. The cathedral trustees, however, prevailed in favoring Gothic. They also wanted plans by the architect that many regarded as the premier living Gothicist, Englishman George F. Bodley. Appreciating the delicacy of choosing a British architect for the U.S. national cathedral, the solution they embraced partnered Bodley with his gifted former pupil, Henry Vaughn, an English-born American citizen. By American standards, Bodley and Vaughn's cruciform, English-style scheme for the Cathedral Church of Saint Peter and Saint Paul was enormous: 476 feet long and 132 feet wide, with a central tower. Still, Bishop Saterlee did not think it as monumental as the national cathedral should be and supported design changes that would make it yet more imposing.[12] Bodley died in 1907, the year the cornerstone was laid, and Henry Vaughn succeeded him. And although Bodley had specified red stone for the cathedral and Vaughn resisted any white stone (even advocating English stone), the building was ultimately rendered in Indiana limestone and boasted a masonry Gothic vaulting system. After Vaughn's death in 1921, the firm of Frohman Robb and Little took over the commission, making alterations to the original scheme such that in many respects it became their design, especially Philip Hubert Frohman's. The National Cathedral's nave was finished in time for the American Bicentennial, in 1976, and the whole structure was completed in 1990.

Progress was also made on the construction of Saint John the Divine in New York. Following architect Heins's death in 1907, his partner, Grant LaFarge, continued the commission. There had been numerous difficulties with many aspects of its structural design as well as unproductive infighting among the project's participants; ultimately, and to his bitterness, LaFarge was dismissed in 1911. He was followed by Ralph Adams Cram, who some thought had plotted devilishly for the post. Cram scorned the former eclectic-style scheme and redesigned the cathedral in Gothic style. The choir and crossing were complete and in use by 1913, and the nave in 1941. Saint John the Divine, whose interior length was now just over 600 feet, exceeded by far that of Saint Patrick's Cathedral. If ever completed, in all it would be the fourth-largest cathedral in the world. The surviving parts of the former non-Gothic crossing and the unrealized work are, paradoxically, not shortcomings: they seem to convey the often irregular stylistic evolution of the great old churches. Even in its unfinished state, or perhaps because of it, Saint John the Divine, of all American cathedrals, may come nearest to its medieval ancestry. The nave by Cram, genius in his handling of Gothic, is awe-inspiring.

An earthquake and subsequent fires destroyed much of San Francisco in 1906, and in their aftermath plans were developed for Grace Cathedral in the city's Nob Hill district. George Bodley also received this 1907 commission but died within a year, succeeded by his English partner, Cecil Hare, who revised the design. The cornerstone was laid in 1910, but the project leadership was eventually turned over to California architect Lewis Hobart, who repositioned the cathedral, giving it an east-west siting. Hobart further revised the plans, which began to be realized in 1928. Grace Cathedral, constructed with a complex earthquake-resistant steel framework, was completed in 1964.

A major Episcopal cathedral project also fizzled. In the high-flying 1920s, the Episcopal Diocese of Pennsylvania made plans for what would have been the largest cathedral in the country, 200 feet longer than Saint John the Divine. Only the Lady Chapel and two side chapels were raised of the Cathedral Church of Christ, in Philadelphia, by the local firm of Watson, Edkins & Thompson, before the Depression snuffed out the project for good.[13]

ARCHITECTURAL PACESETTERS, HISTORICIST AND MODERN

Although not a cathedral for a diocese, the National Shrine of the Immaculate Conception in Washington, D.C., was a highly visible Catholic undertaking begun in 1920 and designed by Charles D. Maginnis and Timothy Walsh. This Boston-based team particularly channeled Cram's ideals for pacesetting Catholic commissions and had a track record of stylistically literate Catholic churches.[14] They were widely regarded as the leading designers for Catholic commissions and were influential in establishing new architectural preferences with their suave Romanesque schemes for Catholic churches.[15] For the National Shrine, Maginnis and Walsh (and later Frederick V. Murphy and Eugene F. Kennedy Jr.) combined Byzantine and Romanesque influences for a grand pilgrimage church in the nation's capital. The planners explained their choice of style by saying that Gothic was too costly for the scale of building they desired and that their design harmonized with the classical architecture normative in the District of Columbia. The choice also differentiated the National Shrine from the Episcopalian's (Gothic) National Cathedral. Within the Newark archdiocese, Maginnis & Walsh produced several works around 1930: a large Gothic church with an impressive flèche for Our Lady of Sorrows in South Orange, a Romanesque design for Saint Vincent de Paul in Bayonne, and a more Byzantine-style church for Holy Name of Jesus parish in East Orange. They also gained a high-profile project for Saint Patrick's Cathedral in New York, producing renovations that included a new main altar and baldachin, completed in 1942. Maginnis won the American Institute of Architects' coveted Gold Medal, the highest honor bestowed by the association, in 1948.

Whereas these major twentieth-century cathedral projects were in various historical styles, progressive American architects and patrons increasingly embraced Modernism. Among the important churches in nonhistoricist modes were Frank Lloyd Wright's 1906 Unity Temple in Oak Park, Illinois, and the work of Eliel and Eero Saarinen, especially the First Christian Church in Columbus, Indiana, of 1942. In an example of revealing coincidence, just as the Newark archdiocese contemplated completing Sacred Heart in the Gothic style, Eero Saarinen's pioneering Christ Church Lutheran in Minneapolis was raised. Barry Byrne responded keenly to the Modernist call in his church work in the Midwest and was arguably the most inventive architect working on Catholic commissions in this period.

PART IV

Completing Sacred Heart

18

Resolve

IT WAS AGAINST THIS MULTIFACETED architectural backdrop that Newark returned to its many-decades-long cathedral project. Within months following V-J Day in 1945, Newark Church officials beckoned architect Paul C. Reilly to the Newark chancery to discuss, in general terms, the future of its cathedral endeavor. Did they consider other architects? Certainly, the Maginnis & Walsh firm had the largest national practice among firms specializing in Catholic buildings, plus three fine demonstrations of their work around Newark, but no formal discussion appears to have been initiated with it or other firms.[1]

Finishing the Job in Newark: Architect Paul C. Reilly Returns

Reilly's involvement began in the 1920s, when he joined Isaac Ditmars on the final phase of exterior construction and to prepare interior schemes that, as we saw, failed to be realized. (Reilly's marriage to a daughter of builder Edward Waldron was another intersection in the personal narratives that at times joined and diverged in the multigenerational effort to raise the cathedral.) Reilly was a practical-minded professional and neither abandoned historical modes nor resisted emerging Modernism.[2] In giving clients what they wanted, Reilly produced very persuasive Gothic and Colonial Revival works, and an unthreatening contemporary style for the more adventurous.[3] He said that he loved the Gothic style and yet made remarks that reveal that he was conscious, when designing it, of working in an antiquarian mode that was then not popular or esteemed in the architectural mainstream. On these occasions, he sounded a little defensive but honest.

Reilly had good reason to be wary of the artistic challenges of designing in Gothic in the mid-twentieth century. Time had exhausted the Gothic Revival as a vital aesthetic movement. It nearly expired after Pugin and Ruskin's direct influence dissipated. Ralph Adams Cram pruned it back to its fundamental principles for a reflowering in America during the first quarter of the twentieth century. But after that, its creative force was not fresh or pervasive. Even so, and amidst the ever more progressive design ideologies of midcentury, Reilly appears never to have suggested (not that the Newark hierarchy would be receptive in the first place) that Sacred Heart's interior be finished in any style but traditional Gothic. As his discussions with the archdiocese unfolded, and his scope of work was clarified, Reilly also quietly accepted that the drawings he had worked on in the late 1920s were rolled up and, moreover, that the interior decorative work was to be turned over to designer Gonippo Raggi, who, in more ways than one, was a Roman Catholic.

An Artistic Roman in New Jersey: Gonippo Raggi

Born in Rome to an artistically inclined family, Gonippo Raggi trained in the academy tradition at the Accademia di San Luca there, claiming prizes for proficiency in composition and the handling of oils.[4] Facile with various historic modes, Gonippo found an interest and market in Christian subjects. Having gained a reputation in Vatican circles, in his twenties he was offered a life-changing commission in Spring Lake, at the Jersey shore.

Martin Maloney, a Pennsylvania native and a utilities magnate who summered in Spring Lake, was devastated when his teenage daughter Catharine died of tuberculosis in 1900. The Count, later Marquis, Maloney (titles of the Papal Court that this Irish American from Scranton savored) immortalized young Kitty and the family name by having Philadelphia architect Horace Trumbauer re-create a jaw-dropping domed Roman Baroque church on a striking site near Maloney's mansion, "Ballingarry," also by Trumbauer.[5] Maloney then brought Gonippo Raggi from Rome in 1904 to paint a program of murals in it.

Saint Catharine Church (the Maloney Memorial) was the first of Raggi's scores of American ecclesiastical interiors.[6] Though his paintings for the Spring Lake church "show some originality, a few inspirations, and many artistic quotations," as a decorative scheme, they formed a convincing whole within the scaled-down, monumental interior.[7] Most vacationers at the

Jersey shore at the time, walking into Saint Catharine, with its penumbral vaults and murals and mysterious crypt, would have been near certain that they had been miraculously transported to Rome. And this is exactly what its patron and artist intended. Fortunately for Raggi, Saint Catharine Church later gained the notice of Bishop Thomas Joseph Walsh, then of Trenton. Bishop Walsh exalted in the Roman manner and, playing Julius II and Paul III, had found his own court artist in Gonippo Raggi. Acting steadily as commissioner and promoter, Walsh secured Raggi to decorate a number of churches under him in the Trenton and Newark sees, which included covering their walls in more artistically rendered murals of a type ubiquitous in Catholic churches of the time.

Raggi's Roman Catholic ties reached to the Vatican stratosphere. His first cousin, Lorenzo Cardinal Lauri, had been a papal nuncio and was made Camerlegno by Pius XI, meaning that he would head the Curia between the death of the reigning pontiff and his successor.[8] And Raggi cultivated a high Roman—and Roman Catholic—aura in the United States. He never mastered English, in part, he said, because he believed that it was not essential to his livelihood. But it was not merely the case that as an artist, his language was visual. He rationalized his broken English in practical terms, explaining that much of his business was with priests, noting that because he spoke Italian and they had to know "Latin, which is very similar . . . I get along without English."[9]

He encouraged the appellations "Professor Raggi" and "the Professor," along with their academic and Old European connotations, and nodded at publicity that rated him America's "foremost ecclesiastical artist in the Catholic Church."[10] If this latter distinction was in a thrice-restricted arena, he never quibbled. Such aggrandizement might have been off-putting had Raggi, a short, animated man, not been cheerful and agreeable and so fervent in trying to widen appreciation of art generally. He deplored the reproduced murals typically found in church decoration and appealed at every turn for clergy to commission skilled artists to provide original work, even if closely derived from Renaissance and Baroque sources.[11] More than that (and like Jeremiah O'Rourke, two generations before), deep faith motivated him. He declared, "In profane art, when an artist finishes a painting the first feeling is generally one of satisfaction and pride. In religious art, however, the first impulse of the painter should be to kneel down and pray. His painting should inspire even himself. He should have the feeling that the figures on the canvas are not the products of his own creative powers."[12]

Raggi winced at art that was not purely representational and thought that modern styles had no place in church work.[13] But he later softened, conceding, "It does not matter what style an artist uses. You can tell quickly enough if he can draw."[14] He himself eventually drew and designed in Gothic, Renaissance, Impressionist, and Modernist styles. Apart from Raggi's artistic abilities, the prime factor driving his appointment to the Sacred Heart Cathedral commission was Archbishop Walsh's patronage. Only the stained glass portion of the commission called for work directly related to that by which he gained his reputation, paintings and murals. Otherwise, the scope of work came heavily to consist of three-dimensional carving and figurative sculpture. Nor was Gothic his natural idiom. What Raggi most brought to the Sacred Heart project was an artistic sensibility that could initiate design schemes and then guide and shape the work of others. Moreover, empowered by a forceful archbishop, he would become a strong liaison between patron and the teams of artists and artisans retained to execute the actual work.

TEAMWORK

Architect Reilly and designer Raggi had collaborated on other projects and enjoyed friendly relations, making them easy, complementary teammates. Reilly had overall architectural control and design responsibility for the interior architectural envelope and carved masonry, such as portal screens.[15] Raggi had a separate contract with the archdiocese to create, and manage the subcontractors for, liturgical furnishings and appointments, and decorative elements: statuary, mosaics, wood-carving, and the stained glass.

Gonippo Raggi's sons, Ernest and Louis, assisted their father at a studio in Orange.[16] Reilly's architectural office was in the Constable Building on lower Fifth Avenue in Manhattan, where Schickel and Ditmars had practiced and Reilly first worked with Ditmars in the 1920s. He handily administered the staff working on Sacred Heart, a dozen at its peak, and the phalanx of technical advisers that it was by then customary to consult on a building of Sacred Heart's complexity.[17] One of Reilly's rare complaints says a lot about architecture at the time. He said that Modernism's ascendance, and the ensuing descent of ornament, required that he search and advertise everywhere before he could assemble a team of draftsmen who could competently prepare the drawings and specifications for a Gothic structure.[18]

Of the many design influences that worked upon Reilly and Raggi at this juncture, the chronologically latest and most detectable were Ralph Adams

Cram's books on Gothic architecture and related arts, which, by then, had a limited, very salutary effect on Catholic architecture. Cram notably influenced Maginnis & Walsh, and this lineal influence reached Reilly and Raggi, informing aspects of Sacred Heart's ultimate interior scheme. Maginnis & Walsh's projects in Saint Patrick's Cathedral in New York of two decades earlier would serve as important models for those now working on Sacred Heart. Although Reilly seems not to have studied original High Gothic specimens extensively in this period, he went on what he called a "check-up" tour in Europe, visiting Spain and Italy.[19]

Target Date and Fund-Raising

Although it took several more years for a project of such magnitude to become practicable, the designers began new conceptual schemes. Ambitious fund-raising plans could also be convincingly prepared. Regarding the latter, nothing was more telling than that Archbishop Walsh, with his colossal will and galvanizing self-confidence, resolved, once and for all, to complete Sacred Heart. Although he delegated management of the cathedral project to auxiliary bishop James A. McNulty, few doubted the outcome with Walsh behind it.[20] This time a momentous target was set—for 1953, the Newark see's centennial. Attesting to the archdiocese's assimilation of corporate and professional methods, it hired a fund-raising firm to manage solicitation. It became a campaign of total victory: Sacred Heart would be finished to the smallest detail. The era of what over the years had been a called a "pay-as-you-go" approach—build as funds are raised—was over.[21]

A forced march to raise $5 million began in 1950. Every parish in the archdiocese was assigned a goal. The solicitation was dignified by an invitation to join the Cathedral Builders Association, suggesting that donors could become latter-day counterparts of the medieval cathedral patrons.[22] The onus fell on church pastors, who were made the association's local treasurers, to assure broad participation. These clergy, on orders from the chancery, mounted their pulpits on the first Sunday of Lent, a liturgical season with a theme of sacrifice, and made the case for completing the cathedral.[23] Not all priests were happy about it, many hated fund raising, and some, though circumspect, thought that the money should be spent on other purposes, especially education and social services. Nonetheless, the campaign meant canvassing the parish and personal calls upon those they thought could be enticed to pledge larger amounts.[24] Parish solicitations thus became a kind of referendum on the effectiveness of pastors. Heftier amounts meant donors could have particular liturgical and decorative features named in their honor or as memorials.[25] There was no clergy exemption. Every priest was required to join the Cathedral Builders Association. Underneath the euphemism of a contribution, pastors had to give $1,600 in four payments over two years and other priests were instructed to come up with $1,200 under the same terms.[26]

Fund-raising brochures made the case that, $3.3 million having been spent on Newark's cathedral, the time had come to truly finish it. An introductory letter over Walsh's signature (in his bold, florid, giant script) began: "My Beloved Brethren: The Cathedral Builders Association provides a golden opportunity for the Archdiocese of Newark to crown a century of Catholic progress. . . . Newark is now one of the outstanding archdioceses of the world and consequently deserves to have a Cathedral that will appropriately represent the fervent faith of the people."[27] Newark pride was in full dress. The brochure also unapologetically fused the symbolic value of architecture and the cult of the prelate, saying that the cathedral would be "truly representative of the greatness of the Archdiocese of Newark and our beloved Jubilarian."

Endorsements by leading laymen addressed the campaign from varied perspectives. A respected layman positioned it in the context of global sociopolitical conditions: "We are not called upon to make the terrible sacrifices that are the fate of our brethren in those sorrowful countries which are under the spell of cruel, atheistic rulers. Therefore we should with a deep feeling of joy take this opportunity . . . to cooperate in this splendid project."[28] An executive spoke about it in terms that borrowed from current business jargon. "We should be glad to safeguard the wise and generous investment made by our predecessors. . . . We are given the fortunate opportunity to finish the job. The sensible and efficient methods proposed by the Cathedral Builders Association are, in my opinion, the up-to-date way to achieve this splendid objective."[29] The promotional material, produced at a time of deep chill in the Cold War, equated the cathedral with remarkable, almost mystical, powers of national defense and well being, declaring that a finished Sacred Heart would stand as "a lighthouse of faith, a bulwark against the inroads of atheistic Communism."[30] The *Advocate*, the Newark archdiocesan newspaper, gave local Catholics a stake in these causes, telling them: "Fortunate indeed will be those who, in days to come, can point to the Cathedral of the Sacred Heart and say to their children, 'I had a part in building the cathedral.'"[31]

In their appeals, Church leaders successfully characterized the cathedral as the principal church for the entire archdiocese, not just those Catholics who lived near it. And because Newark still functioned effectively as the region's urban hub, a city-versus-the-suburbs duality (bringing with it a perception that the cathedral might have a circumscribed role) did not develop. Here it should be noted that however much the City of Newark was changing socially and economically, the archdiocese had within its boundaries many communities—Short Hills, Millburn, South Orange, West Orange, Franklin Lakes, Essex Fells, Montclair, Ridgewood, and Summit among them—that were very affluent and fertile ground for fund-raising. Altogether, fund-raising initiatives received notably broad support and exceeded goals. Moreover, the relative ease with which the archdiocese tapped funding for the cathedral attested to a local and national Catholic culture that was widely flourishing and supremely confident, one that reflected also how fully Catholics, once largely immigrants and marginalized, had won economic station in America.

"Neo-Scholastics" in Newark

The archdiocese's representative on the project, Auxiliary Bishop James A. McNulty, had studied at the august Catholic University at Louvain, Belgium. Ever the diligent student, McNulty, in taking up the cathedral assignment, entered into the medieval mind. He apprehended that to create a genuine Gothic interior and decorative scheme in Newark, he and a committee of clergy working with him needed to understand the theological as well as the structural underpinnings of the old cathedrals. To these moderns, the medieval system of scholasticism represented not only rationalized Christian belief but the underlying principles of the art and architecture of the Middle Ages. Such works as the *Summa Theologica* of Aquinas, the lives of the saints as recorded in the *The Golden Legend* by de Voragine, the *Rationale* of Durandus about churches and liturgy, and the encyclopedic *Speculum maius* (The Great Mirror) of Vincent of Beauvais were viewed as the main pillars of a magisterial construct of faith and learning. Architecture and decorative arts portrayed heaven and earth as the Christian of the Middle Ages understood them.

In this cosmology, Christ was first and last, and the Virgin was almost as universal; indeed, Mary was the patroness of the most important of the High Gothic masterpieces. It began with what Augustine posited—"the Old Testament is nothing but the New covered with a veil, and the New is nothing but the Old unveiled"—continued with the institution of the Church, the example set by holy men and women, and concluded with the Last Judgment. Literal and representative depictions were ingeniously mixed and wondrously referential. Symbolism was everywhere: in symmetry, numerology, ordering, and in an iconographic code for virtually everything in medieval man's City of God. All this brought forth an environment of richness, complexity, and mystery that was meant to delight, edify, admonish, and, especially, instruct.

All this added up to a very tall order in mid-twentieth-century America. If it daunted Auxiliary Bishop McNulty, he never showed it, nor could he afford to. He worked for an archbishop who wanted it done well and done fast. McNulty and his committee, donning the caps of neo-scholastics, poured over volumes on medieval thought and Gothic art and architecture.[32] Having absorbed the principles that informed the visual theology of the cathedrals, they and the designers brought them forward to include later developments and, finally, mapped iconographic themes and subjects for Sacred Heart's vast array of new sculpture, stained glass, and other decorative arts. Newark's own story of faith, which they wanted to convey as part of an ancient continuum, would be told through a program of statues and other carved features of its bishops and popes during the see's nearly one-hundred-year history. What is more, the cathedral was to be, the planners said, a building that also represented the diverse people of the archdiocese and their ethnic heritage. The latter aim was to be expressed principally by chapels commemorating the national and ethnic origins found among Newark archdiocesan congregations, as diverse as any in America.

A half century before, at the Cathedral of Saint John the Divine, its planners also decided to represent the origin of the region's population in chapels radiating from the cathedral apse. They called them "The Chapels of the Tongues," using "tongues" to signify the language and culture of ethnic groups in New York. Those finishing Sacred Heart increasingly looked to New York's Saint John the Divine and Saint Patrick's for prototypes.

19

Interior Scheme

Artistry from Here and Abroad

THE COMPRESSED TIMETABLE FOR COMPLETING Sacred Heart meant that thematic decisions about decorative arts could be deliberate but not overworked. Early in their discussions, priests on the cathedral planning committee stipulated a single-level sanctuary platform and a "liturgical style" (freestanding) altar. Newark's Church leaders were open to progressive ideas encouraging fuller congregational participation in worship, and these arrangements reflected it.[1] The designers then confronted the challenge of how to make the main altar the focal point in Sacred Heart's immense interior. The solution was a large canopy on columns over the altar called a baldachin, or *baldacchino*, as Professor Raggi, in his Italian-inflected English, would almost sing. The model for it, which had been inspired by Robert of Anjou's tomb in S. Chiara in Naples, was in Saint Patrick's in New York, designed by Charles Maginnis and installed in 1942.[2] Looking at Maginnis's bronze baldachin, Raggi rendered a similar one in marble.[3]

The idea of a stone screen, dividing the narthex, or entry, from the nave, germinated in the 1920s, when Isaac Ditmars said it would be "treated similar to a rood screen or a magnificent reredos."[4] Paul Reilly took the design for the one that he and Ditmars had submitted in 1930, and added to it citations to the celebrated sculpted portals of High Gothic cathedrals. Unlike a portal, however, it was to face the inside of Sacred Heart. The inversion would have the effect of elevating the symbolic significance of walking through the narthex screen and departing from the cathedral. An unorthodox idea, Reilly's equally personal extemporization on its models became the interior's most novel feature—the kind of signature that the diagonal towers were on the outside.[5]

STAINED GLASS: THE CHARTRES STANDARD

When the planners set their sights on the glazing for Sacred Heart, they soon declared that it was to be based on the stained glass in Chartres Cathedral. Of the myriad Gothic precedents in Sacred Heart, no historic model was named more openly, save for Ditmars's arcade capitals. With the most spectacular cycle of stained glass surviving from the Middle Ages, Chartres set the enduring standard. The Newark planners embraced Cram's conclusion about the Chartres glass makers: "They reached a point beyond which there was no possibility of progress. . . . With all our boasting, we have added nothing to their work. We cannot even make some of the glass they made. We can make very wonderful substitutes that have certain splendid qualities of their own. All we can do is to use this as they would have used it, following implicitly their principles and their ideals."[6]

F. X. Zettler of Munich received the huge Newark commission, the largest in the firm's history. The impressive nineteenth-century revival of stained glass production in Germany was centered in Munich, and for years the eponymous Munich Style was prized in many quarters around the world, especially the American Catholic church market. Franz X. Zettler founded the firm in 1870s, and it had become a subsidiary of the Franz Mayer Studio in 1939, a little more than a decade before the completion phase of the Newark project began. Both firms shared a lineage stemming from the patronage of King Ludwig I of Bavaria and other proponents of the German religious revival.[7]

The painting of the major portions of Sacred Heart's glass was assigned to Karl Jung and Franz X. Braunmiller, associates of the Zettler firm. Jung was a Munich native who had studied at its Academy of Arts and, more broadly, was a product of Bavaria's formal art culture; Braunmiller was steeped in the same tradition.[8] They, like Raggi, were facile artists capable of turning out a variety of historic modes, as taste and clients' demands shifted throughout their careers. As was also true with Raggi's historically inspired work, few trained eyes could mistake the Munich windows in thirteenth-century style for true medieval glass painting.

After receiving the Newark commission, the principals of the two firms, Oscar Zettler and Adalbert Mayer, along with artists Jung and Braunmiller, visited France to study medieval examples, making the invariably awe-inspiring pilgrimage to Chartres to study the major iconographic schemes and placement of subjects, but especially the painting and coloristic systems. In New Jersey, a committee of clergy under McNulty, having studied the theological and aesthetic premises of the Gothic cathedrals, considered the Newark windows' subject matter with Raggi and his sons. The Raggi firm coordinated this transatlantic exchange of ideas about Sacred Heart's stained glass program and how it would be implemented. Themes became assigned to the cathedral's various spatial zones. The chancel clerestory would hold Old Testament subjects and the Mysteries of the Rosary, the latter probably because the upper windows of the apse at Chartres are devoted to the Glorification of Mary. The transepts' clerestory was for scenes depicting familiar scriptural stories from the life of Christ, and the aisle windows depicted Gospel miracles. The nave clerestory became a gallery for images of the founders of the religious orders serving in the Newark archdiocese or their saint-protectors, other popular holy men and women, and, in general, a "Communion of Saints." Newark's west rose, as at Chartres, would blaze with the Apocalyptic "Coming of the Lord: Last Judgment." With these choices made, the Raggi firm worked up a color sketch for the planning committee to review, ultimately sending an agreed-upon version to Munich.

The Zettler artists translated Raggi's sketches into the visual language of High Gothic, approximating Chartres's figure style, geometric composition, border patterns, and colors, sending to-scale sketches back to their clients in New Jersey.[9] These exchanges had time-honored precedents. In the Middle Ages the sketch was called a *Vidimus* ("I/we have seen"), a similar drawing approved by both patron and artist that bound each to the design before it was consummated in the essentially irreversible product of the easel and kiln.[10]

Once the sketch was accepted, the artists produced a cartoon, a full-scale drawing of the window that was then used to cut the stipulated colored glass. Once the cut glass was temporarily attached to a sheet of transparent glass with wax drops, the whole window was, in effect, a blank—albeit, colored glass—canvas, mounted on an easel. On these Jung and Braunmiller, assisted by staff artisans, painted the decorative and figural details. The sticks and brushes that they used were little different from those of their forerunners in the Middle Ages. Indeed, the salient particulars of stained glass production were remarkably similar to the methods in use seven hundred years earlier. After baking in kilns at over 1,100 degrees Fahrenheit to adhere the designs, the finished glass was assembled using lead joins. Photographs were taken and dispatched to Raggi, who had to approve every window before it was packed (with all of the fastidious care necessary for such fragile material) and shipped to Newark. The huge job at times absorbed the efforts of twenty of Zettler's staff.[11]

The Organ

Two firms submitted complete bids for an organ: the Schantz Organ Company of Orville, Ohio, and Casavant Frères of Quebec. A priest on the committee charged with recommending an organ builder and specifications balked and wanted to consider a company that built mostly electronic organs. Another influential priest thought this was the view of a Philistine and told the archbishop that by no means were such imitative instruments able "to supply the majestic power, brilliance and tone quality required for an edifice as imposing as Sacred Heart Cathedral."[12] Though Casavant was popular in American Catholic circles and Schantz's bid was higher, the latter provided more stops and pipes per dollar and won the commission.[13] The same influential priest also favored Schantz.

The tonal specification developed for Newark was typical of many large American instruments of the previous twenty years and bore the influence of the American Classic Organ, originating most famously with the Aeolian-Skinner Organ Company of Boston. It was a tonal scheme that aspired to create instruments on which all of the major periods of organ repertoire could be played convincingly.

Building Again

The head of steam driving the project brought it rapidly to the point at which the planners were ready to hire a construction company. Attesting to the professionalism regulating archdiocesan practices, proposals from construction companies, including the firm now led by Edward Waldron's descendants, were unsealed during a session of the committee of priests advising the archbishop. The general contract award went to the George A. Fuller Company of New York. Fuller was a big operation that had to its credit more than a half century of blue-chip projects nationwide. Fuller had built the Flatiron Building and Plaza Hotel in New York and the Lincoln Memorial in Washington. Notably, it was the contractor from the early years of the century for the Episcopal Church's Washington National Cathedral, which at the time was still a work-in-progress.

In explaining Fuller's role to the public, Reilly called attention to stipulations that, had they been followed a half century before, would have spared endless woe in Newark: "The architect is the fountainhead from which all things flow and through whose hands all things pass down to the minutest detail."[14] In another statement, he was even more specific. "Everything is absolutely under the architect's control. . . . If we specify granite, the contractor submits a sample of granite. If it meets with our approval as to quality and finish, then we approve it. . . . [If not] the contractor has to get new samples and resubmit them. It must be in strict accordance with the specifications and plans."[15] Addressing an aspect of the general contractor's conduct that had also brought earlier discord to the Newark project, Reilly was firm: "The procedure . . . is to procure a number of estimates for the work of each sub-contract trade and submit them with their recommendation. . . . The saving that he affects in the award of these sub-contracts reverts to the owner and not to the contractor."[16]

The new generation of leaders agreed that the interior should be finished in limestone, which was already covering some of the walls. The amount required was so vast, some 60,000 cubic feet, that the general contractor divided the work among three suppliers in the metropolitan region. They, in turn, procured this ocean of limestone from the Carl Furst Company of Bedford, Indiana, a single source that assured the uniformity of the stone's texture and color.

Reilly's staff produced the reams of scale and full-size drawings for the interior masonry. Some could go directly to the Indiana contractors and carvers. Drawings for more elaborate items were sent for modeling in preparation for carving in Indiana. Rochette & Parzini, which had modeled three-dimensional elements for Sacred Heart beginning early in Ditmars's years as cathedral architect, was retained again to fashion these—statues, traceries, and an array of Gothic devices.

An Endangered Artisanal Class and Its Italian Counterpart

Translating models into carving was no simple matter in the United States in the 1950s. The conditions that led to Reilly's struggle to find designers willing and able to draft Gothic forms had also nearly doomed the careers of specialists in architectural carving. Little demand for this expertise had forced the Furst Company to cease offering it as an in-house service, so a band of these artisans had been organized as a small firm, and it handled the most intricate work for Newark.[17]

With the stone pieces and Rochette & Parzini's models set up in their Indiana workshops, the carvers used a pointing machine, an amazing apparatus that helped transfer the contours of the plaster model to the stone itself.[18] When the basic form of the statue or architectural detail was established with pneumatic hammers and chisels, the carver finished by eye and hand, revealing the depth of his skill. The head of these artisans regarded the Newark commission as the finest and most elaborate he had worked on during a four-decade career.[19]

The planners wanted many of the appointments and finishes to be wrought in marble. On a 1951 trip to Europe, Raggi headed to the northwest of Italy and the region above Pisa bounded by the Alps and the Ligurian Sea. He was in search of Carrara marble for many small statues and Botticino, a light brown, warm-hued marble for altars, including the *mensa* (table) of the principal altar, pulpit, cathedra, baptismal font, and other liturgical furniture and fixtures. He readily found Carrara, white as new snow, in the place from which it takes its name. He also went to nearby Pietrasanta, not as famous as Carrara yet also with a storied history. Michelangelo's *Moses* and the *Slaves* were sculpted from Pietrasanta's Botticino, as were monumental pieces by other artists and designers, including the main altar of Saint Peter's in Rome.

Raggi found a Pietrasanta quarry owner who had just located a large, unusually fine formation of Botticino and purchased large blocks of the new supply in behalf of the archdiocese. If a mother lode of gold had been discovered and secured for Sacred Heart, Raggi's excitement would not have been keener. He provided jubilant reports in Newark about the quarryman's find and his own role in buying it. The Raggis also explained in publicity that even the source of the Botticino had special meaning for its purpose it Newark. The term *pietra santa* means "holy stone" because, they noted, it is "used for altars in churches."[20] This perpetuated a pious myth. Pietrasanta, in fact, was named in the thirteenth century for Guiscardo Pietrasanta, who founded the town.[21]

For many centuries, Carrara and Pietrasanta, and the vicinity around them, begat a cottage industry that produced statuary and decoration for sacred and secular commissions all over the world. In sheds and studios, boys and young men in the region learned carving from fathers and uncles and grandfathers. There, a similar sequence of modeling and carving to that taking place in Indiana ensued. In addition, nine statues for Sacred Heart would be produced in an extraordinary export-import process. The limestone for the statues of the narthex screen was quarried in Indiana, shipped to Italy for carving, and brought to Newark for installation.[22] The Raggi firm provided a sense of the nearly industrial methods of the larger Italian shops: "In these towns where there are marble quarries . . . you will find that everybody in town works in one way or another on marble. . . . The place making [the] altar will have . . . some doing all one kind of work, some doing little columns, some doing the *mensa*, . . . some doing only statues."[23]

The designers in Newark, however, wanted their role in this production known. The Raggis explained: "Detailed drawings have been prepared, showing exactly the design desired. . . . As the work progressed, photographs are made from all angles, and these are submitted periodically to the artists, so that they may judge whether the work is proceeding according to plan. It also enables them to improve the design where possible, to develop some expression, some detail, . . . the face, the hands, the feet, the little things that will make it a beautifully and completely finished statue."[24] (The process described discloses that Sacred Heart's statuary would be the product of a collective artistic process conforming to an overarching decorative scheme rather than expressing the conception and execution either of a single artist or a group of independent artists.)

The Raggis and the archdiocese, telling and retelling the provenance of the cathedral's interior appointments and the religious and historical stories associated with their production, tethered the Newark project in this phase to the Italian cultural tradition. They proudly invoked celebrated names in art history and the splendors of High Renaissance and Baroque Catholicism in Rome and in Italy, generally. A source of national honor for Gonippo Raggi, it also signaled the ties between Newark's churchmen and the Vatican.

Not everyone was happy that the cathedral's statuary and other carved works would be executed for the most part in Indiana and Italy. The president of the New York–based Architectural Sculptors' and Carvers' Association sent a letter to the diocese asking that some of the statuary work be commissioned from its members. "We have at present," he lamented, "only two members out of the whole Association working," and that members had effectively done "all of the outstanding work of art [of this type] in the United States," citing projects at the Riverside Church, Saint Thomas Church, Saint John the Divine, and Saint Patrick's Cathedral in New York, as well as the Lincoln Memorial and the Supreme Court Building in Washington.[25] He pointedly asked the archbishop "in the name of justice to allow us to carve and present to Your Excellency the portrait of you in Indiana limestone as a compliment. Compare our work of art with the statues that come from the quarry in Indiana or elsewhere." The association president also mentioned that the organization had members living around Newark, many of them Catholics who had contributed to the cathedral fund-raising. And a local stone sculptor had these cranky but poignant things to say about the decision to produce Sacred Heart's stone work far afield: "Sending this work out to be done in Indiana and Italy not only has brought harm to these present day craftsmen of the stone-trade and all other business[es] that depend on one another, but the loss of opportunity . . . to transfer our skill and knowledge to the now many students of this art who have already sacrificed so much of their time and efforts to the study of art and architecture. What shall we tell these students when they ask us for an opportunity to fulfill their dreams?"[26]

These claims and appeals, not without some merit, though heard, were not acted on.

Glories Above and Below

Jeremiah O'Rourke first imagined white marble for the cathedral floors. Ditmars settled for terrazzo in the 1920s. In completing the interior, the client approved an array of fine marbles. It consisted mostly of large, light-colored fields broken by contrasting squares and set within geometric borders. Listed in press coverage (with a mix of languages and orthographic accuracy that ranged wildly), the choice Italian and domestic marbles—*Tavernelle* Rose, *Tavernelle Clair*, Bond Pink, Vermont *Verde* Antique, Red *Lavanto*, Alabama Madre Cream, Danby, Westland *Cipolino*, Italian *Cremo*, Belgian Black, *Griotte Belge*, and *Venato*, among others—gave the impression that Sacred Heart was being finished with unlimited resources and in indescribable luxury.

There was no hesitation in completing the remainder of the cathedral with the Guastivino vaulting system installed on the east side of the interior twenty years before. First, however, Reilly and his structural engineer had to solve a problem of the sort that the building team had puzzled over in the 1920s. The new vaulting would create a lateral pressure on the walls. Flying buttresses on the exterior were a hypothetical answer but were never part of Sacred Heart's scheme. The complex engineering solution called for weights and counterweights responding to the dynamic form of the ribs and vaults, the success of which permitted Reilly to keep his promise that, in theory, the roof of the cathedral could be taken off and the vaults would not budge.[27]

As the Guastivino system was constructed, the planners made a point of saying that it was not chosen because it was cheaper than real vaulting. It was preferred for its acoustical effect.[28] Guastivino tile could be made with absorbent material that dampens reverberation within a space as potentially resonant as the cathedral's, thereby rendering speech more intelligible. Happily, here it would not eliminate the resonance that permits music to bloom, and, moreover, the refinement of the Guastivino system added a visual felicity to Sacred Heart's interior.

20

Complete at Last

IN SUMMER 1952, BUILDING CONTRACTORS and subcontractors, artists and artisans all labored furiously. But as this charge raced to the finish, the necrology of those who grasped for the grail of a completed cathedral in Newark lengthened by one name. With an abruptness with which he made many decisions, Archbishop Thomas Walsh died. Sacred Heart's interior—crammed with scaffolding, pallets of stone, crated materials, and laden with the dust of heavy construction—could not be cleaned and readied for his large funeral. After a solemn requiem in Newark's Saint Patrick's, Walsh's remains were interred in the crypt of Sacred Heart.

The death of the archbishop and, to a lesser extent, minor labor problems, meant postponing the cathedral's dedication for a year. The new archbishop, Thomas A. Boland, had been one of Walsh's protégés and most recently was serving as bishop of Paterson. His natural authority and easy manner made him a popular choice in Newark. Boland decided that Sacred Heart's formal opening and dedication should be combined with a ceremony in which he received the sacred pallium, symbol of his new rank.

When that day came in October 1954, the service, which might well have been a triumphalist liturgical drama, was, rather, a decorous, ancient rite for which the newly finished cathedral played a supporting role. As it began, Boland appeared humbled in the presence of the apostolic delegate and the crowds, and in anticipation of the ceremony. The tone he set might have been sounded by his earliest predecessor in Newark, Roosevelt Bayley, who had arrived there a week shy of one century and one year before. In another echo of the past, Archbishop Boland as a youngster had attended

Saint John's Church and School in Orange, both designed by Jeremiah O'Rourke.

A View of the Sanctuary

The organ prelude began with the attention-grabbing arpeggios of César Franck's Third Choral. As they looked around from the pews, the more than two thousand people there could see, at long last, the finished interior. Its staggering elaborateness and the sumptuous materials helped them comprehend what they had been told before examining Sacred Heart for themselves: Newark's cathedral was, at $10 million, the most expensive Catholic church ever built in the United States. That this boast skipped the intricacies of the dollar's fluctuating purchasing power over the years and its effect on the cost of other projects did not matter. What locals understood was that Newark had outspent the country. Newark ranked first.

During the service, Bishop James A. McNulty, who had supervised the cathedral's completion and recently been appointed bishop of Paterson, ascended the pulpit's sinuous stairs to preach. An effusive composition wrought from almost eight tons of marble, the pulpit had an elaborate rostrum that held statues of important scriptural commentators.[1] McNulty told the congregation that a Gothic cathedral "represents the complexity of life and its unity under God. It is a miniature of God's cathedral, which is the universe."[2] During the sermon and throughout the service, the congregation could take in that extraordinary complexity and unity, whose huge symbolic apparatus McNulty had helped to create.

The clergy and congregation that day saw Raggi's baldachin, its four posts supporting a pyramidal roof on which ascending ranks of small statues rose to a crowning finial of a figure of the Sacred Heart. In one of the designer's tricks borrowed from the Italian Baroque, the life-size polychrome marble statue, seen from the main aisle, appeared to support the central bay of the triforium gallery. (About that triforium, Newark partisans pointed out that Sacred Heart's was authentic, whereas Saint Patrick's in New York has a blank triforium in the apse.)

The altar table had been carved from a single block of the marble that Raggi found in Pietrasanta. There was a crucifix of bronze and onyx for which Italian artists carved a corpus from a single piece of Portuguese rose marble that approximated the color of flesh. Symmetric, muscular, serene, the sculpture seemed lifted from a reliquary or decorated binding.[3] Raggi's keen sense of perspective assured that the crucifix was compositionally harmonious with the baldachin and yet could possess the far reaches of the transepts and nave.

Statuary and Woodwork

There was a host of statuary to see. The statues in the (liturgical) south screen (right of the altar) formed a composition that brought together Old and New Testament subjects and symbols with all the invention and certainty of medieval Scholasticism, an especially fruitful example of the planners' Gothic research.[4] Here, on the side of Sacred Heart whose tower holds symbolism of Jesus (just as the corresponding one relates to Mary), a youthful, beardless Christ presides. A trumeau figure of the apostle Paul, as one of the "Founders of the Church," stands between the doors of the right portal.[5] John the Baptist, herald of Jesus, is prominent, as is Mary Magdalene, both commemorated in clothing associated with repentance. The figures of the south screen, through pose, anatomy, and aspect, conveyed their subjects' unique identities and convictions, the sharp undercutting of the limestone vitalizing individual pieces and groups. Statues of John the Baptist and Mary Magdalene, in fact, broke from a Gothic treatment, and derive loosely from works of Donatello.

In the opposite screen, the sculptural program was based on the history of the Church, presided over by Mary, "Mother of the Church." A statue of Saint Peter, the other Founder, is surrounded by likenesses of popes and prelates from the era of the Newark see.[6] It established the Church's continuum from the apostles to the present. A seated figure of Archbishop Walsh, planned before his death, holds a model of the Sacred Heart Cathedral—lest there be doubt about who was its ultimate patron.[7]

For the 129 small Cararra marble statues set within traceried niches in the cathedral's main liturgical pieces (altars, baldachin, pulpit, baptismal font, cathedra), Raggi chose another idiom. They were treated in an attenuated, otherworldly, loosely Gothic manner. Whatever the style, "all the statues," the Raggi firm stated, "represent the saints in devotional expressions." The Raggis suggested that, while the Gothic style was appropriate for the stained glass figures so that they "would conform with the architectural style of the building," they felt released from adhering to a strictly Gothic manner for Sacred Heart's legion of carved figures.[8] And although historical modes are dominant, some figural work hints, too, at a more modern sensibility and properly locates at least some of the vast sculptural program in the twentieth century.

Raggi's appointments held abundant tracery. In addition to the Gothic patterns that aligned with the cathedral structure, it is composed of Flamboyant forms associated with a later Gothic phase. Paul Reilly did likewise in his designs for the interior portal screens and other carving. This gives the impression that Sacred Heart's interior dates later than the exterior construction. It is an effective—indeed, accurate—historicizing device.[9]

Just as the baldachin framed and gave focus to the altar, a screen of honey-hued Appalachian oak, designed by Raggi, wrapped the interior of the apse arcade. All of the woodwork is exceptional, especially the carved-oak statues.[10] And in the screens to the ambulatory are two wonderful references: statues of Saint Honoré and Saint Vincent the Deacon, the saint-protectors, respectively, of breadmakers and winemakers—thus patrons of those who make the bread and wine used in the Eucharist.

Altogether, the colors of marbles, lesser stones, wood finishes, and embellishments in Sacred Heart were chosen for how they would look individually, with each other, and in the larger structural envelope of the earlier marble and masonry choices. Raggi, with a decorator's eye congenitally tuned to the earth tones of Italy, succeeded in providing a limited, warm, and harmonious palette.

Apse Altars and Ethnic Commemorations

At the end of the apse stood the Lady Chapel, dedicated to Mary under the title of Our Lady of Grace. It holds the only altar composed of white Carrara marble, symbolically connoting Mary's purity. And the designers and Church leaders made a point of saying it was not just white Carrara (*Carrara Bianco*), used here, but *pure* white Carrara (*Carrara Bianco P.*).[11] Across from it stood a superb altar dedicated to Saint Luke, patron saint of medical professionals, given by physicians in memory of their deceased colleagues. (At an early point in planning Sacred Heart, this location was intended as a memorial to James Roosevelt Bayley, Newark's first bishop. Its ultimate use as an altar associated with physicians became a quiet tribute to Bayley and also Monsignor Doane, both of whom had studied medicine.)

Five other chapels radiating from the apse ambulatory were dedicated to the saints associated with the lands from which Newark's richly diverse ethnic groups came, giving at the same time a lesson in the history of immigration in the region. This, too, had ancient precedent, as the saint-heroes associated with their localities were commemorated often in medieval cathedrals. Though composed of the same Italian marbles, each chapel in Sacred Heart was different in design from the others.

Saint Patrick, in many respects Newark's proto-patron, presided over the chapel associated with the British Isles. The recent world war had elicited ambivalent feelings toward Germany but could not diminish the contribution German Americans had made to Newark's prosperity and Catholic life, and their country of origin was recognized in a chapel to Saint Boniface. A chapel dedicated to Saint Lucy Filippini marked the strong Italian presence in the region. The Religious Teachers Filippini, an order of religious women originating in Italy, named for Saint Lucy and much admired by Archbishop Walsh, assisted critically in extending the Church's service to Italian Catholics in New Jersey.[12] The Italian chapel also held a window depicting a woman with the strongest claim to saintliness actually demonstrated in Newark. Frances Xavier Cabrini, who once ministered in Newark's Ironbound section, was the first U.S. citizen to be canonized. Of course, all of the Italian-derived stylistic devices that Raggi introduced into Sacred Heart's final interior scheme might also be said to honor what had become New Jersey's dominant ethnic group in the twentieth century.

Another chapel to Saint Stanislaus recognized those of Hungarian, Polish, Lithuanian, and other central or eastern European ancestry. (The Lady Chapel also held an association with this region: its chandeliers are composed of Czechoslovakian hand-cut crystal.)[13] Finally, all other races and groups were gathered into the Chapel of Saint Anne, with stained-glass windows depicting Saint Martin de Porres (for those of both African and South American origins), Martin Wu (for those with roots in Asia), and Teresa of Avila (for Spanish ancestry).

Those honored in the latter chapel, in the next half century, would form the largest modern immigration to northern New Jersey. From South and Central America, Cuba, Puerto Rico, and other islands in the Americas, they would constitute an influx as significant as those in the nineteenth century. For the archdiocese, it called for a response equal to that of the earlier waves. In due course, the archdiocese would create parishes and social services largely dedicated to them, just as Sacred Heart Cathedral would hold liturgies, or mix in prayers and music at its other services, in their own language. In fact, for an even more exalted reference to those of Hispanic origin, all anyone in the cathedral has to do is look up. A Spaniard, Rafael Guastivino, brought from Spain the technology used to create the cathedral's remarkable vaulting system.

Stained Glass

Every window opening in Sacred Heart was filled with stained glass. The color schemes of the large rose windows followed the Chartres model, especially the hypnotic blues and reds of the rose window in Newark's facade. The palette of those in the transepts, also as at Chartres, introduces more yellows, greens, and less-saturated reds and blues, and these are purposefully arranged: the lighters colors of the south transept (geographically facing east) are radiant in the morning light; opposite, fiery reds can be set ablaze by the late afternoon sun.

The two Zettler artists achieved harmonious but quite different results in the figural painting.[14] With a few more pen and brush strokes than Karl Jung, Franz Braunmiller painted saints that are not so much otherworldly beings in human form as simple holy men and women. Braunmiller's expressiveness found other outlets. He freed figures from the architecture-like frames, permitting a hand or foot, elbow or crosier, to extend beyond the patterned borders. These devices had precedent in High Gothic art, and he made clever use of them for Newark. In such ways, and by varying pose and mannerism, Braunmiller, with Raggi's blessing, invigorated his designs. Jung, on the other hand, fashioned frontal, unworldly figures with direct gazes or downcast eyes. He took a more spirited approach in the nave and transept windows depicting Christ's ministry.

Adherence to a medieval mode sometimes made for disjointed compositions. Renaissance- or Baroque-era saints were rendered in the clothing of their day but as seen through a thirteenth-century lens. Modern-era saints such as Mother Cabrini and Pope Pius X have realistic faces drawn from photographs topping Gothic figures. These examples call attention to the artistic perils that can bedevil revival forms. Much medieval glass painting, including Chartres's, depicts people and settings as artists actually saw them, portraying work, home, religious, and court life. Like illuminated manuscripts, they are often pictorially accurate renderings of their time. The Zettler artists, however, deliberately drew from their imaginations, providing an approximation of the old painting but depriving their work, however skilled, of the authentic settings that bring to life much original Gothic painting.[15] By another interpretation, these hundreds of figures and scenes throughout Sacred Heart are made to appear as belonging to an unearthly, heavenly realm. One window, however, captured Newark as it was and would be: high up in the south transept, the window called

"Christ, Friend of the Children" portrays a pastoral Christ surrounded by a racial mix of black, white, and brown young people.

More than anything else, perhaps, Sacred Heart's stained glass offers in extravagant abundance the sensory thrill of seeing light through expertly produced colored glass. If the cathedral lacked all of its other religious and aesthetic merits, it would be still be admired as a framework for the glass-stainer's art.

Other Italian Features

The Way of the Cross, or more familiarly, the Stations of the Cross, would be treated, Raggi had declared, "in an original way," and these fourteen scenes of Christ's Passion were composed in mosaics of *smalti*, small pieces of colored and gold-leafed glass, produced by Zettler. They are set in a reredos over marble altars. In the previous generation, architect Ditmars said that the "stations and confessionals gracefully alternating down the side aisles will overcome any barren effect which has met the eyes of the observer upon entering the side aisles of other cathedrals." Among all of Sacred Heart's appointments, the Byzantine-influenced mosaic panels broke most sharply from the cathedral's Gothic style. Some found this a welcome variant. Others thought them discordant.[16]

Sacred Heart's fourteen bells also came from Italy, cast in a foundry in Padua. Everything about them rang out with an Italian and Roman air.[17] The inscriptions on them were "composed by Monsignor Ameleto Tondini, Vatican Latinist," and before leaving Italy they were formally tested by numerous civic and ecclesiastical commissions. The main portal's bronze doors were also produced in Italy and were still being manufactured when the cathedral was formally opened. They were modeled by Aurelio Mistruzzi, "internationally famous sculptor and official Vatican medalist," as the Raggis described him for local audiences.[18] This celebrated metal sculptor took Raggi's panelized scheme, based loosely on themes found in the main portal of Chartres, and fashioned exquisite reliefs in a format borrowed from Ghiberti, thus blending High Gothic and Italian Renaissance influences. Locals learned of their archbishop's personal interest in them: "While the subject composition and modeling was proceeding in Rome, His Excellency Archbishop Boland personally called to see the work in progress and to express his thoughts and ideas concerning it."[19]

And Newark's designer was on hand when the doors were being finished in Italy: "In Florence, Professor Raggi visited the foundry where the castings for the doors are being made. He personally supervised the metal pouring and had a look at the first door nearing completion"[20] When the doors were installed, Newarkers read about one last instance that again proclaimed a quasi-official Roman imprimatur being placed on the project: "When the center doors were completed, they were exposed in Rome, and they have been viewed and praised by eminent members of the Vatican Curia, by artists and architects, including His Eminence Cardinal Costantini and his brother Archbishop Costantini, both famous experts on matters pertaining to Ecclesiastical Art."[21]

Although totally literal Italianate features were few, the one with the strongest association is the baptistery. For the semi-detached octagonal structure conceived by O'Rourke, Raggi created a font in the same Gothic vocabulary as his altar and pulpit. But above it, the Italian American specified a mosaic ceiling that was northern Italian in both manner and execution—it suggested the most famous baptistery of all, at the Duomo in Florence, although the mosaics were created in Venice.

The rapid production of Sacred Heart's decorative arts, compressed into fewer than four years, gave it a certain aesthetic coherence, yet this circumstance also deprived the interior of the variety and richness that can accrue when such work is added in increments over decades and centuries, as was typical in the Gothic masterworks. In this, it joined company with many revival-style churches here and abroad, Catholic and Protestant. Also, when art is produced in the quantity that it took to complete Sacred Heart, it is fiendishly hard to maintain consistent standards. And whether artists and artisans worked in the United States or abroad, achievements ranged predictably. Yet it must also be said that amidst the vast programs of sculpture and glass in the medieval cathedrals, not every artist's effort produced a masterpiece or a treasure

A Symbol at Departing: The Narthex Screen

Everyone entering the main doors of the cathedral passed through the narthex screen. Facing the nave, it is a monumental assembly of Gothic devices. The setting for its statuary was lifted from Chartres's entryways, as were the canopies and jamb statues and the short columns they stand on. Architect Reilly was thinking of the whole composition when he said proudly that there was "nothing like it anywhere." As part of the screen composition, above the doorways at the head of the aisles, carvings depicted the livelihoods of the Newark archdiocese's people. The precedent came from recognition given to the medieval guilds for financing cathedrals; guild symbols or other devices were often placed in stained glass and sculpture. Here, emblazoned in limestone, are shields holding representations of the diverse ways that Newark's "Cathedral Builders" made a living: a printing press, truck, desk, transmission tower, crane, monkey wrench, pipe, rope, policeman's badge and nightstick, cash register, rails, airplane, even a sheaf of wheat and a plow—New Jersey, industrial as it became, was still the Garden State—among a host of others.

When the long service on that momentous October 1954 day was over, and as the starburst chords of Charles-Marie Widor's Toccata in F sounded from the organ, many in the congregation departed by the main doors. Then, and for all times in the future when worshipers passed through the narthex screen, its unique symbolism was activated. It implied that what lay beyond was no less sacramental than what you experienced within the cathedral: that when you walked out of Sacred Heart, *Civitas Dei* was at your feet. In this regard, this screen was as potent as any symbol in the cathedral.

Epilogue

Finishing Sacred Heart brought a season of applause for Newark clergy, architect Paul Reilly, designer Gonippo Raggi, and the hundreds of workers who labored with them. The latter visited by the dozens to take photographs and give tours to family and friends. Thousands more came to Newark to see the sparkling-clean stone landmark, say a prayer in what many of them helped pay for, and explore its new, story-filled spaces. General interest articles in the New York press compared Sacred Heart to Westminster Abbey in size, said it was taller than Notre Dame in Paris, and spoke admirably, though not knowledgeably, about its "French Gothic construction." The *Illustrated London News* ran photographs with extended captions that credited O'Rourke's contribution, noted that the cathedral could be seen from the Empire State Building, and told an international readership that no Catholic church in the United States cost more.[1] Yet the architectural journals paid Sacred Heart Cathedral no notice, nor did it claim the attention, favorable or otherwise, of mainstream art or architecture critics.

The Brooklyn diocese's newspaper, the *Tablet*, came closest to providing a critical assessment. A well-informed local writer complimented Sacred Heart, though with a reservation: "The interior will be regarded by many as the most beautiful Gothic interior in the United States. The entire nave and apse is enclosed by a row of massive granite piers the like of which cannot be found elsewhere in the country. It is to be regretted however that the highly polished red granite piers encircling the sanctuary are somewhat blurred out by the choir stalls and the high altar at the east end. . . . Because the nave arches are comparatively low, the triforium comes into its own and I do not believe any cathedral on the continent has developed this feature so successfully."[2]

A few years after Sacred Heart opened, attention in the cultural community fixed on it when the Schantz organ was completed and formally dedicated.[3] Pierre Cocherau, destined to become organist of Notre Dame in Paris, came to play the dedicatory recital in 1956. His concert began with an obligatory selection by Bach, in this case, the sublime, perfect Prelude and Fugue in B Minor, dating from this unsurpassed genius's mature years in Leipzig. The program proceeded to music by French composers Vierne, Dupré, and Duruflé and concluded with an improvisation, of which Cocherau was a supreme master. Cocherau's virtuosic playing conjured the French cathedral music tradition, paying homage as well to other French influences found in abundance in Sacred Heart.

Ultramontane, a wonderful word that derives from old French, literally means "beyond the mountains." Figuratively, it stands for the Vatican's influence on Catholic affairs outside of Italy—beyond the Alps. Sacred Heart's interior preserves in amber a moment when an ultramontane spirit reigned in America and Catholicism in the United States was approaching its apogee of social and cultural sway. Within short years of completion, Sacred Heart's interior, descended from medieval and Counter Reformation theological constructs, liturgical practices, and devotions, all rendered in historical modes, seemed the product of an old dispensation.

Ironically, conditions originating in Rome soon displaced many of the assumptions upon which Sacred Heart was designed. The Second Vatican Council, called eight years after the cathedral opened, was the culmination of theological and liturgical reforms that had gathered momentum for generations. It brought radically altered liturgy and devotional norms. The archdiocese slowly and gently responded to directives stemming from Vatican II. In 1976, it removed the tabernacle from the main altar and suspended the altar's crucifix from the baldachin.[4] Yet these and a few other changes were relatively minor, and Sacred Heart was spared the more iconoclastic alterations to Catholic church interiors in that era.

Sacred Heart: Church and Cathedral

As Sacred Heart began to function as the cathedral for the archdiocese and as a parish church, it could hardly have been a more spectacular setting for liturgies and services. Eucharists, confirmations, weddings, ordinations, funerals, anniversaries, ecumenical assemblies of the community, and, later, an annual Christmastime service of music that filled every seat—were dignified and elevated by Sacred Heart's scale, richness, and religious and historical associations. But in other ways, the completed building raised hard questions.

Adjacent Branch Brook Park was a gorgeous foreground or backdrop for the cathedral. In spring, when its acres of cherry trees, the gift of Caroline Bamberger Fuld in 1927, blossomed, it provided views of Sacred Heart as splendid—and iconic—as any cathedral here or abroad. Thousands flocked each year to enjoy both nature and architecture. But the park prevented development in the district north and west of the cathedral, and Newark's economic trajectory altered the nature of its urban development. So the founders' predictions that residences and businesses would cluster around the cathedral proved off the mark. Thus Sacred Heart became a place of destination rather than drawing a sizable core congregation from immediate neighborhoods. In this and other ways that would surely have surprised Bishop Bayley and Monsignor Doane, the cathedral seemed aloof or removed from the place that it had been meant to serve.

Locals were proud of the extraordinary church in their midst, yet some were of two minds. One longtime Sacred Heart parishioner, Emily DiFonzo, was, like many others in the district, born in Italy and came to Newark in the early 1900s. She spoke for others when she said, "We liked the cathedral and were impressed by its beauty and size, but we missed worshipping in the little church; there we could all sit together. In the cathedral we were scattered and it didn't have that homey feeling that we were used to."[5]

Sometimes, more distant echoes were heard. In 1977, Margaret Hoffman of Nutley, New Jersey, wrote to the archdiocese, enclosing a souvenir button from the 1899 cornerstone ceremony and saying:

> My mother passed away two years ago and in going over her keepsakes, I came across this button. She used to tell us all about the day they broke ground for the cathedral. They passed these buttons out showing a picture of the way it was going to look. As we all know, they did change the plans. It was her great day also because she became engaged on this day. I hope you do not think me silly but I wondered if anyone would still be alive and would remember this great day? If you cannot find anyone who wants it just discard it.
>
> Gratefully, Margaret Hoffman[6]

By 1977, few themselves remembered that "great day," but it remained legendary in Newark's collective memory. The archdiocese kept both Margaret Hoffman's note and the treasured souvenir that her mother preserved, commemorating, as it did, personal and broader memories layered over each other.

The Foundation Crisis: What Was Below It?

Statements from the archdiocese at Sacred Heart's official opening glossed over the problems and conflicts that riddled the cathedral's history. The most vexed of these, the O'Rourke and Waldron debacle, was tidied up. Jeremiah's departure was described as a retirement, just as Bishop O'Connor's fateful letter to him in 1910 had said. Has the passage of time or new evidence revealed anything more about that troubled chapter? The hard facts are little different. Distance and dispassion, however, bring new interpretations and understanding.

First, it should be said that Newark officials were right to have been cautious. The intervening years provided reminders that cathedral projects could have serious construction problems. As we saw, at Albany's Catholic cathedral, Patrick Keely originally planned 300-foot spires but reduced them by a third because of fears about unstable soil conditions. In the twentieth century, the cathedral had to be strengthened with steelwork because of a weakening infrastructure. About a half century after the construction of the Hartford cathedral, also by Keely, its stone walls began to crack and fracture, caused by the uneven settlement of the site's subsurface. In the 1930s, the foundations were rebuilt and reinforced with steel at great expense.[7] As we saw, construction flaws in Pittsburgh's cathedral forced extensive repairs and rebuilding, and eventually the structure was replaced. In 1916, the dome of Seattle's Cathedral of Saint James simply collapsed. And the second Buffalo cathedral, designed by Aristedes Leonori of Rome and built between 1912 and 1915 (and for which, ironically, as a young priest Newark's Archbishop Walsh helped with fund-raising), had so many structural problems that it was torn down; the diocese reverted to the old cathedral, still standing.

In Newark, almost certainly, the preparation for, or construction of, Sacred Heart's foundations was imperfect. Even O'Rourke registered doubt about them at one point. Soon after the arbitration report was filed, he resisted but did not refuse to provide revised drawings. He also considered more substantial action to secure the structure: Vicar General Sheppard recorded that O'Rourke "would evidently take down the whole building and readjust it."[8] But if Jeremiah's confidence in the cathedral's stability was shaken, he soon regained it and countered with compelling evidence. Although the arbitration report leads us to believe that the foundations were imperfect, O'Rourke, not a reckless man, in the end took the position that they were adequate. The engineering analysis by Joseph O'Brien, a reliable expert, supported him. In time, everyone conceded that O'Rourke's design was sound and that his structural calculations were defensible. The problem lay in their execution. It is difficult to say how severe those problems were and impossible to guess how bad they might have become.

Despite how poisoned O'Rourke and Waldron's relationship became, nothing in the record points to mischief on the site during the battle, no altering of conditions to support one or the other position. But it remains that once the remedial work was under way, everyone but O'Rourke had incentive to make assurances that the costly action was absolutely necessary, no matter what was found as they deconstructed base after base.

Over the years, these peculiar circumstances gave rise to speculation. Multiple theories were offered to explain the problems. Among them was that the foundations and the bases of the piers and columns may not have settled in the same way, or to the same depth, owing to shifts in the substrata. Along these lines, underground springs or streams feeding bodies of water near the site might have played a part in softening the ground below the bases. But when O'Rourke and others assessed it as a building location in 1870, they saw no reason to worry about water. It is theoretically possible that, because the cathedral lots were cleared and graded by 1875 and left open for a quarter of a century, environmental factors, especially rain and melting snow, disturbed the ground's makeup in the hiatus between clearing the site and building on it.

Another theory held that during excavation, the first contractors mistook large rocks or clusters of rocks for solid bedrock. Foundations built on them might have supported the bases and piers but could have begun to shift under the heavier load of the clerestory. A theory that the site's bedrock is a slanting ledge and that the columns began to "slide" was also proffered. None of these possibilities, even if forensic evidence made them provable, adequately explains the traumatic outcome.

It is a truism in construction that unexpected conditions routinely occur, just as cost and time overruns are common. Conflicts, too, are endemic. These circumstances, to varying degrees, strain relations among those who must join together to raise a building. The least disruptive solution to the problem would have been for O'Rourke and Waldron to have worked together to remedy it. But their relationship, as we saw, by then had deteriorated woefully. If O'Rourke had been able to see beyond Waldron's earlier ethical slips, the builder might have been enticed to meet him halfway and work together to solve the problem. But Jeremiah appears to have been incapable of traversing such a morally ambiguous terrain.

Jeremiah O'Rourke and Edward Waldron, though both Irish-born, Catholic, and successful in their fields, had almost diametric values. O'Rourke was a moral absolutist. Waldron was a pragmatist. O'Rourke, as he demonstrated over and over, abhorred the greater and lesser iniquities of the building trades. Waldron naturally was, or learned to be, pliant in his dealings in a very difficult industry. There were other poles of contrast. Jeremiah could be righteous and preachy; Edward, willful and bluff. O'Rourke consciously lived simply and pursued religious, charitable, and cultural interests. Waldron set out to become a successful businessman and, achieving his goal, was happy to enjoy the good life. And he took others with him on this journey: he came to be regarded as someone who treated his employees and retired employees well, whatever their ethnic origins or race.

Even death revealed pronounced differences between the two. Jeremiah O'Rourke instructed in his last will and testament that he be buried in a plain box and clothed in the robes of a lay Franciscan.[9] Edward Waldron died in 1942 in Palm Beach, a posh Florida resort utterly remote from Jeremiah's psychic geography. (And in another instance where a death said something about a life, when Gonippo Raggi died five years after the opening of Sacred Heart, his funeral was held, not in his parish church or Sacred Heart Cathedral, but in the Italianate splendors of Saint Catharine Church in Spring Lake, the first of his interior schemes in the United States.)

Two other facets of the foundation crisis remain curious. Monsignor Sheppard, while weary of acting as a referee in a nasty fight, registered few doubts about the legality or ethics of Waldron's profit-enhancing substitution of materials. As the battle raged, O'Rourke may have been naive about the monsignor's own ethical tolerance. Sheppard, after all, was a force in Jersey City Mayor Frank Hague's political machine, notorious for its freewheeling approach. Sheppard might also have been susceptible to the largesse of, and averse to alienating, a wealthy Catholic such as Waldron. O'Rourke thought that his client had been cowed by Waldron but would eventually come around and see the situation his way. But he had, by this time, lost Sheppard's confidence. In instances where the client-architect relationship is sundered and other alignments arise, it very often spells trouble for the designer.

In the light of these circumstances, it is irresistible not to conjecture that the outcome might have been better for O'Rourke had Monsignor Doane, having negotiated other diocesan crises, been on the scene during O'Rourke's standoff with Waldron. As with other "what if?" scenarios, it is left to the imagination. It remains, however, that the conflict began shortly after Doane's death and Monsignor Sheppard's ascendancy to the project leadership. And while Sheppard was adept at managing administrative processes, he did not have an aesthetic bone in his body and probably did not care about changes in building materials or design.

A Newark archdiocesan historian and writer, Monsignor Joseph Brady, was the first to closely study the primary sources covering Sacred Heart's history. When writing about the crisis more than forty years after it happened, he stood back from drawing conclusions, admitting, "The writer has not been able to pass judgment on the merits of the feud; evidently, Mr. Waldron retained the confidence of the Bishop, as his firm was kept, while Mr. O'Rourke was discharged, despite the grave charges brought by the architect. The writer, therefore, will enter into the quarrel no more than may be necessary to tell the story of the cathedral."[10]

"Genuine tragedies in the world," an aphorism holds, "are not conflicts between right and wrong. They are conflicts between two rights."[11] Both architect and builder at various moments had been right. And both at times acted wrongly, or at least imprudently. But it played out tragically for Jeremiah O'Rourke.

One more conjecture arises. The final battle between O'Rourke and Waldron began when Jeremiah was more than seventy-five. Aspects of his behavior hint at the possibility that he may have been suffering from the onset of some form of senility or old-age dementia. His conduct was erratic—assenting to one position, then reversing himself, returning to old grievances, and venting in Lear-like outbursts. His own sons, moreover, might be seen as having been in retreat from him during the crisis, as two of the three left the firm in those years.[12] The eighty-three-year-old's death certificate listed cerebral arteriosclerosis as the primary cause of death, symptoms of which could include hardening of the brain's arteries. "Cerebral arteriosclerosis" on a death certificate of this period could be read today as suggesting that there had been evidence of mental impairment or senility.

Also, Sheppard's journal holds such phrases as "I have written to the Bishop that Jeremiah should have a guardian";[13] "Better, I think, to give the old man a chance";[14] "He is getting worse";[15] and "the usual twaddle." And the headline over the *Star-Ledger* report of his funeral read: "Aged Architect's Memory Honored."[16] If, in fact, O'Rourke's mind was troubled or failing, it does not annul the builder's earlier shenanigans or Jeremiah's high-minded intransigence. It does, however, add to the litany of sorrows that grew out of a desire to build a great cathedral in Newark.

Perhaps in the end, the final judgment belongs—borrowing a Latin epigram that Monsignor Sheppard had used—to *Tempus edax rerum* ("time, the devourer of all things"): both O'Rourke and Waldron left a legacy of buildings that have survived the test of time.

A Changed City

When Sacred Heart opened, Newark was radically changed, and still changing, from the place it was through decades of planning and constructing the cathedral. The centrifugal force of suburbanization had worked on the city since the nineteenth century. The thrust outward intensified after the Second World War. In fact, Newark's population peaked, at nearly 450,000, the year that the war ended, in 1945. Businesses, leading and lagging indicators, preceded and followed Newark's people. Although Newark's airport and seaport became international hubs, enterprises based in the city were a fraction of what they had been. Corporations in the area prospered, but most now had a tenuous attachment to the place that had created the conditions from which the region's commerce grew.

This is not the place to recount the events in Newark during summer 1967 that have been called the Riots or, by some, the Disturbances. Whatever one calls them, they were not a spontaneous social upheaval; Newark had been hurtling downward for years. The troubles that awful summer brought four days and nights of turmoil that ended with twenty-six people dead. No flames torched Sacred Heart Cathedral during this murderous time. No horde stormed through it (as the posse of Know-Nothings had done to Saint Mary's Church in 1854). No rioters scared its walls or shattered stained glass. But the cathedral was mute witness to events of immense sorrow.

In 1974, social unrest roiled Newark again, mostly within the disenfranchised Hispanic community. It started in Branch Brook Park, in the shadow of the cathedral, when Puerto Rican American men clashed with police, and festered for four days that brought two deaths and scores of injuries. A *Harper's* magazine article the next year drove Newark's reputation lower, saying that it was unequivocally the worst city in the nation. Other assessments in this vein followed. Newark was an easy target. Residents and intrepid visitors saw decay everywhere: in abandoned houses and buildings daubed in graffiti, yards and empty lots filled with rubbish and weeds, parks gone to scrub, formerly broom-swept neighborhoods littered and laced in chain-link and razor wire. Many were fearful places for their own residents, and others avoided them at all costs. Gone entirely were the stylish downtown department stores that had remained attractions even after their residential customer-base followed the moving vans to the suburbs.

Near the cathedral, the emptied Columbus Homes housing project deteriorated before the eyes of all—Newarkers and those traveling by rail or on highways through the city. Many drove on Interstate 280, whose planners, determined to build a highway spur between Route 80 and the New Jersey Turnpike, plowed its path alongside the old Morris & Essex rail line, creating a paved moat between Newark's center and the city's northwest quadrant and its principal landmark, Sacred Heart Cathedral.

It took decades and the determination of a new generation of leaders and creative public and public-private initiatives, to halt and then reverse the downward spiral. Recovery moved stepwise rather than in leaps, and with sometimes painful setbacks on the way forward. Among the firmer steps was the exceptional service that the Archdiocese of Newark continued to provide. It neither abandoned nor curtailed its ministries and social mission in the city, nor the architectural monument that symbolized both. In this period, the cathedral might well have been neglected by its owners or its maintenance deferred. Succeeding archbishops, Peter Leo Gerety, Theodore E. McCarrick, and John Joseph Myers, countenanced neither, giving the cathedral unstinting care. Beginning in 1986, Sacred Heart was illuminated nightly, thereby both day and night radiating a sense of religious purpose and high culture.

Papal Visit: Basilica

Sacred Heart had its greatest public moment when Pope John Paul II visited the cathedral in 1995. In the weeks leading up to it, the media made recognizance trips to Newark. Journalist after journalist repeated the incredulity that the building often induces. What in the world is it doing in

Newark? When was it built? Who designed it? How much did it cost? Who paid for it? A writer from the *New York Times*, Frank Bruni, was the most probing of those astonished to discover it and quickly gathered information about the cathedral's origins and reported on the structure, the current scene in Newark, and the approaching papal visit. Two days before the pope's arrival, Bruni wrote in the *Times*, "When the Pope travels these streets on Wednesday, the first of four days in the New York metropolitan region, what he will glimpse is a troubled urban landscape that would be decidedly worse off if not for the church's presence. Sacred Heart Cathedral, a breathtaking French Gothic structure that is among the finest cathedrals in the country, provides an apt metaphor for the church's grand hopes for Newark and its refusal to let them wither."[17]

Newarkers for once had no cause to cavil about condescending treatment by New Yorkers or demeaning comparisons to Manhattan. The papal visit had a huge television audience, which saw many views of the cathedral's exterior and interior. John Paul, then on the crest of his long papacy, arrived at the airport in Newark and traveled through the city's streets to Sacred Heart. At the start of a late afternoon prayer service there, the pope walked down the main aisle as the enthralled congregation sustained steady applause. Many held out their hands to the pope, who took some into his own. President Bill and First Lady Hillary Clinton were in a front pew amid rows of national dignitaries. Before leaving that evening, the pope designated Sacred Heart a minor basilica, a distinction reserved for churches of religious or historic importance. It was the building's proudest hour. There were few prouder days in Newark's remarkable history.

Questions, Yet Pride, Still

After changes in leadership and architects, after spasmodic fund-raising campaigns, after fitful starting and stopping, after skirmishes and battles, after the fatal accidents of workers and the deaths of all those who first dreamed about it, after a five-generation commitment and exertion, after unimaginable changes in Newark, one wonders, was it worth it? Was it worth it to raise a great cathedral in Newark?

During the city's saddest years, hovering above acres of poverty and neglect, the elaborate cathedral was to some shameful, a conspicuous trophy of its patrons' vanity and a venal use of funds that more than ever might have aided the poor. To these people, devoted Catholics among them, it mocked the Gospels.

For others, the hard times imparted on Sacred Heart Cathedral Basilica an unexpected transcendence. To them, it looked not merely like a Catholic church or a Christian building, both of which it manifestly was. It became a symbol of the persistent longing to create something beautiful and enduring. It suggested that Newark's future might be better than the recent past. Sacred Heart induced in them the same awe that George Hobart Doane felt on seeing the Gothic chapel in England that he and Jeremiah O'Rourke visited when they were planning a cathedral. And the expression that came to Monsignor Doane a century earlier matched what they felt in Newark all those years later: it was "like a bit of Heaven let down upon earth."

APPENDIX A

The Cathedral's Materials, Dimensions, and Plan

A. Principal Materials

Exterior

Walls	New Hampshire granite
Ornamental stone at portals	Vermont granite tympana and small columns of Connecticut granite
Foundation	Pennsylvania brownstone
Roof	Slate
Flèche	Copper
Window tracery	Terra cotta
Main doors at facade	Bronze (modeled and produced in Italy)

Interior

Walls	Sheathed in Indiana limestone
Base molding	Massachusetts granite
Vaulting	Guastivino Akoustolith tile; limestone arches, ribs, and bosses
Narthex, transept screens	Indiana limestone
Flooring	American and European marbles
Woodwork	Appalachian white oak
Stained glass	F. X. Zettler (Munich, Germany)
Columns	
All capitals	Maine granite
Apse shafts	Maine granite
Apse bases	Massachusetts granite
Nave shafts	Vermont granite
Nave bases	Vermont granite
Altars	Italian Botticino marble, except for the Lady Chapel altar of Italian Carrara (pure white) marble
Baldachin and cathedra	Italian Botticino marble ornamented with Venetian mosaic work; statues of Italian Carrara marble

Pulpit and baptismal font	Italian Botticino marble ornamented with Venetian mosaic work; statues of Italian Carrara
Cross	Bronze with onyx inlays
Corpus	Portuguese rose marble, with loin cloth of Italian Carrara
Sacred Heart statue	Portuguese rose marble, other polychrome marbles
Aisle altars	Italian Botticino marble ornamented with Venetian mosaic work; statues of Italian Carrara
Stations of the Cross	Subjects in Italian mosaics (fabricated by F. X. Zettler, Munich, Germany) and set in aisle altars
Organ	Schantz Organ Company (Orville, Ohio)
Bells	Colbachini & Figli (Padua, Italy)

B. Principal Dimensions

Exterior

Length	365 ft.
Width, including transepts and porches	165 ft.
Height to top of tower roofs	232 ft.
Height to top of flèche	260 ft.

Interior

Length from main doors to Lady Chapel window	340 ft.
Length from interior narthex screen door to main altar	175 ft.
Width at crossing and transepts	135 ft.
Width, nave and aisles	85 ft.
Height, nave floor to vaulting	100 ft.
Facade rose window	34 ft. in diameter
Transept rose windows	32 ft. in diameter

sources: Dimensions derive from measurements of Donald W. Geyer, Newark, "licensed Professional Planner and Architectural Historian," in consultation with Paul C. Reilly, for nominating Sacred Heart to the National Register of Historic Places, Newark Public Library and Flanagan Papers. Also architectural drawings in the storage room of Sacred Heart Cathedral.

C. Plan

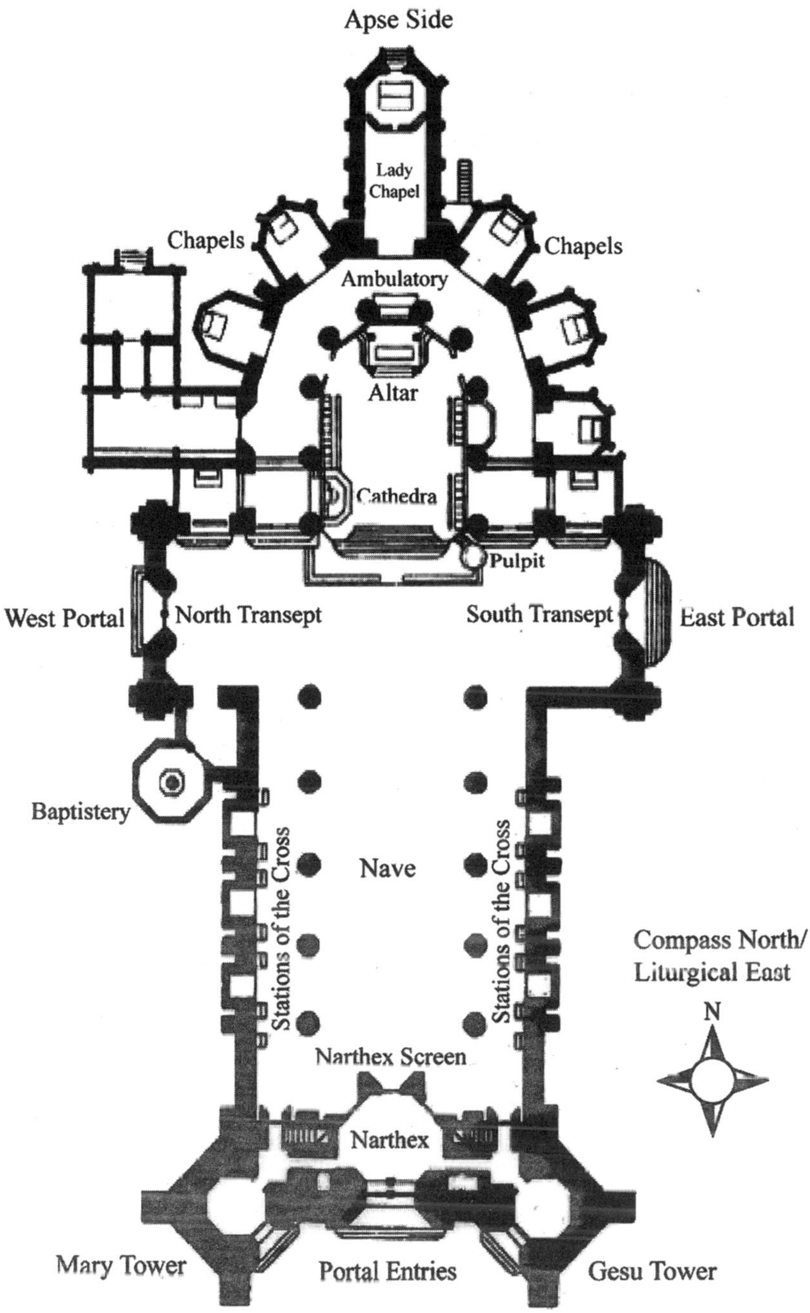
Apse Side
Lady Chapel
Chapels
Chapels
Ambulatory
Altar
Cathedra
Pulpit
West Portal
North Transept
South Transept
East Portal
Baptistery
Stations of the Cross
Nave
Stations of the Cross
Compass North/
Liturgical East
N
Narthex Screen
Narthex
Mary Tower
Portal Entries
Gesu Tower

APPENDIX B

Chronology of the Newark Cathedral Project

1853	Diocese of Newark established, serving the state of New Jersey. James Roosevelt Bayley becomes first bishop of Newark. Saint Patrick's Church in downtown Newark becomes the cathedral (the pro-cathedral) for the new diocese.
1855	George Hobart Doane received into the Catholic Church and is ordained a priest two years later.
1859	Cathedral site at High and Kinney Streets purchased.
1866	Second cathedral site purchased, across from South Park (later Lincoln Park).
1868	Father Doane appointed pastor of Saint Patrick's Pro-Cathedral parish.
1870	Father Doane and architect Jeremiah O'Rourke travel abroad to study church architecture and meet with English architects. Plans begun for a new cathedral designed by English architects Goldie and Child, with O'Rourke as local architect. Cathedral Chapel of Our Lady and Saint Patrick, the dedication intended for the future cathedral, opened. Third and final (current) site chosen in the Eighth Ward (now North Ward).
1872	Drawings completed by Goldie and Child. Bishop Bayley leaves Newark to become archbishop of Baltimore.
1873	Michael A. Corrigan becomes second bishop of Newark. Panic of 1873 and crisis at Saint John's Church in Orange.
1875	Cathedral site graded. Cathedral project suspended indefinitely.
1880	Father Doane named Domestic Prelate, with title of monsignor. Bishop Corrigan leaves to become bishop, later archbishop, of New York.
1881	Father Winand Wigger becomes third bishop of Newark.
1891	Sacred Heart parish organized and church erected on the southwest corner of the future cathedral site.

1893	Jeremiah O'Rourke appointed supervising architect of the United States.
1895	Planning of Branch Brook Park begins.
1897	Formal discussion of the cathedral project renewed. Four architects invited to submit designs for a new cathedral. O'Rourke firm chosen.
1898	Excavation and foundations completed by Peter Boyle's firm, which also constructs the first course of the water table the next year.
1899	Cathedral cornerstone ceremony; dedication is to the Sacred Heart. E. M. Waldron & Company hired as contractors.
1901	Death of Bishop Wigger. John J. O'Connor becomes fourth bishop of Newark.
1905	Death of Monsignor Doane. Monsignor John Sheppard becomes diocesan representative for cathedral project. Controversy begins between Waldron and O'Rourke, principally over substitution of materials and payments. The nave and transept walls are well advanced by 1905; towers completed to 84 feet. The plan and profile of the cathedral as it would appear are clearly visible.
1908	Controversy over the stability of foundations for the piers.
1910	O'Rourke separated from the project. Architect Isaac Ditmars retained. Scheme modified and plans for spires eliminated.
1916	Exterior masonry completed.
1917	United States enters World War I
1919	Flèche and slate roof completed.
1924	Carved relief sculpture at portals completed. Structure entirely enclosed.
1926	Paul C. Reilly joins Ditmars's architectural practice.
1926–1928	Walls of sanctuary and ambulatory, sheathed in limestone with a granite base. Guastavino vaulting installed in the same area. Limestone wainscoting completed throughout interior.
1927	Death of Bishop John O'Connor.
1928	Bishop Thomas J. Walsh of Trenton becomes fifth bishop of Newark. Installation ceremony held in unfinished cathedral. The Waldron firm completes its final contract for the cathedral.
1930	Ditmars and Reilly continue preparing designs for the interior scheme.
1937	Newark becomes an archdiocese, and Bishop Walsh is appointed archbishop.
1938	Archbishop Walsh receives the pallium, symbol of an archbishop, in the unfinished cathedral.
1941	United States enters World War II.

1946 Architect Paul C. Reilly consulted about renewing construction.

1951 Paul C. Reilly awarded contract to complete Sacred Heart, work that includes the design of narthex and transept screens. Gonippo Raggi awarded contract for appointments, furnishings, and stained glass.

1952 General contract awarded to George Fuller Construction Company.
Death of Archbishop Walsh.

1953 Thomas A. Boland becomes sixth bishop and second archbishop of Newark.

1954 Sacred Heart Cathedral completed and consecrated.

1956 Bronze main doors installed.
Schantz pipe organ dedicated.

1976 Sacred Heart listed on the National Register of Historic Places.

1995 During his visit on October 4, Pope John Paul II designates Sacred Heart a minor basilica.

NOTES

Books and manuscript sources that are listed in the bibliography are cited in these notes in shortened form.

Abbreviations

AABN	*American Architect and Building News*
ADN	Archdiocese of Newark Collection, Monsignor William Noé Field Archives & Special Collections Center, Seton Hall University
Advertiser	*Newark Daily Advertiser*
Avery	Avery Architectural and Fine Arts Library, Columbia University
Call	*Newark Sunday Call*
Evening News	*Newark Evening News*
Flanagan Papers	Research and assembled papers related to the history of Sacred Heart Cathedral and other New Jersey churches by Bernard A. Flanagan of Maplewood, N.J. Papers cited here are part of the author's research collection.
NA	National Archives, Washington, D.C.
NPL	Newark Public Library: Charles F. Cummings New Jersey Information Center, Sacred Heart Cathedral files.
RG	Record group
SHC	Sacred Heart Cathedral
Sheppard, "Journal"	ADN, RG 2, box 6: Vicar General John A. Sheppard Papers, in Bishop O'Connor Papers

Last names are used for frequently cited persons.

Bayley	James Roosevelt Bayley
Corrigan	Michael A. Corrigan
Ditmars	Isaac E. Ditmars
Doane	George Hobart Doane
O'Connor	John J. O'Connor
O'Rourke	Jeremiah O'Rourke
Sheppard	John A. Sheppard
Waldron	Edward M. Waldron
Wigger	Winand M. Wigger

1. Destination: Newark

1. Pierce M. McCarthy, "Sermon on the Permanency of Catholic Faith, Preached at the Laying of the Corner Stone of the New Cathedral Chapel, Newark. Nov. 21, 1869. P. M. McCarthy," ADN, RG 2.1, box 11. Also following quotation.

2. In 1850, the national average was six Irish for every one German immigrant; in New Jersey the average was three to one, or about 31,000 Irish and 11,000 Germans.

3. Estimates placed the number of Catholics in New Jersey in 1853 at forty thousand.

4. In 1850, only 23 of the 814 churches in New Jersey were for Catholic congregations. Dougherty, *Bishops of Newark 1853–1978*, 6. Among the larger churches in Newark was Trinity Church, an 1809 structure in the manner of the Englishman James Gibbs and typical of the classical-inspired English and later American churches when it was built; in the twentieth century, it became the cathedral for the Episcopal diocese based in Newark.

5. Newark archdiocese historians have traditionally estimated the population of Newark at the diocese's 1853 founding by taking the population in 1850 and adding three-tenths of the population growth between 1850 and 1860.

6. Wister, "*St. Patrick's Pro-Cathedral, Newark, New Jersey*, 1.

7. For a discussion of Saint Patrick's Pro-Cathedral's style, see Decker, "Grand and Godly Proportions," 86–92. Decker explains that the ahistoric Gothic mode represented by Saint Patrick's Pro-Cathedral was found in Protestant churches in Ireland dating to the early nineteenth century and, a little later, in Catholic churches. Saint Patrick's needle spire had abundant Irish models from the same period.

8. Yaeger, *Life of James Roosevelt Bayley*, 103; quoted in Kupke, *Living Stones*, 55.

9. "Newark Diocesan Scrapbook, 1855–1872," ADN, RG 2.1, box 24. Quoted in Quinn, *The Irish in New Jersey*, 82.

10. Paul V. Flynn, *History of Saint John's Church, Newark*, 105–106.

11. Quoted in Quinn, *The Irish in New Jersey*, 84.

12. Bayley to Corrigan, August 19, 1873, Archives of the Archdiocese of New York, C-1. Quoted in Curran, *Michael Augustine Corrigan and the Shaping of Conservative Catholicism in America, 1878–1902*, 43n, 47.

13. Dougherty, *Bishops of Newark*, 14.

14. *Antiques* 102 (August 1972): 256–261. The cathedra by Jelliff remains in the sanctuary of Saint Patrick's Pro-Cathedral in Newark.

15. See Joseph M. Flynn, *Catholic Church in New Jersey*, 601, for another local example of employing an intermediary to purchase land for Catholic use. It involved the transaction of the South Orange real estate for Seton Hall.

16. Bayley, "Episcopal Register," February 19, 1859, entry 69, ADN, RG 2.1, box 3.

17. South Park was renamed Lincoln Park in 1869. The second site was irregular in shape, with 400 feet on Broad Street and 271 feet on Lagrange Street (sometimes called Lagrange Place and sometimes with an uppercase G). It constituted the small block immediately south of the public park. The diocese paid $10,000 for the first site, $52,000 for the second, and $60,000 for the third and final site, on a lot bounded by Fifth and Sixth Avenues (now Park Avenue and Victoria Avenue, respectively) and Clifton Avenue and Ridge Street. See also Brady, "The Cathedral of the Sacred Heart in Newark, New Jersey," 7–9.

18. *Northern Monthly* (September–November 1867). Quoted in Cunningham, *Newark*, 169–170.

19. Bayley, "Pastoral Letter, February 4, 1867," ADN, RG 2.1, box 6.

20. Bayley, "Circular Letter, March 31, 1869," Bishop Bayley Papers, ADN, RG 2.1, box 6. Quoted in Yaeger, *Life of James Roosevelt Bayley*, 248.

2. Gothic and the Context of American Cathedral Building

1. Pugin, *True Principles*, 42.

2. Ibid., 1.

3. Ecclesiologists disseminated their views in an eponymous journal and through pamphlets, books, and published drawings.

4. They thought that a church, at minimum, must have a place for the celebration by the clergy of the mass and other rites (the chancel) and a space set apart for the laity (the nave); to these could be added transepts, a tower, a sacristy, and other embellishments as need required and funding permitted.

5. Pugin, *True Principles*, 30.

6. Quoted in Stanton, *Pugin*, 92.

7. Newman was less interested than most Victorians in the externals of religion and, as it related to architecture, never saw the English Middle Ages as a golden era to be revived.

8. Atterbury, *A.W.N. Pugin: Master of Gothic Revival*, especially Barry Bergdoll's essay, "The Ideal of the Gothic Cathedral in 1852," 103–135.

9. The Irish round tower for Our Lady of Grace in Avondale (Saint Mary's parish in what is now Nutley, N.J.), designed by James Renwick and for which O'Rourke appears to have served as local architect, was a rare instance of citing historic Irish building. Architectural acculturation was more the norm among Irish Americans. A photograph of Our Lady of Grace, built in the 1870s and subsequently razed, appears in Joseph M. Flynn, *Catholic Church in New Jersey*, 459.

10. Keely's works in New Jersey included Saint Patrick's Pro-Cathedral (built as a parish church), Saint Mary's, and Saint James in Newark; Saint Michael's, Saint Mary's, Saint Patrick's, and Saint Bridget's in Jersey City; Saint Mary's in Trenton; Saint Peter's in New Brunswick; and Saint John's and Saint Joseph's in Paterson, among others.

11. For a concise assessment of Keely's approach, see Atterbury, *A.W.N. Pugin: Master of Gothic Revival*, 207–208.

12. Decker, "Grand and Godly Proportions," 99.

13. Farnsworth et al., *Stained Glass in Catholic Philadelphia*, 70–71.

14. Architect John Notman also worked on the Philadelphia cathedral.

15. Cited in William H. Pierson Jr., *Technology and the Picturesque, the Corporate and the Early Gothic Styles*, vol. 2 of *American Buildings and Their Architects*, 249.

16. Farley, *History of Saint Patrick's Cathedral*, 141; and Thomas J. Shelley, *Bicentennial History of the Archdiocese of New York* (Strasbourg, France: Éditions du Signe, 2007), 404.

17. Accounts of the size of the future Brooklyn cathedral varied. Some reported it was to be 352 feet in length, others a little longer. Local newspaper reports said the spires would reach 350 feet, but an account in the *American Builder* in 1876 said they would reach 400 feet. Keely's scheme is discussed briefly and illustrated in Stern et al., *New York 1880*, 888.

18. Bayley to Corrigan, March 20 and 27, 1870, Archives of the Archdiocese of New York, C-2. Quoted in Yaeger, *Life of James Roosevelt Bayley*, 249.

19. Bayley to Corrigan, March 20, 1870, Archives of the Archdiocese of New York, C-2. Quoted in Yaeger, *Life of James Roosevelt Bayley*, 249.

20. "Consecration of the South Park Cathedral Chapel," newspaper clipping in Diocesan Scrapbook, 1855–1872, ADN, RG 2.1, box 24. The church dedication of "Our Lady and Saint Patrick" was also popular in England and Ireland at the time.

21. Bayley to Archbishop Martin John Spalding, March 20, 1869. Baltimore Cathedral Archives, Baltimore, Md. Quoted in Yaeger, *Life of James Roosevelt Bayley*, 244.

22. The New York archdiocese attempted to soften this criticism by adding a Catholic, William Rodrigue, to the design team.

23. *New-York Freeman's Journal and Catholic Register*, June 27, 1868.

24. Doane to Bernard McQuaid, September 13, 1869. Quoted in Brady, "The Sacred Heart Cathedral in Newark, New Jersey," 8.

25. *AABN*, March 6, 1880.

26. Another practical incentive to consider a change had also emerged. The cathedral lot (the second site) was about to be assessed for street improvements.

27. Farley, *History of Saint Patrick's Cathedral*, 122; quoted in Decker, "Grand and Godly Proportions," 129.

28. Evelyn Carole Voelker, "Charles Borromeo's Instructions for the Building of Churches (*Instructiones Fabricae Ecclesiasticae et supellectilis ecclesiasticae*), 1577, Book 1 and Book 2, A Translation with Commentary and Analysis" (PhD diss., Syracuse University, 1977; Ann Arbor, Mich., 1977), 1:1–2.

3. Gothic Passions: The Doane Family

1. Hills, *History of the Church in Burlington*, 545. The quotation is from a sermon by Cortlandt Van Rensselaer, a Presbyterian minister.

2. Stanton, *Gothic Revival*, 31. Doane was the second North American patron member elected; a Canadian was elected previously. Stanton amply chronicles Bishop Doane's important role in the Gothic Revival in America.

3. Ibid., 45. Riverside was erected between 1837 and 1839. The villa was razed in 1961, despite efforts to save it.

4. English ecclesiologists opposed outright copying of medieval buildings but made an exception for those who wanted a Gothic church outside England, where they were concerned that locals would not have the ability to produce the style correctly. Bishop Doane, intent on having a proper Gothic edifice, invoked this architectural dispensation and had Upjohn mimic a specific medieval church, Saint John's Church, Shottesbrook in Wilshire.

5. Eliza Doane was the widow of James Perkins. Her full name after her marriage to Doane became Eliza Greene Callahan Perkins Doane. Eliza had five children with Perkins.

6. The Inman portrait of the Doane sons is in the collection of the Newark Museum. It is illustrated in Lurie and Mappen, *Encyclopedia of New Jersey*, 407.

7. George Hobart Doane and William Croswell Doane were named after two of their father's friends, John Henry Hobart and William Croswell, also leading figures in the Episcopal Church.

8. Hills, *History of the Church in Burlington*, 578.

9. Doane authored a journal article arising from his medical training abroad: "Comparative Advantages of Vienna and Paris, as Places for Medical Study, with Some Remarks on the Operation of Extraction for the Removal of Cataract," *New Jersey Medical Reports* 7 (1854): 17–20.

10. Hills, *History of the Church in Burlington*, 516.

11. Quoted in Paul V. Flynn, *History of Saint John's Church, Newark*, 132.

12. Flynn, "The Conversion of George Hobart Doane," *History of Saint John's Church*, 121–139. Doane's apologia, in the form of a letter to Bishop Bayley, was published posthumously in Flynn's 1908 book.

13. Quoted in Hills, *History of the Church in Burlington*, 513; and 513–517 for an account of this episode from Bishop Doane's perspective.

14. Quoted in Hills, *History of the Church in Burlington*, 517.

15. For a discussion of the conversion phenomenon in this period, see Patrick Allitt, *Catholic Converts: British and American Intellectuals Turn to Rome* (Ithaca, N.Y.: Cornell University Press, 1997), chaps. 1–4; also D. J. Scannell-O'Neill, *Distinguished Catholic Converts to Rome in America* (Saint Louis: B. Herder, 1907).

16. Quoted in Hills, *History of the Church in Burlington*, 513.

17. The Collegio Pio was founded for English clergy who joined the Roman Catholic Church from other denominations. Its name was changed to Pontifio Collegio Beda in 1899.

18. After his own ordination, Bishop Bayley had been made secretary to Bishop John Hughes of New York.

4. Father Doane and Jeremiah O'Rourke: Architectural Collaborators

1. The Gothic Revival flowered vigorously in Ireland. Pugin's Irish cathedrals and the parish churches in Wexford are among the best architecture the movement produced anywhere. The Irishman J. J. McCarthy secured Pugin's influence in Ireland. Called the Irish Pugin, he founded the Irish Ecclesiological Society in 1849. Although McCarthy made Pugin's case for an Irish Catholic audience, his influence on O'Rourke before his emigration was only general. For a study of McCarthy, see Jeanne Sheehey, *J. J. McCarthy and the Gothic Revival in Ireland* (Ulster: Ulster Architectural Heritage Society, 1977).

2. John Turpin, *A School of Art in Dublin since the Eighteenth Century: A History of the National College of Art and Design* (Dublin: Gill & Macmillan, 1995), 104–106. Shortly later, the society was reconstituted and renamed as the Government School of Design. The Government School of Design was for all intents and purposes a continuation of the Royal Dublin Society School of Drawing, begun in the eighteenth century. O'Rourke was there during the transition phase from the Dublin Society school to the Government School of Design. Professor John Turpin to Bernard A. Flanagan, September 29, 1982, Flanagan Papers. Records at the Dublin institution indicate that Jeremiah O'Rourke enrolled in 1849. Royal Dublin Society Library e-mail to author, February 24, 2011.

3. In the late 1840s, the Dublin Society's aesthetic emphasis remained on the classicism that prevailed when the schools were set up in the eighteenth century. In this, it held to a preference that broader developments, especially the Gothic Revival would sweep away—as O'Rourke's career will illustrate.

4. Upjohn, *Richard Upjohn*, 138–140. Everard Upjohn provides a helpful account of the working methods used in the offices of architects and building designers in this period.

5. *Advertiser*, July 23, 1852.

6. In 1820, there was only one Catholic church in all of New Jersey, in Trenton. Thirty years later, the year of O'Rourke's immigration, there were twenty-three. In the next thirty years, that number would grow to 190, or an average of more than 5 churches each year. In the Diocese of Newark alone, during the subsequent twenty years new churches increased by more than 85 percent. These numbers capture the number of new parishes or missions started, which implied erecting a church or adapting a building to

serve as one. Sometimes individual congregations grew so swiftly that within these periods a larger church replaced the original building, making actual church-building activity even greater.

7. O'Rourke later moved the office to 756 Broad Street.

8. Saint James the Less in Philadelphia (1846–1848) was among the first in the Early Pointed style on American soil and drew upon the same English sources as Christ Church, Newark.

9. *The New York-Ecclesiologist* 2, no. 1 (October 1849): 18; cited in Stanton, *Gothic Revival*, 181–183.

10. Christ Church is located at 76 Prospect Street and is currently (2011) the Pan American C.M.A. Church parish center; it has been extensively altered.

11. Saint Joseph's Church in Mendham dates from 1858–1859. The building contract is in the parish records and is currently displayed at the church. Saint Philip and Saint James Church in Phillipsburg was built in 1860–1861; J. O'Rourke, "Phillipsburg Church," expense table, undated, with "Rev. G. H. Doane" written on verso, copy in ADN, RG 10.5: Phillipsburg. A sketch of O'Rourke's design appears in "History of Saint Philip & Saint James Church, Phillipsburg, 1858–1989," 10. ADN, RG 10.5: Phillipsburg.

12. The scheme for the chapel for Seton Hall also included an unrealized detached bell tower.

13. Doane to Bayley, July 24, 1861, ADN, 2.1.9.

14. Pugin, *True Principles*, 34.

15. The crossbeam, open timber roof resembles that in Pugin's Saint Giles Church, Cheadle, as well as Saint Mark's in Philadelphia.

16. Bayley, "Episcopal Register," July 21, 1866, ADN, RG 2.1, box 3. The Church of Immaculate Conception became the cathedral of the Diocese of Camden when it was established in 1937.

17. *New-York Freeman's Journal and Catholic Register*, January 14, 1871. The pastor was the Rev. Patrick Byrne.

18. *Advertiser*, September 24, 1866.

19. The tower, unlike that of Saint Giles Church, fronts the north aisle. This and other design features reflect O'Rourke's reading of Pugin and the ecclesiologists as their philosophy of church design evolved. In place of an open timber roof, O'Rourke chose plaster vaults. Although anathema to the ecclesiologists, imitative materials were frequent substitutions in the United States, including in Richard Upjohn's much-admired Trinity Church in New York. And contemporaneous with the Orange church's planning, the decision was made to abandon Renwick's plan for masonry vaulting in his Saint Patrick's Cathedral. Although cost had been a factor in these decisions, another reason applied: it would have been virtually impossible to find masons in this country able to construct Gothic vaulting.

20. Quoted in Stanton, *Pugin*, 108. Newman was not otherwise fully persuaded of the merits of reviving Gothic.

21. Pugin, *True Principles*, 42.

22. J. & R. Lamb of New York provided interior furnishings and decoration.

23. *Advertiser*, October 11, 1869.

24. *Saint Paul's Church Centennial 1844–1944* (Princeton, N.J.: Saint Paul's Church, 1944), 41.

25. Ibid., 37. Saint Paul's was one of the first instances of the use of structural polychrome in Princeton. For illustrations of these churches and other buildings, see Constance Greiff et al., *Princeton Architecture: A Pictorial History of Town and Campus*

(Princeton, N.J.: Princeton University Press, 1967); O'Rourke's Saint Paul's Church is illustrated on page 139, illustration no. 136.

26. Other features of the Princeton church were an amalgam of contemporary American church design and the midcentury Irish churches of Pugin and his followers; antecedents of the distinctive buttressed tower were found in England, Ireland, and America in this period. Probable influences are two churches in Ireland, in Dingles and Feries in County Kerry, by J. J. McCarthy from the early 1860s. An illustration of Keely's Saint Vincent Ferrer Church appears in John Gilmary Shea, *Goulding's Catholic Churches of New York City* (New York: Goulding & Co., 1877), 717. Saint Paul's Church in Princeton was remodeled in 1912 by architect James H. Jackson, who altered the facade and replaced the original tower.

27. Ann Taves, *The Household of Faith: Roman Catholic Devotions in Mid-Nineteenth-Century America* (Notre Dame, Ind.: University of Notre Dame Press, 1986), 125.

28. Although Catholic churches were different in internal arrangements, during the nineteenth century there was a cultural exchange among Christian denominations regarding church design and appointments. For a discussion of this dynamic, see Smith, *Gothic Arches, Latin Crosses.*

29. O'Rourke to Corrigan, November 5, 1878, ADN, RG 2.2, box 3. To the Pugin reference, O'Rourke added, "See *Dublin Review,*" mentioning the publication that carried some of Pugin's most important writing. O'Rourke probably meant "Apology" rather than "Plea." O'Rourke's comments were in response to a request by the diocese to review the plans for a proposed church, because others had doubts about them as well.

30. Pugin, *True Principles*, 36.

5. Newark's Gothic Pilgrims Abroad

1. *Advertiser*, September 2, 1870. Letter dated "Durham, August 12, 1870."

2. *Advertiser*, September 12, 1870. Letter dated "Dublin, August 22, 1870."

3. Melrose Abbey was constructed of red sandstone, a type of stone found in New Jersey.

4. *Advertiser*, September 12, 1870. Letter dated "Dublin, August 22, 1870."

5. Quoted in Stanton, *Pugin*, 11. Pugin's original uses the old spelling, "antient."

6. *Advertiser*, September 12, 1870, and subsequent quotations in the paragraph. Letter dated "Dublin, August 22, 1870."

7. *Advertiser*, May 30, 1870, this and subsequent quotation. Letter dated "Oscott College, near Birmingham, May 15, 1870."

8. Ibid.

9. Ibid.

10. *Advertiser*, September 16, 1870. Letter dated "Dublin, August 22, 1870."

11. *Advertiser*, May 30, 1870. Letter dated "Oscott College, near Birmingham, May 15, 1870."

12. O'Donnell, *The Pugins and the Catholic Midlands*, 118–119. The chapel is described and illustrated.

13. *Advertiser*, May 30, 1870. Letter dated "Oscott College, near Birmingham, May 15, 1870."

14. *Advertiser*, July 27, 1870. Letter dated "Cadenabbia, Lake of Como, July 9, 1870." The rector of the Pontifical North American College, Silas Francis Chatard, accompanied Doane during his private audience with Pius IX.

15. Pugin, *Contrasts*, 18.

16. *Advertiser*, July 7, 1870. Letter dated "American College, Rome, June 12, 1870."

17. *Advertiser*, August 8, 1870. Letter dated "Geneva, July 17, 1870."

18. Doane's album of *cartes de visite* is preserved in the Newark archdiocese's archives (ADN, RG 2.1, box 25).

19. Doane, *To and From the Passion Play*, 283.

20. Atterbury and Wainwright, *Pugin: A Gothic Passion*, especially Roderick O'Donnell's essay, "The Later Pugins," 259–271. For a discussion of the younger Pugins' work in America, see Atterbury, *A.W.N Pugin: Master of Gothic Revival*, 208–212.

21. Architects' files: George Goldie (1828–1887). British Architectural Library, Royal Institute of British Architects, London.

22. Goldie's work included Sligo Cathedral and Saint John's College, overlooking the city of Waterford; Our Lady of Victories in Kensington, dated from 1867 to 1869; and Saint Wilfrid's in York, 1862–1864. An article, with drawings, about the latter appeared in *Building News*, May 9, 1873. The Kensington church was destroyed in the Second World War.

23. *Advertiser*, September 2, 1870. Letter dated "Durham, August 12, 1870."

24. Charles Edwin Child, Goldie's former pupil and assistant, joined Goldie in partnership in 1867. Goldie's son, Edward Goldie, joined the partnership in 1881.

25. *Advertiser*, September 12, 1870.

26. Ibid.

27. *Architectural Review* (October 1899): 117.

28. Doane to Corrigan, January 17, 1880, ADN, RG 2.2, box 4.

29. *Advertiser*, September 16, 1870.

6. "The Newark Cathedral": Gothic Pilgrims at Home

1. *Advertiser*, September 15, 1870, and following quotations from this article. The poet quoted by Doane is Thomas Moore.

2. *Newark Evening Courier*, September 15, 1870.

3. *Advertiser*, September 16, 1870 (quoting the London *Tablet*).

4. Bayley quotation from a *Call* article, October 1, 1916. It noted, "Nearly half a century has rolled by since the September day in 1870 when the European cable bore a message from the Rt. Reverend James Roosevelt Bayley (The Roman Catholic Bishop of Newark) to Jeremiah O'Rourke. It said, "Heartily approve your selection," and referred to the site chosen by the architect of the New Cathedral of the Sacred Heart." The property was formally purchased from Peter T. Doremus and Hiram M. Rhodes on January 2, 1871. In May 1871, the cathedral chapel was moved to Thomas Street, where it later served Saint Columba's parish.

5. O'Rourke, "Report on Property of Messrs. Rhodes & Doremus, Situated on Mount Prospect, Newark, N.J.," October 11, 1870, ADN, RG 10.5, box 140.

6. Ibid.

7. *Advertiser*, December 14, 1871.

8. Joseph M. Flynn, *Catholic Church in New Jersey*, 294.

9. *Advertiser*, July 5, 1872, and following quotations in this paragraph. Such Rayonnant window traceries were also like those planned for Saint Patrick's Cathedral in New York.

10. *Advertiser*, July 5, 1872. The length was reduced from 300 feet to 270 feet; the width remained about the same. The taller of the two spires was reduced from 300 feet high to about 200 feet.

11. *Advertiser*, July 5, 1872.

12. *Advertiser*, September 16, 1870, quoting the *Tablet* (London).

13. *Building News*, June 20, 1873.
14. Eastlake, *History of the Gothic Revival*, 348. Also, the following quotation.
15. The trustee was probably O'Rourke's father-in-law, William Dunn.
16. Cited in Tuttle, *How Newark Became Newark*, 67.
17. Tuttle, *How Newark Became Newark*, 63–68.
18. *Advertiser*, August 24, 1872.
19. In a 1902 letter to Newark's Bishop John J. O'Connor, O'Rourke explained that the drawings of the Cathedral of Our Lady and Saint Patrick were sent to the Brooklyn residence of Bishop Charles McDonnell. They had been requested by McDonnell in relation to Brooklyn's own cathedral plans, and O'Connor had instructed O'Rourke to provide them. One imagines that O'Rourke did so reluctantly; as it is, they have not since been found in Newark, Brooklyn, or elsewhere. O'Rourke to O'Connor, December 20, 1902, ADN, RD 10.5, box 140.
20. *Building News*, July 31, 1885. The design published here was modified, and Charles Edwin Child and Edward Goldie succeeded to the commission after George Goldie's death in 1887.
21. The Plainfield church's cornerstone was laid in 1875, and the church opened in 1880. O'Rourke also used this roof system for Saint Aloysius Church in Newark, opened in 1881.
22. The gestalt of Saint Mary's in Dover owes a debt to Pugin's churches in Wexford, particularly those at Barntown and Tagoat, whereas details descend from his English parish churches. The Marian symbolism of the stained glass is close to that in Pugin's Saint Giles Church. The unrealized spire is in the style of Frank Wills, the English-American associated with the Doanes. O'Rourke's drawings for the Dover church survive in the parish archives. They were apparently sent to the parish when the O'Rourke firm proposed interior renovations in 1908. Never returned to the firm, they are among the rare complete sets of drawings by O'Rourke to survive.
23. *Iron Era* (Dover, N.J.), November 8, 1873.
24. Ibid.
25. The Jeremiah window, as well as all of the others in Saint Mary's, was almost certainly produced by a firm connected with Stephen Slack and Charles Booth, English-trained stained glass artists with a studio in Orange; Slack is the more likely artist of Saint Mary's figural windows.
26. *Iron Era* (Dover, N.J.), November 8, 1873.

7. Bust: Crisis and a Grand Hope Deferred

1. Mahoney and Wosh, *Diocesan Journal of Michael Augustine Corrigan*, 3.
2. Although it may seem unusual that Hickey, a young man in good health, should do so, it was not unusual in this period for pastors to purchase life insurance policies for the value of the outstanding mortgage on a new church.
3. Other calculations place the value of the debt at $265,000. Existing records make it hard to calculate a precise amount.
4. "Minute Book," Saint John's Church, Orange, New Jersey, February 7, 1873, 46.
5. Institutional lenders included the Bank of Orange, Mutual Benefit Life Insurance Company of Newark, Shamrock Provident Society of Orange, and Republic Trust Company. Individual lenders included Martin Burne, who made money in the grocery business in Newark and was president of the Hibernia Fire Insurance Company; William Dunn, O'Rourke's prosperous father in law; Daniel Coghlan, a Catholic leader of the paper mill industry in Whippany, to whom Wigger appealed for help; George V. Hecker,

New Yorker and brother of the priest who preached at Saint John's dedication; Joseph M. Smith, whose firm did the church's carpentry and a director of the North Ward National Bank of Newark; George Spottiswoode, who started out in the coal and lumber yard business and founded Half-Dime Savings Bank; and Marcus L. Ward of Newark. The largest individual creditor by the time of the restructuring of the debt was John O'Rourke, contractor for the church. "Records of the Trustees of Saint John's Church, Orange, New Jersey" (Minute book), 1872–1875, parish archives, Saint John's Church, Orange, N.J.

6. *Advertiser*, February 12, 1874.

7. Mahoney and Wosh, *Diocesan Journal of Michael Augustine Corrigan*, 31.

8. Corrigan, Circular Letter, February 21, 1874, ADN, RG 2.2, box 5. Corrigan's circular letter also survives among the parish records of Saint John's; it is inserted in "Records of the Trustees of Saint John's Church, Orange, New Jersey." It was reprinted in the *Newark Daily Journal*, February 24, 1874.

9. Corrigan's later boast that it was accepted unanimously and that "the very best feeling prevailed" perhaps underestimates the pressure his clergy felt to capitulate to his wishes (Mahoney and Wosh, *Diocesan Journal of Michael Augustine Corrigan*, 39).

10. Corrigan, Circular Letter, April 21, 1874, ADN, RG 2.2, box 5.

11. The floating debt of the parish was not entirely paid until the 1890s.

12. The bonding materials used for the walls had been of poor quality, and the construction technique was inadequate. "Records of the Trustees of Saint John's Church, Orange, New Jersey," July 21, 1880.

13. Paul T. Carew, *The Story of a Mother Church: Saint John's Orange, N.J. 1851–1934* (Brooklyn, N.Y.: published by the author and printed by Braunworth & Co., 1934), 45–46. Carew wrote: "Mr. O'Rourke as he lay dying in his Newark home was visited by the reporter of a New York newspaper and was asked which of all his works he thought the loftiest example of his art. He replied without hesitation, 'Saint John's Church in Orange.'"

8. O'Rourke in Washington

1. O'Rourke also served on the board of the State Psychiatric Hospital in Morris Plains, various City of Newark commissions and boards, and the cathedral parish's Saint Vincent de Paul Society, dedicated to the relief of the poor.

2. *AABN*, July 30, 1887, and quoted in Lee, *Architects to the Nation*, 3.

3. W. Coleman Nevils, *Moulder of Men* (New York: Apostleship of Prayer, 1953), 12. *Moulder of Men* includes memoirs of Rev. John H. O'Rourke, S.J., Jeremiah O'Rourke's nephew.

4. *AABN*, April 15, 1893.

5. *AABN*, September 23, 1893.

6. O'Rourke to Carlilse, January 13, 1894. National Archives, RG 56, General Records of the Treasury Department Received from the Supervising Architect.

7. Paradoxically, the American Institute of Architects vigorously opposed competitions as a method for choosing architects for private-sector work, because the economies of entering them were stacked against architects.

8. *AABN*, April 7, 1894.

9. "The Correspondence between the Secretary of the Treasury and the President of the American Institute of Architects," Daniel H. Burnham to John G. Carlisle, *AABN*, April 7, 1894.

10. O'Rourke to Daniel Burnham, February 6, 1894. Quoted in "Washington," *AABN*, March 31, 1894.

11. O'Rourke proposed to Carlisle a reorganization that included a new educational division (or department) within the office, writing that "the office . . . is capable of being made the nucleus of a National Academy of Architecture and Fine Arts." He also asked that "I be authorized to form a permanent Post-graduate class of from six to twelve young draughtsmen of superior taste and ability, graduates of Institutions of Technology, or Offices of reputable Architects, who after a few years practical experience in this Office would give the country a supply of thoroughly trained Architects of high professional tone and character." O'Rourke to John G. Carlisle, January 13, 1894, Letters Received from the Supervising Architect, National Archives, RG 56.

12. Nevils, *Moudler of Men*, 12–13. The episode is recounted in O'Rourke's nephew's autobiographical sketch.

13. O'Rourke to John G. Carlisle, September 17, 1894, Letters Received from the Supervising Architect, National Archives, RG 56.

14. Senator Smith could be of no help, as he was apparently out of the country when O'Rourke was dismissed.

15. O'Rourke to John G. Carlisle, dated "Wednesday morning," received February 26, 1894, Letters Received from the Supervising Architect, National Archives, RG 56.

16. J. R. McPherson to Secretary Carlisle, September 21, 1894, National Archives, RG 56.

17. Paul G. Botticher to W. J. Edbrooke, November 16, 1891, National Archives, RG 56.

9. Monsignor Doane

1. *Newark Evening Journal*, September 30, 1869.

2. Bayley, "Newark Diocesan Scrapbook, 1855–1872," ADN, RG 2.1, box 24.

3. *Advertiser*, May 8, 1870.

4. *Advertiser*, October 8, 1879.

5. Mahoney and Wosh, *Diocesan Journal of Michael Augustine Corrigan*, 218–219. Also, following quotations in this paragraph.

6. Bayley to Martin John Spalding, March 20, 1869, Baltimore Cathedral Archives, 36-A-A2, and following quotations in this paragraph. Quoted in Yaeger, *Life of James Roosevelt Bayley*, 244.

7. Wister, *Stewards of the Mysteries of God*, 63.

8. McQuaid had a bleak upbringing at home. His mother died when he was four. His father was killed in a fight five years later. A bitter, short time as the ward of his stepmother ended with Bernard's spending the remainder of his youth in a Catholic orphanage in New York. Drawn to the Church, he became a feisty warrior for it.

9. Dougherty, *Bishops of Newark 1853–1978*, 50.

10. Wister, *Stewards of the Mysteries of God*, 62–66. Wister accounts for the peculiar circumstances of Wigger's nomination and appointment.

11. Wigger understandably perceived that Doane's natural authority would make the cathedral a difficult stage to share. But when he sought to remove Doane as pastor of Saint Patrick's Cathedral parish on the grounds that the bishop was its rightful pastor, bringing with it the rectory and pastor's salary, it endeared him to no one. A priest fighting with Wigger over other issues taunted, "I know what the Propaganda already thinks of your action toward Monsignor Doane" and Rome's "opinion of your prudence" (Patrick Corrigan to Wigger, April 1, 1884, from Hoboken, N.J., ADN, RG 2.3, box 3). Wigger later nipped at Doane's heals, once or twice questioning the amount of

Doane's entertainment expenses at the rectory, but largely he left him alone and treated him with decency. Doane acted with scrupulous deference.

12. Patrick Corrigan (no relation to the bishop) was the pastor of Our Lady of Grace in Hoboken. For these controversies, see Dougherty, *Bishops of Newark 1853–1978*, 52–55; and Kupke, *Living Stones*, 119–122.

13. *Call*, March 30, 1902.

14. Doane, *To and From the Passion Play*, 301.

15. *Advertiser*, August 17, 1870.

16. *Call*, October 5, 1904.

17. *Call*, May 15, 1902.

18. *Call*, October 18, 1904.

19. William Croswell Doane became the Episcopal bishop of Albany in 1868.

20. The first purpose-built cathedral in the Episcopal Church is disputed, with the 1869 Cathedral of Our Merciful Savior in Fairbault, Minnesota, designed by James Renwick, making a strong claim; another is Saints Peter and Paul Cathedral in Chicago, from 1862 and destroyed by fire in 1921. A legislative charter establishing New York City's Cathedral Church of Saint John the Divine was made in 1873, but actual construction came later in the century.

21. Cram, *Church Building*, 176.

22. Quoted in Paul V. Flynn, *History of Saint John's Church, Newark*, 134.

23. Doane to Wigger, November 25, 1889, ADN, RG 2.3, box 6.

10. Stilled Project, Ceaseless Change

1. Newark's Wigger was in a minority of bishops of German origin. Although the Irish did not constitute half of the U.S. Catholic population, two-thirds of the bishops were Irish Americans.

2. In the next decade, new immigration to the diocese from Italy raised the number of immigrant Italians to nearly eighty-five thousand, part of more than three million Italian immigrants to the United Sates between 1900 and 1920.

3. Kupke, *Living Stones*, 141.

4. Quoted in Lurie and Mappen, *Encyclopedia of New Jersey*, 415–416.

5. During Bishop O'Connor's era (1901–1927), twenty-six Italian parishes were added.

6. Quoted in Dougherty, *Bishops of Newark 1853–1978*, 64.

7. After the organization of the Diocese of Trenton, the number of churches in the Diocese of Newark dropped to 83; by 1901, it rose to 155.

8. Sr. Mary Agnes Sharkey, *New Jersey Sisters of Charity and Mother Mary Xavier Mehegan* (New York: Longmans, Green, 1933), 1, 162. Quoted in Quinn, *The Irish in New Jersey*, 93.

9. Denis Robert McNamara, *Heavenly City: The Architectural Tradition of Catholic Chicago* (Chicago: Archdiocese of Chicago, Liturgy Training Publications, 2005), 2–4.

10. Louis-Auguste Boileau used cast iron for columns and other structural elements for the Church of St-Eugène-Ste-Cécile in Paris (1854–1855), as well as later churches. Architectural professionals deprecated the results, but, as in Boston, good sight lines were achieved.

11. The friend of Doane's was Father Augustine Hewitt.

12. *AABN*, June 24, 1876.

13. O'Rourke to Isaac Hecker, June 19, 1876, Archives of the Church of Saint Paul the Apostle, New York.

14. Father George Deshon, a West Point graduate trained in military engineering, took over.

15. See Helene Barbara Weinberg, "The Work of John La Farge in the Church of Saint Paul the Apostle," *American Art Journal* 6, no. 1 (1974): 18–34.

16. O'Rourke found opportunity to rework his design for the Paulists for the Church of the Holy Cross in Harrison, N.J., and it anticipated his 1897 Sacred Heart Cathedral scheme. The spires O'Rourke planned for Holy Cross were not built when the church was dedicated in 1890. (A lithograph of O'Rourke's scheme survives at the Harrison church. It was also illustrated in the *Call*, January 8, 1888.) Towers designed by another hand were built in the 1920s.

11. Newark's Rise and the Project's Revival

1. Brady, "The Cathedral of the Sacred Heart in Newark, New Jersey," 9–10. The small church was to serve a new parish separated from Saint Michael's Church in 1889. The building was started in 1890 and finished in February 1891. The new parish was incorporated as the "Church of the Sacred Heart" on February 19, 1891. The incorporating document is preserved in ADN, RG 10.5, box 141.

2. In 1873, the Diocese of Newark had been placed under the patronage of the Sacred Heart, along with the others in the New York Province. Pius IX made the Sacred Heart a universal feast of the Roman Catholic Church in 1856; in 1889, it became "double the first class" (the highest ranking for a feast day); and in 1899, the year of the Newark cathedral's cornerstone laying, Leo XIII consecrated all humanity to the Sacred Heart. During the battle to save Saint John's in Orange, Bishop Corrigan suggested that if the diocese prevailed, the parish would be renamed "Sacred Heart"; it was not. Corrigan, Circular Letter, April 28, 1874, ADN, RG 2.2, box 5.

3. "Old Office of the Sacred Heart," eighteenth century, translated by Father Edward Caswall (1814–1878); it appeared in many Catholic hymn books, including *The Saint Gregory Hymnal* (Philadelphia: Saint Gregory Guild, 1920), no. 67.

4. Ann Taves, *The Household of Faith: Roman Catholic Devotions in Mid-Nineteenth Century America* (Notre Dame, Ind.: University of Notre Dame Press, 1986), 32–36.

5. Quoted in Kupke, *Living Stones*, 433. Wigger's letter is in the Archives of the Archdiocese of New York.

6. Wigger to Doane, "Letterbook," 4, 50, dated October 1897, ADN, RG 2.3, box 12. Quoted in Hinrichsen, "History of the Diocese of Newark 1873–1901," 408–409.

7. Doane to Wigger, October 14, 1897, ADN, RG 2.3, box 12.

8. Binding, *High Gothic*, 228–231. Binding provides a table with the construction duration for the major medieval cathedrals.

9. Doane to Wigger, July 12, 1897, ADN, RG 2.3, box 12.

10. William P. O'Rourke joined his father's practice in 1898. Joseph B. and Louis J. came to help in 1901.

11. Among Schickel's other prominent commissions were the Benedictine monastery in Latrobe, Pennsylvania; a building at Saint Vincent's Hospital in Greenwich Village; and Stern's dry goods store, a downtown Manhattan emporium.

12. Lawrence J. O'Connor's New Jersey churches include Saint Mary's, South Amboy; Saint Joseph's, Newton; Saint Mary's (Star of the Sea), Bayonne; and Church of the Assumption, Morristown. Usually composed in brick, O'Connor's designs show a less sculpted, more rectilinear, manner influenced by Ruskinian Gothic; relative to O'Rourke's churches of comparable size, O'Connor's were less costly.

13. George Audsley, a prolific polymath, wrote and illustrated books on the history of design, architecture, and Oriental art, in addition to a four-volume work on the pipe organ. For a discussion of his architecture, see David H. Fox, "Audsley Architecture in America," *Tracker* 39, no. 3 (1995): 25–30.

14. Some accounts of the competition mistakenly refer to the firm as Ansley Brothers.

15. Appointed to the committee were Monsignors Doane and Seton, Dean McNulty, and Fathers John O'Connor (future bishop of Newark), Hugh Flemming, Maurice O'Connor, Bernard Ter Woert, and Martin Gessner.

16. The drawings of the Audsley submission are in the Architectural Archives of the University of Pennsylvania. The nave facade has a rose window with tracery copied from Chartres's west rose and large turrets framing the main gable; matching towers and spires are detached from the body of the nave. One page of Schickel & Ditmars submission is preserved at Sacred Heart Cathedral. (It is currently located in oversized files in a basement storage room.) It is a pen-and-ink drawing on oversize card stock, at a scale of one inch equaling six feet, depicting a transverse section at the transept and showing the chancel, Decorated window tracery, tall cresting, and a squat flèche. O'Connor and Metcalf's submission, which Brady states included a printed description, is not known to survive.

17. Quoted by Joseph A. Brady in a letter to Stephen Welsh, October 4, 1960 (in response to Welsh's inquiry about the first cathedral scheme of the 1870s), ADN, RG 10.5, box 159.

18. *Call*, November 21, 1897.

19. Brady, "The Cathedral of the Sacred Heart in Newark, New Jersey," 14. The firms not awarded the commission were each paid $250 for expenses incurred.

20. Ibid. O'Rourke and the diocese considered the difference a contribution to the building fund.

12. The Cathedral of the Sacred Heart

1. O'Rourke perhaps chose red tile because of the color red's association with the symbolism of the Sacred Heart.

2. Early newspaper accounts indicated that the roof would be red or blue tile, though the rendering published in *AABN*, July 28, 1906, shows a raised-seam metal roof, probably intended to be copper. The coverage given by this journal was one of growing body of reports on Catholic church architecture in America, which architectural journals in the nineteenth century had largely ignored.

3. "Journal of Proceedings, American Institute of Architects, 1896," 74. Avery.

4. The rebuilding of Saint Ouen's facade occurred from 1846 to 1851. The architect was Henri Grégoire.

5. Fergusson, *History of Architecture in All Countries*, 2:157.

6. Ibid., 2:157–159.

7. Ibid.

8. Keely used the diagonal tower device for a chapel scheme (unrealized) at the University of Notre Dame in Notre Dame, Indiana, and for the Church of the Gesu in Montreal, which still stands, spireless. For a frame church he designed for Saint Joseph's in Washington, New Jersey (1871), Keely set a centered belfry at the diagonal two years after O'Rourke used the device in Saint Paul's, Princeton. Edwin F. Durang angled the tower of the Church of Our Lady of Good Counsel in Bryn Mawr, Pennsylvania (1887). There are other examples in North America and abroad.

9. It is tempting to link O'Rourke's use of the Brooklyn cathedral's conspicuous design feature to Keely's death in 1896, and the abandonment of his plans for it shortly after, but this remains conjecture. Brooklyn never built a new cathedral.

10. Bishop Charles E. McDonnell to Archbishop Michael Corrigan (Archives of the Archdiocese of New York), quoted in John K. Sharp, *History of the Diocese of Brooklyn, 1853–1953* (New York: Fordham University Press, 1954), 61. The fates of the Newark and Brooklyn projects brought other coincidences. At the turn of the century the two dioceses were on courses that reversed those of a generation earlier, when Brooklyn opted for the local Patrick Keely and Newark forged an Anglo-American partnership between George Goldie and O'Rourke. Now Newark found who it wanted in O'Rourke, and Brooklyn in the same period began working with the Englishman J. F. Bentley. And in another turnabout, Bentley was the architect for the new Westminster Cathedral that would replace the pro-cathedral designed by Goldie, earlier selected to design Newark's cathedral.

11. Fergusson, *History of Architecture in All Countries*, 2:158.

12. *Evening News*, November 18, 1897.

13. This seminal Gothic Revival church in Philadelphia was almost certainly known to Doane and O'Rourke.

14. The band also appears in Saint Wilfrid's plans published in *Building News*, May 2, 1873.

15. At Saint Colman's Cathedral the nave arcade, triforium passage, and clerestory cross the transepts. "Here, more than in any other Irish work, the architects intuited that sense of structure as a web of voided wall to which modern historians have given pre-eminent place as the distinguishing characteristic of medieval Gothic" (Douglas Richardson, *Gothic Revival Architecture in Ireland*, 502).

16. Modern commentators have cited this treatment approvingly as well. See C. M. Smart Jr., *Muscular Churches: Ecclesiastical Architecture in the High Victorian Period* (Fayetteville: University of Arkansas Press, 1989), 136–141. Note especially the Church of Saint Augustine, Kilburn Park, Paddington, London, designed by John Loughborough Pearson.

17. *Advertiser*, November 19, 1897. Also following quotation.

18. *Call*, March 30, 1902.

19. The rumor that Doane responded to probably related to possible land acquisition plans. See Kelsey, *First County Park System*, 82–87, 100–103, 150. Kelsey's informative screed about the Essex County Park system provides one perspective of this episode.

20. *Call*, March 30, 1902.

21. Quoted in Kelsey, *First County Park System*, 150. Doane's letter is dated January 9, 1897.

22. Kelsey, *First County Park System*, 286.

23. *Call*, October 5, 1904. This and the other *Sunday Call* letters quoted in this chapter also appear in *Letters of Monsignor George Hobart Doane* (Newark: Schultz and Gasser, 1905).

24. *Call*, March 30, 1902.

25. Doane to Wigger, July 12, 1897, ADN, RG 2.3, box 12.

26. *Call*, October 13, 1903.

13. Progress and Setbacks

1. *Evening News*, November 18, 1897. O'Rourke earlier enunciated the procedures for this type of work in his paper delivered at the 1893 World Congress of Architects in Chicago and reprinted in *AABN*, September 23, 1893, 183.

2. *Call*, March 5, 1899. The foundation walls are Pennsylvania brownstone, from Whitehaven or Hummelston, and more likely Whitehaven. A review of the cathedral's structural stonework is provided in Bernard A. Flanagan, "Survey of Stonework," January 28, 2011, Flanagan Papers.

3. The *Advertiser* reported that the parade was the largest public demonstration in the history of the city, aside from military marches. The *Evening News* of June 12, 1899, provided a detailed account of the cornerstone ceremony and preceding events.

4. *Evening News*, June 12, 1899, and following quotations of Bishop McQuaid at the cornerstone ceremony.

5. See the epilogue, and reference to Margaret Hoffman's note of February 7, 1977.

6. *Evening News*, June 10, 1899.

7. Separate contracts were given to another firm to supply and build the cathedral's steel work.

8. *Evening News*, January 31, 1942. Information about Edward Waldron's birthplace (in Ballyhaunnis, County Mayo) was provided by Elizabeth Waldron Mitchell. E-mail to author, May 14, 2011.

9. Norcross Brothers was eventually dropped in favor of Emerson Troy. In 1913, Webb Granite and Construction Company of Worcester became the granite supplier. Some of the confusion over the granite sources for Sacred Heart's principal walls occurs because in the historical record numerous quarry owners, agents, and operators are named without sufficient reference to their precise role; all were part of a supply chain traceable back to granite quarries in southern New Hampshire. Notably, Fitzwilliam granite would also be used in the new Howard Savings Institution building (1899), on whose board of managers O'Rourke served, and Newark City Hall (opened in 1906), constructed by Waldron's firm.

10. O'Rourke to O'Connor, September 30, 1902, ADN, RG 10.5, box 140.

11. Waldron to O'Connor, April 14, 1903, ADN, RG 10.5, box 159.

12. The bid was $317,841. The earlier contract was closed out; the balance to Waldron on that contract was $233,650.

13. *Call*, August 12, 1903.

14. *Call*, January 22, 1905, and the following quotations in this paragraph.

15. *Advertiser*, January 23, 1905.

16. *Advertiser*, January 25, 1905.

17. *The New Museum, Selected Writings by John Cotton Dana* (Newark, N.J: The Newark Museum; Washington, D.C.: American Association of Museums, 1999), 113.

18. This plan was indeed realized in a brick Tudor Revival building designed by the O'Rourke firm.

19. *New York Times*, February 24, 1902, and May 6, 1902.

20. Waldron substituted granite from Dummerston, Vermont.

21. O'Rourke to O'Connor. July 4, 1905, ADN, RG 10.5, box 140.

22. O'Rourke to O'Connor, August 17, 1905, ADN, RG 10.5, box 140.

23. O'Rourke to O'Connor, August 16, 1905, ADN, RG 10.5, box 140.

24. O'Rourke to O'Connor, August 12, 1905, ADN, RG 10.5, box 140.

25. O'Rourke to O'Connor, September 20, 1905, ADN, RG 10.5, box 140.

26. Joseph M. Flynn, *Catholic Church in New Jersey*, 347.

27. "Investiture Dinner for Monsignor Sheppard, October 18, 1903," ADN, RG 2.4, box 6: Vicar General John A. Sheppard Papers in Bishop O'Connor's Papers.

14. The Great Foundation Controversy

1. Quoted in Brady, "The Cathedral of the Sacred Heart in Newark, New Jersey," 23.

2. Ibid., 24.

3. The substituted material was Waldoboro, Maine, granite from quarries operated by Booth Brothers and Hurricane Island Granite Co.

4. O'Rourke to O'Connor, March 4, 1908, and O'Rourke to Waldron, December 1, 1908, ADN, RG 10.5, box 140. O'Rourke called it "illegitimate profit" in both letters.

5. In the period of the foundation crisis, Sheppard mediated two nasty entanglements over church building in other quarters. Both involved George Audsley, another competitor for the cathedral commission. In one, Waldron played a role. At parishes in Elizabeth and Bayonne, pastors retained Audsley, later deciding not to work with him, use his plans, or pay fully for his services. In Bayonne, the pastor settled on Audsley's design and was in conversation with, or had already hired, the Waldron firm to construct the church. For reasons that are unclear, the priest backed out of the Audsley agreement, and then Waldron helped find another architect for him. "Waldron it appears is the go-between, sending him the new architect, Poole & Co. of New York," Monsignor Sheppard wrote. "I guess this secures Waldron the work at least, or so this is how it appears to me. Waldron certainly is clever." Sheppard, "Journal," February 11, 1910.

6. O'Rourke to O'Connor, May 8, 1908, ADN, RG 10.5, box 166. Quoted in Brady, "The Cathedral of the Sacred Heart in Newark, New Jersey," 24. The original completion date was January 1908. It was postponed.

7. O'Rourke to Waldron, December 29, 1908, ADN, RG 10.5, box 166. Quoted in Brady, "The Cathedral of the Sacred Heart in Newark, New Jersey," 25.

8. One of Ditmars's buildings was the Church of the Immaculate Conception in Montclair, opened in 1907.

9. Sheppard to O'Connor, June 27, 1908, ADN, RG 10.5, box 166.

10. Brady, "The Cathedral of the Sacred Heart in Newark, New Jersey," 26.

11. O'Rourke to Sheppard, February 20, 1909, ADN, RG 10.5, box 166. Quoted in ibid.

12. Sheppard, "Journal," March 17, 1909.

13. Sheppard, "Journal," March 20, 1909.

14. Sheppard, "Journal," June 20, 1909. Sheppard mentioned a church in High Bridge and the Paulist Church in New York. But his hunt for evidence that supported his allegations was apparently unfruitful.

15. Sheppard, "Journal," April 7, 1909. This and the following quotations from Sheppard.

16. "Report Embodying the Decisions and Recommendations of Messrs. I. E. Ditmars and Fred L. Metcalf upon the Questions Referred to Them in the Agreements Made on the Twelfth Day of January 1909, between the Roman Catholic Diocese of Newark and the Right Reverend John J. O'Connor, D.D., Bishop of Said Diocese, Hereinafter Designated as the Owners, and Messrs Edward M. Waldron and Samuel P. Waldron, Co-partners, Trading as E. M. Waldron & Co., Hereinafter Designated the Contractors." Report dated April 6, 1909, ADN, RG 10.5, box 159.

17. The failures included the Ireland Building in 1895 and the Darlington Apartments in 1904, both in New York. See Donald Friedman, *Historical Building Construction: Design, Materials, and Technology* (New York: Norton, 1995), 41–50.

18. "Report Embodying the Decisions and Recommendations of Messrs. I. E. Ditmars and Fred L. Metcalf," 10–11.

19. Isaac Ditmars and Fred Metcalf, "Memoranda Supplementary to the Report of April 6, 1909," 3. ADN, RG 10.5, box 159.

20. Ibid.

21. Sheppard, "Journal," July 9, 1909.

22. Ibid., this and the following quotation.

23. Ibid.

24. Ibid.

25. Sheppard, "Journal," July 14, 1909.

26. Sheppard, "Journal," July 15, 1909.

27. Sheppard, "Journal," July 19, 1909.

28. Sheppard, "Journal," July 22, 1909.

29. Sheppard, "Journal," August 21, 1909.

30. Sheppard, "Journal," September 9, 1909.

31. Quoted in Sheppard, "Journal," September 11, 1909.

32. Sheppard, "Journal," September 13, 1909.

33. This included findings of the Foundation Company, based in New York.

34. Sheppard, "Journal," October 1909. The exact date is unclear: the entry falls between those on September 27 and October 26, 1909.

35. Sheppard, "Journal," November 12, 1909.

36. *Evening News*, November 15, 1909.

37. Paul C. Reilly, "Architects for the Cathedral of the Sacred Heart, Newark, New Jersey. Footnote(s) 6," n.d., ca. 1971, 3. ADN, RG 10.5, box 141.

38. After Ditmars's death in 1934, his children gave a gift of art in memory of him and his wife, Isabel Peck Ditmars, to Saint Paul's Episcopal Church (Flatbush) in Brooklyn, suggesting that Ditmars or his wife (or both) were Episcopalians. *Brooklyn Daily Eagle*, May 5, 1934.

39. Sheppard, "Journal," December 23, 1909.

40. Sheppard, "Journal," January 26, 1910. Sheppard cites the letter from Bishop O'Connor to O'Rourke.

41. Sheppard, "Journal," January 31, 1910.

42. Sheppard, "Journal," February 3, 1910. Also following quotation.

43. Sheppard, "Journal," February 11, 1910.

44. The sons were probably Joseph and Louis O'Rourke.

45. O'Brien was an employee of Westinghouse, Church-Kerr, a leading engineering firm retained for the Pennsylvania Station project. He had worked on the project since the start of construction.

46. *Evening News*, February 22, 1910.

47. Sheppard, "Journal," February 23, 1909. Also following quotation.

48. *Evening News*, February 22, 1910.

49. Ibid. Also following quotations in this paragraph.

50. Ibid. Also following quotations in the paragraph.

51. Ibid.

52. Sheppard, "Journal," February 23, 1910. Also following quotation.

53. Sheppard, "Journal," February 26, 1910.

54. Sheppard, "Journal," March 5, 1910.

55. Quoted in Brady, "The Cathedral of the Sacred Heart in Newark, New Jersey," 29.

56. Sheppard, "Journal," April 22, 1910.

57. Quoted in Brady, "The Cathedral of the Sacred Heart in Newark, New Jersey," 29.

58. Sheppard, "Journal," April 30, 1910.

59. Sheppard, "Journal," May 4, 1910.
60. *Evening News*, July 29, 1910.

15. New Architect and New Era

1. "Specifications of Work and Materials to Be Furnished for Taking Down the Granite Shafts, Bases, and Foundation Piers of the Nave and Chancel Columns of the Cathedral of the Sacred Heart at Newark, N.J., the Roman Catholic Diocese of Newark, Owner, and Rebuilding Same as Herein-after Specified and in Accordance with Drawings Prepared by I. E. Ditmars, Consulting Architect, 111 Fifth Avenue, New York City," ADN, RG 10.5, box 159.

2. As built, Sacred Heart's main columns are composed of the following: all capitals are granite from Waldoboro, Maine; apse shafts are granite from Jonesport, Maine (Moose à bec red); apse bases are granite from Rockport, Massachusetts (sea green); the nave shafts and bases are granite from Dummerston, Vermont.

3. Doane, *To and From the Passion Play*, 283.

4. Photographs of the capitals that served as models can be found in Paul Vitry, *La cathedrale de Rheims: Architecture et sculpture* (Paris: Librarie Centrale des Beaux-Arts, 1919), 2; plate 96, "Chapiteau d'un des piliers de la nef." Reference Collection, Morgan Library & Museum. The photography for this two-volume work preceded the war.

5. I. E. Ditmars, "The Cathedral of the Sacred Heart, Newark, New Jersey," *Architectural Record* 59, no. 6 (June 1926): 502.

6. Ibid.

7. Schickel's Saint Patrick's Church in Elizabeth, whose facade is a reduction of Cologne Cathedral and its imitations, showed a similar willingness to mimic specific models. Ditmars's later references to Sacred Heart's architecture as "French-Irish-Medieval Gothic" created a hybrid that commentators over the years seized on to describe the cathedral's style, but it is confusing and inaccurate terminology.

8. The photograph is preserved in NPL, Sacred Heart Cathedral photography files, and is reproduced in this book. After a long, fruitless search for a photograph of architect Isaac Ditmars, the author visited the Holland Society of New York, where he had been a member. The energetic response of a librarian there, Mary Collins, resulted in contact with Ditmars's descendant, John R. Ditmars, and through him it was possible to identify Isaac Ditmars in this historic photograph.

9. The bishop's portrait medallions were replaced in a later phase, though photographs of Walsh's work show it to be equal or superior to what replaced it. The photographs are preserved in NPL, Sacred Heart Cathedral photography files.

10. Building progress was marred by two fatal accidents. Late on a winter afternoon in 1913, Alexander Johnson, a stonecutter and the representative of the granite company in Worcester, who was in charge of the stonework, lost his footing and plunged 40 feet. In pitiable condition, but conscious and adrenalin-filled, he gave his office keys to the foreman and told those huddled around him what work should be done; he died the next morning in City Hospital. In 1914, a twenty-three-year-old laborer, Daniel Sullivan, dropped from a spot 30 feet above the ground. Taken unconscious to Saint Michael's Hospital, he died the same night. His requiem was sung a few days later in the little Sacred Heart Church, a stone's throw from where he fell. The Johnson accident occurred about March 13, 1913; the Sullivan accident occurred September 22, 1914. Newspaper clippings, NPL.

11. Among O'Rourke's last projects was the Church of Saint Vincent Martyr in Madison, inspired by Pugin's Saint Barnabas Cathedral (which Doane and O'Rourke had

visited in 1870) and Ralph Adams Cram's writing; also a church for Saint Elizabeth's parish in Avon by the Sea that reprised the style he favored for his earliest commissions.

12. *Star-Ledger*, April 27, 1915 and quotations in the next sentence.

13. *Star-Ledger*, May 20, 1915.

14. Dominic Walsh of Belleville, N.J., hoped to receive the commission for doing future modeling, but Ditmars was not satisfied with his work and engaged Rochette & Parzini. Walsh's letters of appeal to Ditmars from 1911 to 1912 are in files held in a storage room in Sacred Heart Cathedral's basement.

15. Thomas E. Hergert was specified as the designer in the Rochette & Parzini contract for roof ornamentation, including the figures on the flèche.

16. The diocese regarded the cathedral-in-progress as protected from property tax on the grounds that, as a religious institution, it was tax-exempt. It based its claims on the intended use of the building, the fact that the cornerstone blessing had been a religious service, and the occurrence of an annual event held on site by the Church-affiliated Holy Name Society. When court action failed, diocesan interests advanced a bill in the state legislature to spare taxes on such buildings while under construction. Pushed through the Assembly by sympathetic legislators, it was defeated in the Senate. The diocese therefore planned the annual services for parochial schoolchildren.

17. *Evening News*, May 1, 1914.

18. *Sunday Call*, clipped article notated "1916," without month or day. Flanagan Papers.

19. In 1908, a connection to Manhattan via Hoboken was opened, and by 1910, a Manhattan–Jersey City–Newark link was established.

16. Boom and Bust Again

1. *Evening News*, November 26, 1922.

2. The roundels over the portal doors of the tower carry reliefs of Christ crowned with thorns on the Gesu tower and Our Lady of Sorrows on the Mary tower.

3. Brady, "The Cathedral of the Sacred Heart in Newark, New Jersey," 38. Forwarded to the diocese were evaluations from the Bureau of Standards of the Department of Commerce in Washington that gave disinterested support for the argument, describing terra cotta as "permanent if not more so as any other structural material . . . particularly . . . in large tracery windows." See "Bibliography of Architectural Terra Cotta," Architectural Conservation Laboratory, Graduate Program in Historic Preservation, University of Pennsylvania, 2001.

4. Ditmars to O'Connor, April 16, 1921, ADN, RG 10.5, box 166.

5. Ibid.

6. Quinn, *The Irish in New Jersey*, 163.

7. Ditmars to Sheppard, November 15, 1924, ADN, RG 10.5, box 166.

8. *Evening News*, January 20, 1925. See also *Evening News*, January 21, 22, and 31, 1925.

9. Brady, "The Cathedral of the Sacred Heart in Newark, New Jersey," 46–47. This episode with Cram is described in Brady's manuscript, but the correspondence on which it is based has not been found by the author. Brady was a meticulous researcher and writer; it is likely that the letters have been misplaced or lost. There are no documents in the Cram archive at the Boston Public Library. However, the exchange between Duffy and Cram may have been partially off the record, in that Duffy was seeking expert guidance and perhaps without the knowledge of Ditmars. Brady states that contact was made with Cram beginning in January 1926.

10. "Paul C. Reilly, Architect and a Catholic Lay Leader," *New York Times*, September 13, 1984.

11. Paul C. Reilly joined Ditmars in 1926.

12. Brady, "The Cathedral of the Sacred Heart in Newark, New Jersey," 48.

13. Fine and Peterson, who also worked on the Cathedral of Saint John the Divine in New York, were the engineering consultants and would be called in again during a later building phase.

14. The crypt altar was provided by the Benziger firm of New York.

15. Brady, "The Cathedral of the Sacred Heart in Newark, New Jersey," 44. Bishop Wigger was buried in Holy Sepulcher Cemetery; his remains were transferred to Sacred Heart Cathedral's crypt in 1989. Monsignor Sheppard looked to the crypt in Saint Patrick's in New York as a model for Newark, though Ditmars found it less satisfactory.

16. Bishop O'Connor died May 25, 1927.

17. Quoted in Brady, "Sacred Heart Cathedral in Newark, New Jersey," 53.

18. I. E. Ditmars, "The Cathedral of the Sacred Heart, Newark, New Jersey," *Architectural Record* 59, no. 6 (June 1926): 501–511.

19. *Star-Ledger*, April 8, 1928. Also following quotations.

20. Cram, *Church Building*, 164–165. The altar was replaced in 1942 and then adapted for use in the Fordham University Chapel.

21. Brady, "The Cathedral of the Sacred Heart in Newark, New Jersey," 56. Fathers John A. O'Brien, Cornelius Clifford, and Edward O'Malley were the clergy. According to Brady, the architects who reviewed the plans were Wilfrid E. Anthony, E. Durang (probably F. Ferdinand Durang Sr., formerly partner with his father, Edwin F. Durang, who died in 1911), Robert J. Reilly, and Joseph Shanley. Gonippo Raggi was among the designers agreed on in a preliminary meeting, but he appears not to have reviewed the plans.

22. Wister, *Stewards of the Mysteries of God*, 195.

23. The settlement payment was shared with Paul Reilly. Ditmars clearly felt he was owed more by the diocese. Although he may have felt financially squeezed at various times, he was not without means. He sent his son to Phillips Exeter and Harvard; his daughter married a successful attorney. At probate, Ditmars's estate was valued at $137,322; his wife had died less than a year before him, and her estate may have increased his own. *Herald Statesman* (Yonkers, N.Y.), January 18, 1935.

17. Regional Developments and Twentieth-Century Cathedral Building

1. The numbers of new parishes by county were as follows: twelve in Bergen County, nine in Passaic, eight in Essex, six in Union, three in Morris, and only two in Hudson, which included Jersey City. In the five years after 1921, most of the new parishes in the diocese were founded in newly settled or rapidly growing places.

2. Donald Wolf, *Crossing the Hudson: Historic Bridges and Tunnels of the River* (New Brunswick, N.J.: Rutgers University Press, 2010), 106–150.

3. At one time, 20 percent of all jobs in New Jersey had been in Newark; now 5 percent were.

4. Leonard Ellinwood, *The History of American Church Music* (New York: Morehouse-Graham Co., 1953), 228. Nicola A. Montani (1880–1948) founded the Society of Saint Gregory, dedicated to fostering Catholic liturgical music in the spirit of the reforms of Pius X's *Motu Proprio*. He edited and contributed to the popular *Saint Gregory Hymnal*. Montani offered educational programs on sacred music to Newark's priests and seminarians and religious sisters, who, in turn, brought what they learned to their parishes and schools.

5. Archives of the Diocese of Pittsburgh, e-mail to author, October 26, 2011. The Diocese of Pittsburgh spent another $155,000 on art, sacred vessels, vestments, and other appointments.

6. Whitney Warren of New York succeeded Masqueray as architect. Maginnis and Walsh also worked on the Minneapolis cathedral. Early estimates state that it was intended to cost $1.2 million, but much more was spent before it was ostensibly complete.

7. Archives of the Archdiocese of St. Paul and Minneapolis, e-mail to author, October 26, 2011.

8. The Cathedral of Saint Cecilia in Omaha is large: 244 feet long, 158 feet wide, with a tower reaching 222 feet. When finished in 1959, about $2 million had been spent on it.

9. Archives of the Diocese of Toledo, e-mail to author, October 25, 2011.

10. Archives of the Archdiocese of St. Louis, e-mail to author, October 24, 2011.

11. Archives of the Diocese of St. Helena, e-mail to author, October 27, 2011. The cathedral opened in 1914; by 1917, $645,000 had been spent on it. It was consecrated in 1924.

12. Morgan, *The Almighty Wall*, 73–85.

13. The small portion of the Philadelphia project that was completed eventually became a local Episcopal parish, Saint Mary's Church, Andorra; a retirement center called Cathedral Village was later also developed on the site. Saint Mary's Church, Andorra (Philadelphia) e-mail to author, October 21, 2010.

14. James F. O'Gorman, ed., *The Makers of Trinity Church in the City of Boston* (Amherst: University of Massachusetts Press, 2004), 175–177.

15. Saint Catherine of Genoa Church in Somerville, Mass., became especially influential.

18. Resolve

1. Charles Maginnis was by now advanced in years, though he remained active in the practice and new principals had joined the firm; Timothy Walsh had died in 1934.

2. "Many Sided Architect," *Newark Sunday News*, September 19, 1954.

3. Reilly worked very effectively in Gothic for the schemes of Our Lady of Good Counsel in Newark and Saint Paul's Church in Clifton, N.J., and in Colonial Revival for Queen of Peace Church in North Arlington, N.J.

4. The Accademia Nazionale di San Luca is the modern successor of the institution where Raggi studied. Raggi's entry in the *American Catholic Who's Who*, presumably supplied by the designer himself, states that he graduated from "Saint Luke's Royal Academy" in 1897 and later taught at "Saint Michael's Institute of Art," also in Rome. *American Catholic Who's Who*, 1950 and 1951 ed. (Gross Pointe, Mich.: Walter Romig—Publisher, 1951), 9:385. Biographical information on Raggi is also found in Patricia Colrick, ed., *A Centennial History of Saint Catherine Church* (Franklin, Tenn.: Providence House Publishers, 2001), 45–47; and Margherita Marchione, M.P.F., *A Pictorial History of the Saint Lucy Filippini Chapel* (Edizioni Del Palazzo, 1992), 48–50.

5. Colrick, *Saint Catherine Church*, 23–27. Also, Thomas J. Shahan, *Saint Catharine's* [*sic*] *Church: Maloney Memorial* (New York: William H. Sandler, 1928).

6. Raggi's other major commissions include Saint Josephat Basilica, Milwaukee, Wis.; and Saint Peter's Cathedral, Scranton, Pa. Bishop Walsh recommended Raggi for a commission at the shrine of Our Lady of Victory in Lackawanna, N.Y. Locally, Raggi decorated Our Lady of Good Counsel Church, Saint Lucy's Church, and Saint Patrick's

Pro-Cathedral in Newark; the archdiocesan seminary chapel at Darlington; Saint Aloysius Church in Jersey City; and the Saint Lucy Filippini Chapel at Villa Walsh in Morristown.

7. Cecilia D. Iannaccone, "Artistry and Inspiration of Saint Catharine Church," in *Centennial History of Saint Catharine Church*, ed. Colrick, 45. Raggi's contributions to Saint Catharine's decorative scheme spanned several decades.

8. *New York Times*, April 1, 1934. For many years, Cardinal Lauri was a theology professor in Rome who taught, and later helped advance the careers of, two young men who went on to become among the American Church's most powerful cardinals, George Mundelein and Dennis Dougherty. Pertinent to this story about Newark, Dennis Cardinal Dougherty was a mentor of Thomas Walsh.

9. *Citizen* (Orange, N.J.), February 19, 1942. Also Flanagan Papers.

10. *Evening News*, newspaper clipping dated October 8, 1941, NPL.

11. "Raggi, Back from Rome, with New Honors, Pleads for More Originality in Church Art," *New York Times*, April 1, 1934. His interview for this article was one of many media opportunities that Raggi took to promote a higher level of artistry in church commissions; they were aimed at artists and also meant to encourage clergy to fund commissions.

12. Newspaper clipping, n.d., c. 1935 about Raggi's work at Saint Peter's Cathedral in Scranton, Flanagan Papers.

13. Ibid.

14. Citizen (Orange, N.J.), February 19, 1942.

15. Reilly was thus also responsible for the statuary in the three interior portals, although production of other statuary came under Raggi's supervision.

16. Ernesto (Ernest) and Luigi (Louis) Raggi were the given names of the Raggi sons. The Raggi studio was in the former Masonic Building, at 235 Main Street.

17. "Many Sided Architect," *Newark Sunday News*, September 19, 1954.

18. *Newark Sunday News*, September 19, 1954.

19. It is hard to account for Reilly's reference to visiting Spain for study. However, Ralph Adams Cram was beguiled by Spanish Gothic and wrote persuasively about it; Cram's design for Sacred Heart Church in Jersey City referred to Spanish Gothic. Also, as noted, a Spanish historicist style was used for cathedrals in Omaha and Toledo. But if there is any influence from Spanish Gothic on Reilly's Newark cathedral work, it is highly nuanced.

20. The auxiliary bishop who had oversight of the cathedral project in the previous phase of active work, John A. Duffy, left Newark in 1933 to become bishop of Syracuse.

21. Paul C. Reilly, "Architects for Cathedral of the Sacred Heart, Newark, New Jersey," c. 1971, 4–5, typescript, six pages, ADN, RG 10.5, box 141.

22. The minimum contribution for membership in the Cathedral Builders Association was $60.

23. "Campaign Procedures," March 25, 1950, and accompanying, "Suggested Outline for Sermon for the Cathedral Builders Association," ADN, RG 10.5, box 140.

24. "Campaign Procedures," March 25, 1950. Files related to the campaign hold items reflecting some degree of dissonance about the cathedral fund-raising, particularly dustups in Fort Lee and Hackensack, ADN, RG 10.5, box 140.

25. "A Personal Message," 4–6. Published in *The Lay Memorial Committee of the Cathedral Builders Association*, pamphlet, eight pages, ADN, RG 10.5, box 140. The largest gifts available for naming were the organ ($75,000), the nave rose window ($57,400), and the main altar ($50,000); the smallest memorial gifts eligible for naming

were individual pews ($500 each). Ultimately, these features were underwritten by the fund-raising campaign but carried no permanent named designations.

26. January 30, 1950, memorandum from the Archdiocesan Committee to clergy about a meeting held on January 24, 1950. Also a memorandum dated March 30, 1950, ADN, RG 10.5, box 140. See also Wister, *Stewards of the Mysteries of God*, 152–155; Wister provides an account of Archbishop Walsh's approach to the earlier fund-raising for Immaculate Conception Seminary, upon which the cathedral campaign was generally patterned.

27. *A Golden Jubilee Message*, n.d., 2, pamphlet, four pages, ADN, RG 10.5, box 140.

28. Ibid., 3, passage credited to Hon. John J. Breslin.

29. Ibid., passage credited to John J. McManus Jr.

30. *A Golden Jubilee Message*, 4.

31. *Advocate*, March 22, 1952.

32. Sacred Heart's iconographic schemes suggest that the planners almost certainly studied Emile Mâle's influential scholarship on the art and architecture of the Middle Ages. Mâle's seminal work was *L'art religieux du XIIIe siècle en France*, a thesis dating from 1899 and translated into English as *The Gothic Image: Religious Art in France of the Thirteenth Century; A Study in Medieval Iconography and Its Sources of Inspiration* (London: Dent & Co., 1910, 1913; reprint, New York: Icon Editions, 1972). The Flanagan Papers contain diverse materials related specifically to Sacred Heart Cathedral's iconography.

19. Interior Scheme: Artistry from Here and Abroad

1. The reredos-style altar had been intended to be placed above the main level of the sanctuary.

2. Erwin Panofsky, *Tomb Sculpture* (London: Phaidon Press, 1992), fig. 398.

3. The canopy on the cathedra in Saint Patrick's Cathedral in New York, as well as its sanctuary screen, appear to have also served as a starting point for Raggi's designs for their counterparts in Newark.

4. I. E. Ditmars, "The Cathedral of the Sacred Heart, Newark, New Jersey," *Architectural Record* 59, no. 6 (June 1926): 511.

5. The plan of the narthex screen resembles the late Gothic portal of Saint-Maclou in Rouen, France. The changes from the 1930 design, bringing a multiplication of Gothic devices, spreading canopies, and a thickening of the individual masonry ornaments (fleurs de lis and crocketing, for example), expanded substantially on the original conception.

6. Cram, *Church Building*, 144.

7. Raguin, *Stained Glass from Its Origins to the Present*, 200–210. Also, *Stained Glass* 48, no. 2 (Summer 1953): 105–106. And, Bernard A. Flanagan's correspondence with the German stained-glass artisans or their descendants, Flanagan Papers.

8. Braunmiller lived from 1905 to 1993; Karl Jung was born in 1908 and died in 1989. Flanagan Papers.

9. "Louis Raggi, Professor Gonippo Raggi," February 29, 1952. Copy of typescript, five pages, ADN, RG 10.5, box 141.

10. Sara Brown, *Stained Glass: An Illustrated History* (London: Studio Editions, 1992), 22.

11. In discussions and written materials about the cathedral project, Raggi tended to make opaque the role played by the Zettler artists, as he did other artists and artisans who worked on the cathedral project under his supervision, with the exception of Aurelio

Mistruzzi. The design development and production process for the windows was detailed in a long series in the *Advocate*, the archdiocesan newspaper, and in voluminous publicity about finishing the cathedral, but the German artists who painted every stroke and wash of Sacred Heart's windows appear to have passed unrecognized.

12. Adrian A. Maine to James A. McNulty, October 22, 1951. Quoted in Gubernat, "Histories of Sacred Heart Cathedral," 81.

13. Schantz's bid called for 149 stops and 8,689 pipes for $138,324; Casavant's included 109 stops and 6,412 pipes for $129,000.

14. Paul C. Reilly, "By Mr. Paul C. Reilly, Architect," October 23, 1952, 1. Copy of typescript, five pages, ADN, RG 10.5, box 141.

15. "Paul C. Reilly, Architect." February 29, 1952, 13. Copy of typescript, thirteen pages, ADN, RG 10.5, box 141.

16. "By Mr. Paul C. Reilly," 4.

17. Bowden and Hitchcock was the specialty carving firm.

18. *Stone: The Magazine of the Natural Building Stone Industry* (December 1953). The trade journal dedicated an entire issue to the Newark project, covering stone sources, design, and production details; photographs helpfully illustrate the carving process.

19. "Indiana Limestone Work Important in Cathedral Job," October 9, 1954, newspaper clipping, NPL.

20. Louis Raggi, "Notes from Louis Raggi and His Father on Main Altar, Sacred Heart Cathedral," n.d., 3. Copy of typescript, eight pages, ADN, RG 10.5, box 141.

21. Eric Scigliano, *Michelangelo's Mountain: The Quest for Perfection in the Marble Quarries of Carrara* (New York: Free Press, 2005), 192. Scigliano provides a vivid history of the quarrying of statuary marble in northwestern Italy.

22. Eight of the Italian-carved statues of Indiana limestone are in the screen facing the nave; the ninth, Our Lady of Victories, is in the narthex proper.

23. Louis Raggi, "Notes from Louis Raggi and His Father on Main Altar, Sacred Heart Cathedral," n.d., 7. Copy of typescript, eight pages, ADN, RG 10.5, box 141.

24. Floyd Anderson, "The Main Altar: Sacred Heart Cathedral," newspaper clipping from the *Advocate*, 1954, NPL.

25. Joseph Campo to Thomas A. Boland, November 25, 1953, ADN RG 10.5, box 141; also following quotation. By the time Campo made this appeal, the sculpture was effectively complete.

26. Fred Tangorra to Francis Cardinal Spellman, June 1, 1953; the letter was forwarded from Cardinal Spellman's office in New York to the Newark Chancery, ADN, RG 10.5, box 141.

27. Reilly described the engineering solutions in general terms in Paul C. Reilly, "Answers to Mr. Donald W. Geyer's Questionnaire and Letter Dated October 6, 1971 Concerning the Cathedral of the Sacred Heart, Newark, N.J.," 2–3. Copy of typescript, eight pages, ADN, RG 10.5, box 141; "Paul C. Reilly, Architect," February 29, 1952, 9, ADN, RG 10.5, box 141. Reilly gave credit for this structural solution to R. D. Fine, who had worked with Fine and Peterson on Sacred Heart in the 1920s. (Donald Geyer was preparing material for nominating Sacred Heart Cathedral to the National Register of Historic Places.)

28. This explanation is also given in Reilly, "Answers," 3.

20. Complete at Last

1. The form of the pulpit's tester or canopy may descend from one in the choir of Canterbury Cathedral

2. James A. McNulty, homily at the dedication of Sacred Heart Cathedral, October 19, 1954. Quoted in John O'Hara, *Cathedral of the Sacred Heart, Newark, N.J.* (Newton, N.J.: C. Harrison Conroy Co., n.d.), 2.

3. Assertions soon arose that the marble had been worked so that a vein running through it represented the crucified Christ's pierced side, but the designer and the carvers did not make this claim.

4. Bernard Flanagan suggests that the theme for the south transept (geographically facing east) derives from the Canticle of Saint Luke (Luke 1:68–79), in Catholic use, a prayer indicated for the morning office. This would be appropriate for the side of the cathedral on which the sun rises.

5. Bernard Flanagan correctly notes the similarity of the Saint Peter and Saint Paul statues in the transept screens with figures in the Scott Memorial on the facade of Saint Thomas Church, Fifth Avenue, New York. The latter were sculpted by Theodore Barbarossa, associated with Rochette and Parzini, pointing to him as possibly participating in the figural sculpting of Sacred Heart's transept screens. See J. Robert Wright, *Saint Thomas Church Fifth Avenue* (Grand Rapids, Mich.: William B. Eerdmans Publishing Co.; New York: Saint Thomas Church, 2001), 188–189.

6. The north transept screen occasioned difficult choices because it mixed living and deceased prelates, and all were essentially modeled from photographs, sometimes not doing full justice to the distinct personalities it honors. The homogeneity of these stone portraits is exaggerated by rendering the standing figures in cassocks draping to the base of the sculpture.

7. Bernard Flanagan observes that the cathedral model that Walsh holds does not have the two types of Gothic arches that rise on the actual towers.

8. Louis Raggi to Anne Mae Buckley, *Advocate* reporter, October 15, 1959, ADN, RG 10.5, box, 141.

9. Ditmars, as described in chapter 15, had done something similar in his treatment of the design of the towers.

10. The woodwork was part of Raggi's contract. But as with the stained glass artists, the artisans passed unrecognized by the Raggis and the archdiocese. The record points to the involvement of the firm of Irving & Casson—A. H. Davenport, Co. of Boston and New York. Two small drawings and notations by this firm for a pew detail and choir seating are among the Raggi files in ADN, RG 10.5, box 166, labeled "DWG 200" and "DWG 201." Irving & Casson executed Sacred Heart's pews; it probably executed the screens; and may well have sculpted the wooden statues. It did a similar screen in the sanctuary of Saint Patrick's Cathedral in New York, installed in 1929 and designed by Maginnis and Walsh and local architect Robert J. Reilly (not Paul C. Reilly) as well as producing the woodwork for Saint Patrick's organ case, including six large angel figures. The elaborate screen and woodwork in the chancel of Saint Thomas Church, Fifth Avenue, installed in the 1920s, was also executed by Irving & Casson to designs of Bertram Goodhue.

11. Raggi's intention to convey symbolism in the Lady Chapel's appointments was expressed in the altar's slender form and intense whiteness, and in crystal chandeliers. Also, the statue's manner is in the vein of Marian piety descending from nineteenth-century devotional Catholicism; Raggi here did not exercise the emotive restraint with which he composed the other chapels.

12. The Religious Teachers Filippini first came to New Jersey in 1910, to the Diocese of Trenton, when Thomas Walsh was bishop there. Their motherhouse in Morristown was later renamed for their patron-bishop as Villa Walsh.

13. The idea to use crystal chandeliers in Newark may have been partially inspired by a large one hanging in the ambulatory of Saint John the Divine in New York, a gift of the Czechoslovakian government in 1927.

14. Oscar Zettler and his son Michael to Bernard A. Flanagan, February 10, 1991, Flanagan Papers. The Zettlers wrote: "Karl Jung drew the three large rose windows, the nave windows with group scenes, the five sanctuary windows, the Lady Chapel windows, and the upper nave windows, with ornaments. Franz Xaver Braunmiller drew the large figures of saints below the three large rose windows, all the figural windows in the chapels, and the cartoons for the fourteen large stations of the cross, executed in glass-mosaic." The correspondence between Zettler and Flanagan also speculates on which artist worked on the various windows in addition to the major groupings.

15. Karl Jung to Michael Zettler, forwarded to Bernard A. Flanagan, June 4, 1988, in response to a April 22, 1988, inquiry by Flanagan, Flanagan Papers. Jung stated that he used no models.

16. The design for these altar stations appears to derive from Maginnis & Walsh's 1927 shrine altar of Saint Teresa of the Infant Jesus, in Saint Patrick's Cathedral in New York. Although the barren effect Ditmars hoped to avoid in the previous generation was indeed forestalled, one could claim that the altar-station solution unnecessarily crowds the nave aisles and that these altars are of uncertain sacramental purpose.

17. The largest bell is 5 feet in diameter and weighs more than 4,500 pounds. The lowest note of the set is B-natural, followed by a chromatic octave from C to C. The fundamental tone of each bell is favored above its overtone series, making them ideal for playing hymns and other melodies.

18. Gonippo Raggi, press release, April 17, 1956, "Subject: Bronze Doors at Main Entrance and at the Towers." Typescript, one page, ADN, RG 10.5, box 141. Biographical information on Mistruzzi is found in Elvira Eliza Clain-Stefanelli, "Italian Coin Engravers since 1800," *Publications of the United States National Museum*, Bulletin no. 29: Contributions from the Museum of History and Technology, Paper 33 (Washington, D.C.: Smithsonian Institution, 1970), 55–59; and in his obituary in the *New York Times*, December 27, 1960.

19. Gonippo Raggi, press release, April 17, 1956, "Subject: Bronze Doors at Main Entrance and at the Towers." Typescript, one page, ADN, RG 10.5, box 141.

20. *Advocate*, April 3, 1954.

21. Gonippo Raggi, press release, April 17, 1956.

Epilogue

1. *New York Herald Tribune*, March 20, 1954. Claims over the years that Sacred Heart is larger than Saint Patrick's Cathedral in New York are unfounded.

2. James F. Johnson, "Newark Archdiocese Cathedral Completed," *Tablet* (Brooklyn, N.Y.), n.d., 1954, newspaper clipping, Flanagan Papers. The Flanagan Papers also contain letters from Johnson to Flanagan with opinionated, though discriminating, commentary about historic and twentieth-century American Catholic church architecture.

3. The cathedral rectory, also designed by Paul C. Reilly, was also completed after the cathedral's 1954 opening.

4. The tabernacle was given to Our Lady of Mount Carmel Church in Ridgewood.

5. Bernard A. Flanagan, transcript of interview with Emily DiFonzo, June 3, 1980, Flanagan Papers.

6. Margaret Hoffman to the Archdiocese of Newark, February 7, 1977, ADN, RG 10.5, box 140.

7. The 1930s remedial project on the Hartford cathedral totaled $1 million and included the addition of exterior features. The cathedral was totally destroyed by fire in 1956.

8. Sheppard, "Journal," June 15, 1909.

9. O'Rourke's burial instructions were found too late to be honored.

10. Brady, "The Cathedral of the Sacred Heart in Newark, New Jersey," 21.

11. Attributed variously to the philosopher G.W.F. Hegel and playwright C. F. Hebbel.

12. Louis O'Rourke left the firm in 1905 to form Kitchell & O'Rourke, Architects. William P. O'Rourke left in 1907 to head the City of Newark's Building Department.

13. Sheppard, "Journal," May 27, 1909.

14. Sheppard, "Journal," December 17, 1909.

15. Sheppard, "Journal," December 29, 1909, and following quotation.

16. *Star-Ledger*, April 27, 1915.

17. *New York Times*, October 2, 1995.

GLOSSARY

See appendix A for a floor plan of Sacred Heart Cathedral.

aisle. Part of a church parallel to the nave and divided from it by an arcade of columns, thus providing a passageway.

altar. Stone or wood table that is the most important item in a church because the Eucharist is celebrated on it.

ambulatory. A processional aisle around the apse, surrounding the altar and giving access to chapels.

apse. Part of a church projecting from the east or altar end, semicircular or polygonal in shape. *See also* chancel.

arcade. Series of arches supported by columns.

arch. Masonry construction for spanning an opening and supporting the weight above it. Arches can be rounded or pointed. Pointed arches are found in Gothic architecture.

archbishop. Head of an archdiocese.

archdiocese. Diocese under an archbishop's jurisdiction, usually with general oversight of other dioceses.

baldachin. Ornamental canopy over an altar.

baptistery. Portion of a church for conducting the sacrament of baptism, the initiation rite for Christians; it contains the font used in performing the rite.

Baroque. Style of architecture in Europe during the seventeenth and eighteenth centuries. Based on Renaissance style, it is more ornamental and elaborate.

bay. Unit of division marking the space between columns or vertical elements.

Beaux Arts. Style of architecture influenced by the teaching at the École des Beaux-Arts in Paris, often monumental, with elaborate classical features. Popular in the United States beginning in the late nineteenth century.

bell cote. Small structure over the gable of a church for holding a bell.

boss. Projecting ornament covering the intersection of the ribs of a vault at its apex.

buttress. Vertical element supporting or giving stability to a wall, tower, or other structural feature.

capital. Projecting, carved feature on the top of a column or similar vertical element.

cathedral. The mother church of a diocese in which the bishop's chair, or *cathedra*, is located.

chancel. The east end of a church, which holds the main altar. It usually has a flat east wall. *See also* apse.

chapel. Larger Catholic churches have secondary altars, and if these are located in a separate space, they are called chapels. Also, a church for use by a distinct community, such as a school or college.

clerestory. Upper stage of the walls of a church holding glass, usually stained glass.

colonnade. Series of regularly spaced columns giving support to a structure over it.

column. An upright member supporting the structure above it. It transmits, through compression, the weight above it to structural elements below, such as foundations.

crocket. Carved projections in the form of leaves found on Gothic spires and pinnacles.

crossing. Where the transepts cross a church's main axis.

cruciform. Building in the shape of a Latin cross.

crypt. In cathedrals, chamber located beneath the sanctuary in which deceased bishops are entombed.

curvilinear tracery. Later Gothic tracery of more complex, curving forms than geometric tracery.

Decorated Gothic. Style of architecture characterized by its window *tracery*, simple at first (geometric) and more flowing (curvilinear) in later Gothic.

diocese. The territory over which a bishop has ecclesiastical jurisdiction.

ecclesiastical. Of, or related to, the Church.

ecclesiology. In an architectural context, the study of medieval church buildings associated with nineteenth-century Ecclesiological Societies. These groups promoted the revived use of Gothic style.

facade. The face of a building, usually the front, though sometimes the sides or rear.

finial. Ornament on the top of a gable, spire, pinnacle, and the like.

Flamboyant. A style of elaborate tracery found in late French Gothic architecture. Amiens Cathedral's rose window is Flamboyant. Some of the tracery in Sacred Heart's interior screens and other carving is Flamboyant.

flèche. Tall, slender spire, usually of copper, rising from the ridge of a church roof.

floriated. Treated with flower-like ornament.

gable. Upper part of a wall, triangular in shape, and carrying a pitched roof. Also, a feature of similar shape.

geometric tracery. Gothic tracery of simple patterns, using bars and devices based on the circle.

Gothic construction. Architectural form and style that flourished in Europe from the twelfth through fifteenth centuries. Pointed arches, rib vaulting or exposed roof supports, and window tracery are its chief architectural features. Also, later buildings in this style.

hammerbeam. Cantilevered beam supporting a roof structure.

iconography. Traditional symbolic forms or imagery associated with a subject.

lancet. Slim window ending in a simple pointed arch.

liturgical. Having to do with the worship services of a church.

liturgical east, west, north, south. Within a church, tradition places the altar at the east end, making the west end usually the location of the main entry. Facing the altar, north is to the left and south to the right.

lobe. A rounded or circular projection. A quatrefoil has four lobes.

mass. Also called the Eucharist, it is the Catholic Church's principal act of worship, instituted at and recalling the Last Supper.

member. Any component of a structure, such as a beam or a column.

mensa. The table of a consecrated altar.

mosaic. A pictorial representation or decorative pattern formed from various colored glass, marbles, or stones.

mullion. Post dividing windows or doors into two or more openings.

narthex. Enclosed entry or vestibule of a church in front of the nave.

nave. Main body of a church.

niche. Recess in a wall intended for a statue.

ogee arch. Pointed arch formed by a pair of S curves.

pier. Vertical structural support that can take varied forms. Used in chapter 14, the structural work above the foundations and below the columns.

pinnacle. Small, narrow, ornamental tower crowning spires, buttresses, and the like.

pointed arch. Arch formed by two parallel vertical elements that turn toward each other, creating a point.

polychrome. Composed of or having multiple colors.

prelate. A high-ranking ecclesiastic, such as a bishop or archbishop.

pulpit. Elevated platform from which the Gospel is proclaimed and sermons given.

quatrefoil. In Gothic tracery, a form created by four circles or near circles, called lobes. A trefoil has three lobes, a cinquefoil has five lobes.

Rayonnant. Tracery patterns found in French Gothic architecture. A Rayonnant rose window has a central roundel with bars radiating from it; quatrefoils often figure in the composition. Rheims Cathedral's rose window is Rayonnant, as are Sacred Heart's.

reredos. Decorative screen of wood or masonry behind an altar.

rib. Narrow projecting element that strengthens or supports a vault.

rose window. A circular, stained-glass window with mullions and tracery.

roundel. Circular window or carved feature.

Ruskinian Gothic. Later phase of the Gothic Revival influenced by John Ruskin. Characterized by polychrome masonry, brickwork, and roof tiles. Generally more massive, it departed from a strict interpretation of medieval Gothic.

sanctuary. Part of a church holding the altar and the central space for holding liturgical ceremonies.

screen. Carved in stone or wood, a large composition with openings that sets off major portions of a church. Sacred Heart has screens between the narthex and nave, at the transept portals, and surrounding the sanctuary.

see. Jurisdiction or center of authority of a bishop. Another word for diocese or archdiocese.

shaft. Trunk or main part of a column or pillar.

smalti. Italian word for colored glass and glass incorporating gold. Cut into small pieces, it is assembled into a pictorial representation or decoration. It is associated with Byzantine medieval art and its later use or influence in Europe, especially in Italy.

spire. Tapering structure on the top of a building, especially a church tower. Essentially symbolic, its pointing form and height gives prominence to itself and the building to which it belongs.

stage. Story or level of a building or structure.

Stations of the Cross. Fourteen meditations on Christ's Passion, depicted in churches by pictorial scenes.

tabernacle. In a church, enclosure for the Reserved Sacrament. Also, a semienclosed or protected construction on towers and other places, often holding a statue.

terra cotta. Clay molded into shapes and baked in a kiln. The durable material used for Sacred Heart's window tracery.

tracery. Multicurved openwork forms in windows and other features, often holding stained glass in the former.

transept. The arms of a cruciform plan.

triforium. An arcaded gallery above the main arcade, opening into the church and often holding a small passageway. In Sacred Heart, it is below the clerestory.

trumeau figure. Statue in the trumeau (mullion) dividing a doorway. In Sacred Heart, they appear in the exterior and interior portal screens.

turret. Small tower or tower-shaped element.

tympanum. Space between the lintel (horizontal structure over a door or portal) and the arch above it. In Gothic architecture they are often sculpted. In Sacred Heart, they appear above the three main portals.

vault. Arch or several arches together covering a space. In Sacred Heart, they are composed of limestone and Guastivino tiles.

vicar general. After the bishop, the highest-ranking official of a diocese.

BIBLIOGRAPHY

Libraries and Archives

Archdiocese of Newark Collection. Monsignor William Noé Field Archives & Special Collections Center. Seton Hall University, South Orange, N.J. (ADN)
Architectural Archives. University of Pennsylvania, Philadelphia.
Avery Architectural and Fine Arts Library. Columbia University, New York.
Boston Public Library, Special Collections. Boston.
British Architectural Library. Royal Institute of British Architects, London.
Brooklyn Public Library, Brooklyn, N.Y.
Canadian Centre for Architecture, Montreal.
Charles F. Cummings New Jersey Information Center. Newark Public Library, Newark, N.J. (NPL)
Cleveland Public Library, Cleveland, Ohio.
Dover Free Public Library, Dover, N.J.
English Heritage: National Monuments Record, Swindon, England.
Flanagan Papers. Author's research collection.
Irish Architectural Archive, Dublin.
Morgan Library & Museum, New York.
National Archives, Washington, D.C.
Newark Museum, Newark, N.J.
New Jersey Historical Society, Newark, N.J.
New York Public Library, New York.
North Jersey History and Genealogical Center. Joint Free Public Library of Morristown and Morris Township, Morristown, N.J.
Royal Dublin Society Library, Dublin.
Saint Mark's Library. General Theological Seminary, New York.
Scott Memorial Library. Thomas Jefferson University, Philadelphia.
Spring Lake Public Library, Spring Lake, N.J.
Sterling Memorial Library. Yale University, New Haven, Conn.
Thomas J. Watson Library. Metropolitan Museum of Art, New York.

The following churches and institutions (in New Jersey unless otherwise noted) provided access to their buildings and archives:

Cathedral Basilica of the Sacred Heart, Newark (Monsignors John Doran and Richard Groncki and Bishop Manuel Cruz).

Church of Saint Paul the Apostle, New York (Fathers Charles Kullman and Gilbert Martinez).

Diocese of Paterson Archives, Paterson (Monsignor Raymond Kupke).

Holy Cross Church, Harrison.

Our Lady of Mount Carmel Church, Boonton.

Sacred Heart Church, Camden (Father Michael Doyle).

Saint Dominic's Convent, Stone, England (Sister Angela Leydon, prioress, and Sisters Cecily, Hugh, and Henry).

Saint John's Church, Orange (Father Robert Patterson and Mr. Vincent Clarke).

Saint Mary's Church, Dover (Fathers John DeMattia and Richard Oliveri and Monsignor Richard Rusconi).

Saint Patrick's Pro-Cathedral, Newark (Monsignor Neil Mahoney).

Saint Paul's Church, Princeton.

Saint Vincent Martyr Church, Madison.

Books

Atterbury, Paul, ed. *A.W.N. Pugin: Master of Gothic Revival*. New Haven, Conn.: Yale University Press for the Bard Graduate Center for Studies in the Decorative Arts, New York, 1995.

Atterbury, Paul, and Clive Wainwright, eds. *Pugin: A Gothic Passion*. New Haven, Conn.: Yale University Press in association with the Victoria and Albert Museum, 1994.

Bergdoll, Barry. *European Architecture 1750–1890*. Oxford: Oxford University Press, 2000.

Binding, Günther. *High Gothic: The Age of the Great Cathedrals*. Cologne: Taschen, 1999.

Byrne, William, et al. *History of the Catholic Church in the New England States*. Vols. 1 and 2. Boston: Hurd and Everts, 1899.

Brady, Joseph H. *The Most Reverend Thomas Joseph Walsh*. Newark, N.J.: Privately printed by Geiger Bros., 1950.

Ciccarino, Christopher. *Seeds of Faith, Branches of Hope: Archdiocese of Newark Sesquicentennial 1853–2003*. Strasbourg, France: Editions du Signe, 2003.

Cram, Ralph Adams. *Church Building: A Study of the Principles of Architecture in Their Relation to the Church*. 3rd ed. Boston: Marshall Jones Co., 1924.

Cunningham, John J. *Newark*. Newark: New Jersey Historical Society, 1988.

———. *New Jersey: America's Main Road*. Garden City, N.Y.: Doubleday, 1966.

Curran, Robert Emmett. *Michael Augustine Corrigan and the Shaping of Conservative Catholicism in America, 1878–1902*. New York: Arno Press, 1978.

Dixon, Roger, and Stefan Muthesius. *Victorian Architecture*. London: Thames and Hudson, 1978.

Doane, George Hobart. *Letters of Monsignor George Hobart Doane*. Newark, N.J.: Schultz and Gasser, 1905.

———. *Rome and the Sovereign Pontiff as They Really Are: Being the Substance of a Lecture Delivered in Library Hall, Newark, New Jersey*. New York: D. & J. Sadlier & Co., 1865.

———. *To and From the Passion Play*. Boston: P. Donahoe, 1872.

Dolan, Jay P. *The American Catholic Experience: A History from Colonial Times to the Present*. Garden City, N.Y.: Doubleday, 1985.

Dougherty, John J., et al. *The Bishops of Newark 1853–1978*. South Orange, N.J.: Seton Hall University Press, 1978.
Eastlake, Charles L. *A History of the Gothic Revival*, 1872. Reprint, New York: Humanities Press, 1970.
Farley, John M. *History of St. Patrick's Cathedral*. New York: Society for the Propagation of the Faith, Archdiocese of New York, 1908.
Farnsworth, Jean, et al. *Stained Glass in Catholic Philadelphia*. Philadelphia: St. Joseph's University Press, 2002.
Fergusson, James. *A History of Architecture in All Countries*. Vol. 2. 3rd ed. London: John Murray, 1893.
Flynn, Joseph M. *The Catholic Church in New Jersey*. Morristown, N.J., 1904.
Flynn, Paul V. *History of St. John's Church, Newark*. Newark: Press of the New Jersey Trade Review, 1908.
Frankl, Paul. *Gothic Architecture*. Revised by Paul Crossley. New Haven, Conn.: Yale University Press, 2000.
Germann, George. *Gothic Revival in Europe and Britain: Sources, Influences and Ideas*. Translated by Gerald Onn. Cambridge, Mass.: MIT Press, 1973.
Greiff, Constance M. *John Notman, Architect, 1810–1865*. Philadelphia: Athenaeum of Philadelphia, 1979.
Hill, Rosemary. *God's Architect: Pugin and the Building of Romantic Britain*. New Haven, Conn.: Yale University Press, 2009.
Hills, George Morgan. *History of the Church in Burlington, New Jersey*. Trenton: W. S. Sharp Printing Co., 1885.
Howe, Jeffrey. *Houses of Worship: An Identification Guide to the History and Style of American Religious Architecture*. San Diego, Calif.: Thunder Bay Press, 2003.
Howell, Peter, and Ian Sutton, eds. *The Faber Guide to Victorian Churches*. London: Faber and Faber, 1990.
Kelsey, Frederick W. *The First County Park System*. New York: J. S. Ogilvie Publishing Co., 1905.
Kennedy, Roger G. *American Churches*. New York: Stewart, Tabori & Chang, 1982.
Kervick, Francis. *Architects in America of Catholic Tradition*. Rutland, Vt.: Charles Tuttle Company, 1962.
———. *Patrick Charles Keely: A Record of His Life and Work*. South Bend, Ind.: Privately printed, 1953.
Kieckhefer, Richard. *Theology in Stone: Church Architecture from Byzantium to Berkeley*. Oxford: Oxford University Press, 2004.
Kowsky, Francis R. *Frederick Clarke Withers and the Progress of the Gothic Revival after 1850*. Middletown, Conn: Wesleyan University Press, 1980.
Kupke, Raymond J. *Living Stones: A History of the Catholic Church in the Diocese of Paterson*. Clifton, N.J.: Diocese of Paterson, 1987.
Landau, Sarah B. *Edward T. and William A. Potter: American Victorian Architects*. New York: Garland Publishing, 1979.
Leahy, Walter T. *The Catholic Church of the Diocese of Trenton*. Princeton, N.J.: Princeton University Press, n.d., c. 1906.
Lee, Antoinette J. *Architects to the Nation: The Rise and Decline of the Supervising Architect's Office*. New York: Oxford University Press, 2000.
Liptak, Dolores. *Immigrants and Their Church*. New York: Macmillan, 1989.
Little, Brian. *Catholic Churches since 1623*. London: Robert Hale, 1966.

Lurie, Maxine N., and Marc Mappen, eds. *Encyclopedia of New Jersey*. New Brunswick, N.J.: Rutgers University Press, 2004.

Mahoney, Joseph F., and Peter J. Wosh, eds. *Diocesan Journal of Michael Augustine Corrigan, Bishop of Newark, 1872–1880*. Newark: New Jersey Historical Society; South Orange: New Jersey Catholic Historical Records Commission, 1987.

Martin, Christopher. *A Glimpse of Heaven: Catholic Churches of England and Wales*. Swindon, U.K.: English Heritage and Catholic Bishops' Conference of England and Wales, 2006.

Meagher, James L. *The Great Cathedrals and Most Celebrated Churches in the World*. New York: Russell Bros., 1884.

Morgan, William. *The Almighty Wall: The Architecture of Henry Vaughan*. Cambridge, Mass.: MIT Press; New York: Architectural History Foundation, 1983.

Morris, Charles. *American Catholic*. New York: Times Books, 1997.

O'Brien, David J. *Isaac Hecker: An American Catholic*. New York: Paulist Press, 1992.

O'Donnell, Roderick. *The Pugins and the Catholic Midlands*. Birmingham, U.K.: Gracewing and the Archdiocese of Birmingham, 2002.

Panofsky, Erwin. *Gothic Architecture and Scholasticism*. New York: New American Library, 1976.

Pecklers, Keith F. *The Unread Vision: The Liturgical Movement in the United States of America 1926–1955*. Collegeville, Minn.: Liturgical Press, 1998.

Pierson, B. T. *Directory of Newark*. City directories, published 1835–1862. Newark Public Library.

Pierson, William H., Jr. *Technology and the Picturesque, the Corporate and the Early Gothic Styles*. Vol. 2 of *American Buildings and Their Architects*. Oxford: Oxford University Press, 1978.

Pugin, A.W.N. *An Apology for the Revival of Christian Architecture in England*. London: John Weale, 1843.

———. *Contrasts; or, A Parallel between the Noble Edifices of the Middle Ages, and Corresponding Building of the Present Day, Shewing the Present Decay of Taste, Accompanied by Appropriate Text*. London: Charles Dolman, 1841.

———. *The True Principles of Pointed or Christian Architecture*. London: John Weale, 1841.

Quinn, Dermot. *The Irish in New Jersey: Four Centuries of American Life*. New Brunswick, N.J.: Rutgers University Press, 2004.

Quirk, Howard E. *The Living Cathedral: Saint John the Divine*. New York: Crossroad, 1993.

Raguin, Virginia Chieffo, ed. *Glory in Glass: Stained Glass in the United States; Origins, Variety, and Preservation*. New York: American Bible Society, 1998.

———. *Stained Glass from Its Origins to the Present*. New York: Abrams Books, 2003.

Richardson, Douglas S. *Gothic Revival Architecture in Ireland*. New York: Garland Press, 1983.

Richardson, George Lynde. *William Croswell Doane, First Bishop of Albany*. Hartford, Conn.: Church Missions Publishing Co., 1933.

Shand-Tucci, Douglass. *Church Building in Boston 1720–1970, with an Introduction to the Work of Ralph Adams Cram*. Concord, Mass. Rumford Press, 1974.

———. *Ralph Adams Cram: An Architect's Four Quests; Medieval, Modernist, American, Ecumenical*. Amherst: University of Massachusetts Press, 2005.

———. *Ralph Adams Cram: Life and Architecture; Boston Bohemia, 1881–1900*. Amherst: University of Massachusetts Press, 1995.

Shea, John Gilmary. *Catholic Churches of New York City*. New York: Lawrence J. Goulding, 1878.

Simson, Otto von. *The Gothic Cathedral: Origins of Gothic Architecture and the Medieval Concept of Order*. Princeton, N.J.: Princeton University Press, 1988.

Smith, Ryan K. *Gothic Arches, Latin Crosses: Anti-Catholicism and American Church Designs in the Nineteenth Century*. Chapel Hill: University of North Carolina Press, 2006.

Stanton, Phoebe. *The Gothic Revival and American Church Architecture: An Episode in Taste, 1840–1856*. Baltimore: Johns Hopkins University Press, 1968.

———. *Pugin*. Preface by N. Pevsner. London: Thames and Hudson, 1971.

Stern, Robert A. M., et al. *New York 1880: Architecture and Urbanism in the Gilded Age*. New York: Monicelli Press, 1999.

Stoddard, Whitney. *Art and Architecture in Medieval France*. New York: Icon Editions, 1972.

St. Patrick's Cathedral. Published on the occasion of the consecration of the high altar in Saint Patrick's Cathedral, May 9, 1942. New York: Archbishopric of New York, 1942.

Tuttle, Brad R. *How Newark Became Newark: The Rise, Fall, and Rebirth of an American City*. New Brunswick, N.J.: Rutgers University Press, 2009.

Upjohn, Everard M. *Richard Upjohn: Architect and Churchman*. New York: Columbia University Press, 1939.

White, James F. *Roman Catholic Worship: Trent to Today*. New York: Paulist Press, 1995.

William, Peter W. *Houses of God: Region, Religion, and Architecture in the United States*. Urbana: University of Illinois Press, 1997.

Williams, Jeremy. *A Companion Guide to Architecture in Ireland 1837–1921*. Dublin: Irish Academic Press, 1994.

Wister, Robert James. *Stewards of the Mysteries of God: Immaculate Conception Seminary, 1860–2010*. South Orange, N.J.: Immaculate Conception Seminary, 2010.

Woods, Mary N. *From Craft to Profession: The Practice of Architecture in Nineteenth Century America*. Berkeley: University of California Press, 1999.

Yaeger, Sister M. Hildegarde. *The Life of James Roosevelt Bayley, First Bishop of Newark and Eighth Archbishop of Baltimore, 1814–1877*. Washington, D.C.: Catholic University Press, 1947.

Zwierlein, F. J. *The Life and Letters of Bishop McQuaid*. Rochester, N.Y.: Art Print Shop, 1925–1927.

Manuscripts, Pamphlets, and Dissertations

Brady, Joseph H. "The Cathedral of the Sacred Heart in Newark, New Jersey." 1950. Brady's manuscript is a history of the Newark cathedral project through 1950. It was transcribed and notated by Michael E. Gubernat and included in "The Histories of Sacred Heart Cathedral: A Research Document." 2nd ed. 1996 (see below). Citations in the notes refer to Gubernat's pagination. Copies in ADN, NPL.

Decker, Kevin F. "Grand and Godly Proportions: Roman Catholic Cathedral Churches of the Northeast, 1840–1900." PhD diss., University of Albany, State University of New York, 2000.

Gubernat, Michael E., ed. "The Histories of Sacred Heart Cathedral: A Research Document." 2nd ed., 1996. Copies in ADN and NPL.

Hinrichsen, Carl D. "The History of the Diocese of Newark 1873–1901." Ph.D. diss., Catholic University of America, 1962.

O'Hara, John. "Cathedral of the Sacred Heart, Newark, N.J." Newton, N.J.: C. Harrison Conroy Co., n.d. Copy in ADN, NPL.

Sullivan, Edwin V. "An Annotated Copy of the Diary of Bishop James Roosevelt Bayley, First Bishop of Newark, New Jersey, 1853–1872." PhD diss., University of Ottawa, 1956. Copy in ADN.

Wister, Robert J. *St. Patrick's Pro-Cathedral, Newark, New Jersey: An Historical Reflection 1850–2000*. Newark, N.J.: Privately published by St. Patrick's Pro-Cathedral, 2000. Also available at http://pirate.shu.edu/~wisterro/hoc/History_page.htm.

INDEX

ABOUT THE AUTHOR

BRIAN REGAN, deputy director of the Morgan Library & Museum, is coauthor of *The Making of the Morgan from Charles McKim to Renzo Piano*. He is a graduate of Wesleyan University and Harvard University and held a Watson Fellowship for study in England. A New York City resident, he is also a classical musician and active in historic preservation.

The fonts used in this book are Scala and Scala Sans Serif, both designed by Martin Majoor in 1990 and 1992, and named for the Teatro alla Scala in Milan.